Short Takes

Short Takes
Model Essays for Composition

Sixth Edition

Elizabeth Penfield
University of New Orleans

 LONGMAN

An imprint of Addison Wesley Longman, Inc.

New York • Reading, Massachusetts • Menlo Park, California • Harlow, England
Don Mills, Ontario • Sydney • Mexico City • Madrid • Amsterdam

Editor-in-Chief: Patricia Rossi
Publishing Partner: Anne Elizabeth Smith
Associate Development Editor: Karen Helfrich
Marketing Manager: Ann Stypuloski
Supplements Editor: Donna Campion
Project Coordination and Text Design: Ruttle, Shaw & Wetherill, Inc.
Cover Design Manager: Nancy Danahy
Cover Designer: Rubina Yeh
Cover Photos: Digital Stock, Incorporated
Full Service Production Manager: Joseph Vella
Electronic Page Makeup: Ruttle, Shaw & Wetherill, Inc.
Printer and Binder: R. R. Donnelly & Sons Company
Cover Printer: The Lehigh Press, Inc.

For permission to use copyrighted material, grateful acknowledgment is made to the
copyright holders on pp. 317–319, which are hereby made part of this copyright page.

Library of Congress Cataloging-in-Publication Data
Penfield, Elizabeth, 1939-
    Short takes : model essays for composition / Elizabeth Penfield. —6th ed.
        p.   cm.
    Includes index.
    ISBN 0-321-01470-7
    1. College readers. 2. English language—Rhetoric. I. Title
    PE1417.P43 1998   97-44941
    808'.0427—dc21   CIP

Please visit our website at http://longman.awl.com

ISBN 0-321-01470-7

1 2 3 4 5 6 7 8 9 10—DOC—01 00 99 98

CONTENTS

Thematic Guide

Scenes and Places

The Individual

Relationships

Gender

Society

Education

Language

Science and Technology

Popular Culture and the Media

Preface

*T*his book combines the old and the new. Back when the first edition was only an idea, I was teaching freshman English in a highly structured program that emphasized both the rhetorical modes and the final product. My dilemma then was one that many teachers still face: how to incorporate the modes with invention and the whole tangle of the writing process. But once I focused on the aims of discourse, the modes fell into place as means, not ends, and as patterns of organization used in combination, not just singly. There remained the problem of the textbooks, many of which contained essays of imposing length and complexity, essays that intimidated and overwhelmed many a student. Often, any essay that was short was so because it was an excerpt. *Short Takes* was the result of my frustrations. The sixth edition of *Short Takes* still reflects the rhetorical framework of the first one, but it is a flexible framework. You can even ignore it and use the thematic table of contents. But if you find the modes useful, you'll see them here.

This edition remains a collection of short, readable, interesting essays written by professionals and students, and the commentary continues to focus on reading and writing as interrelated activities. But much is new. You'll find new introductions for each chapter, introductions that focus primarily on students and the writing process, as well as the kinds of choices and decisions all writers face. Much else is new as well. Ideas for writing in journals supplement the ideas for writing essays, and there are more suggestions for writing than in previous editions. As for the essays, you'll still find a large number, all of which are complete—no excerpts here. Each author's background and the context for the essay, as well as "What to Look For," the brief description of a notable feature of the writer's style, have been updated and expanded. "Key Words and Phrases," a feature that alerted readers to allusions and vocabulary, has been moved to the Instructor's Manual to allow more space for the explanatory introductions that begin each chapter. Back by popular demand is "Freeze Frame," an initial essay that sets the tone for the book by emphasizing reading and writing as active and interrelated processes, a concept reinforced in each chapter's introduction and apparatus.

If you are familiar with previous editions, you'll also notice that the sequencing of the chapters has changed. Description, narration, and example are still at the beginning, but they are now followed by definition because it plays such an important role in expository and argumentative writing. Each chapter builds on the previous one and leads to the one that follows, culminating in argument, but argument with a difference. The chapter on argument is a basic introduction, an extension of the kind of emphasis on thesis and evidence that exists throughout the text. Within each chapter, the essays are presented in order of difficulty. All the supplementary information—the chapter introductions, background information, notes on style, questions on the essays, and suggestions for writing—balance process and product, working on the premise that the two, like reading and writing, are so closely interrelated that one cannot be considered without the other.

THE ESSAYS

This edition contains fifty-four essays, twenty-one of which are new. All are indeed short—about one thousand words at most—and as such should easily lend themselves to scrutiny and emulation, since most of the papers assigned in composition courses fall in the four hundred to one thousand word range. A few of the essays are longer and rely on the kind of research that students may be asked to carry out. And a few illustrate forms that differ from the classic short essay: the question/answer organization found in how-to or advice columns; a fully developed rhetorical situation calling for the student to respond by adopting a particular persona; and an opinion piece followed by two letters to the editor. Two essays also serve as a basic introduction to the Modern Language Association's system of documentation. All of the essays also represent complete pieces, not excerpts, illustrating the basic aims of discourse and standard rhetorical modes.

To write is to choose among alternatives, to select the most appropriate organization, persona, diction, and techniques for a given audience and purpose. Each of the essays included in this edition was chosen because it exemplifies the author's choices, and the apparatus emphasizes those choices and alternatives. Thus the essays serve as illustrative models of organization and stylistic techniques available to the writer. The essays were also chosen because their authors represent different genders, ages, and cultures; as a result, the subjects of the essays are accessible and their perspectives are lively, qualities that also allow them to serve as sources of invention, as jumping-off places for students to develop their own ideas in their own styles.

RHETORICAL MODES AND THE AIMS OF DISCOURSE

Anyone who has used a reader with essays arranged by mode has probably run into two problems: first, few essays are pure examples of a single mode; second, most collections of essays treat argument—an aim of writing—as though it were the equivalent of description, comparison/contrast, and so on. *Short Takes* addresses these inconsistencies by emphasizing the difference between mode—how an essay is organized—and purpose—how an essay is intended to affect the reader— and by pointing out how writing frequently blends two or more modes.

Because essays usually employ more than one mode, the essays here are grouped according to the *primary* rhetorical pattern that guides their organization; the questions that follow each essay go on to point out the subordinate modes. As for the aims of discourse, the essays represent the various purposes for writing. The writers' self-expressive, informative, and persuasive purposes are underscored in the discussion questions. In addition, the apparatus connects academic writing and the kind of writing found outside the classroom.

Example, description, or other standard modes are used in developing all kinds of nonfiction prose—self-expression, exposition, and argument. Of these three types of writing, self-expression is the easiest and argument the most difficult. For that reason, argument has its own special chapter. Of the eleven pieces in that chapter, eight are interrelated: an essay and two letters focusing on anti-intellectualism, three essays on hunting, and two on the role of African-American studies within the college curriculum. All of these interrelated essays are written from very different perspectives. And while chapters 1–8 contain some essays intended to persuade, those in chapter 9 exemplify the classical appeals: to reason, to emotion, and to the writer's credibility.

APPARATUS FOR READING AND WRITING

The apparatus makes full use of the essays. Each chapter begins with a brief introduction aimed at the student and depicts the mode or purpose under discussion, showing how it can be used in formal essays and in practical, everyday writing tasks. The introductions go on to point out specifically how the modes can be shaped by considerations of audience, purpose, particular strategies, thesis, and organization, ending with advice on finding a subject, exploring a topic, and drafting a paper. This division of the writing process approximates the classic one of invention, arrangement, and style, but is not intended to imply that these are separate stages.

To emphasize both what a text says and how it says it, each essay is preceded by background information on the author and the text and a brief discussion of a stylistic strategy. Two sets of questions—"Thesis and Organization" and "Technique and Style"—follow the essay. Then ideas for journal and essay writing are presented. Throughout, process and product, as well as reading and writing, are interrelated, emphasizing the recursive nature of the act of writing. Writers constantly invent, organize, and revise; the lines that distinguish those activities are narrow, if not downright blurred.

The suggestions for writing following each essay contain a number of options for both journal entries and essays, all related by theme, organization, or ideas to the work that has just been read. The assignments allow a good deal of flexibility: some lend themselves to general information or personal experience, some to research papers, and some to the classic technique of imitation. Once students select a subject, they will find flipping back to the introduction helpful. There the section "Exploring the Topic" shapes questions so that no matter what type of paper they are writing, students can generate information about it. "Drafting the Paper" then helps students organize the material and points out some of the pitfalls and advantages inherent in a particular mode or aim.

ACKNOWLEDGMENTS

I have many people to thank for their help in bringing this book to publication: Karen Helfrich for her good advice and flexibility; Hope Rajala and Leslie Taggart for their able assistance with past editions; and Theodora Hill for her sound recommendations, patience, and help with the more mundane aspects of preparing a manuscript. Susan McIntyre's careful copyediting of this edition is much appreciated. Dené Breakfield,

Boise State University; Nancy Cox, Arkansas Tech University; Susan Doonan, Pennsylvania Institute of Technology; Maurice Hunt, Baylor University; James Murphy, Southern Illinois University at Edwardsville; James Postema, Concordia College; and Nancy J. Schneider, University of Maine at Augusta all provided guidance and advice that improved the manuscript.

ELIZABETH PENFIELD

Short Takes

Freeze Frame:
Reading and Writing

This Book

1 **I**n filmmaking, a "short take" is a brief scene filmed without interruption. Similarly, short essays move quickly, with only the small breaks caused by paragraph indentations, toward their conclusions. Those are the kinds of essays you will find in this book, short essays that explain, argue, express the writer's feelings, or simply entertain. The essays carry out their purposes by drawing on various patterns of organization: description, narration, example, division, comparison, process analysis, causal analysis, and definition. These essays can serve as models for you when you write your own papers.

2 And just as the essays collected here are "short takes," this essay is a "freeze frame," as though you had stopped the film on one particular shot to get a better look at the details. That's just what this essay will do, stop and take a close-up look at what goes on when you read and when you write.

The Writing Process

3 Essays can be deceptive. What you see on the printed page resembles the writer's work about as much as a portrait photograph resembles the real person. What you don't see when you look at printed pages are all the beginnings and stops, the crumpled paper, the false starts, the notes, the discarded ideas, the changed words. Instead, you see a finished piece—the result of the writer's

choices. Don't let that result intimidate you. The process most writers go through to produce their essays is very like your own. The writer Andre Dubus puts it another way: "There is something mystical [about writing] but it's not rare and nobody should treat it as though this is something special that writers do. Anybody born physically able in the brain can sit down and begin to write something, and discover that there are depths in her soul or his soul that are untapped."

4   Both writers and readers tap into those depths, depths that help make meaning of the world we live in. The making of meaning is the heart of the essays contained in this book, together with its explanations, questions, and suggestions for writing. Stated concisely, this book reinforces a basic assumption: reading and writing are highly individual processes that are active, powerful, and interrelated ways to discover meaning. To check out that statement, think of one day within the last week when something memorable happened to you. Isolate that incident so it's clear in your mind. Now think of all the other details of the day, from the time your eyes opened in the morning to the time they closed at night. That's a lot of detail, most of it insignificant, meaningless. Those are the bits and pieces of information you would probably discard if you were to write about that day. What you would be left with is that memorable thing that occurred and a few details directly related to it, some preceding it, a few following. In writing about that day, you would reshape events, evaluating, selecting, and recreating what happened so that what was most meaningful comes through clearly. As a result, someone reading your description would be able to experience at a distance what you experienced firsthand. To write, then, is to create and structure a world; to read is to become part of someone else's world. And just as reading makes a better writer, writing makes a better reader.

The Reader

5   What's a good reader? Someone who interacts with the words on the page. Just as the writer reshapes, evaluates, selects, and recreates events, so too the reader reshapes, evaluates, selects, and recreates the text on the page. After all, as a reader you have your own world, one made up of everything you have experienced, from your first memory to your last thought—all of which you

bring to what you read. An essay about why people love to walk on beaches, for example, will remind you of any beaches you know, and your associations will probably be pleasurable. As you begin the essay, you discover that the writer's associations are also pleasant ones, reinforcing yours. You read on, constantly reassessing your ideas about the essay as you add more and more information to your first impression. Now and then, you may hit a sentence that doesn't make much sense at first, so you stop, perhaps to look up an unfamiliar word, perhaps to go back and review an earlier statement, then read on, again reevaluating your ideas about what the author is saying and what you think of it. The result is analytical, critical reading—not critical in the sense of being a harsh judge but critical in the sense of questioning, weighing evidence, evaluating, comparing your world to the one the writer has created on the page.

6   If you've done much writing, the process summarized above must sound familiar. Most people find that writing is a form of discovery, that writing about an idea helps clarify it. In your own experience, you have probably found that you usually don't have a clear grasp of your main point until you've written your way into it. Odds are you start with an idea, a general focus that becomes clearer as you rethink your choice of a particular word or reread what you've put on the page to get a sense of what should come next. And on you go, sometimes speeding, sometimes creeping, constantly revising, until you finish. Even the idea of finishing is a shaky notion; many writers will continue to revise right up to their deadlines. This idea of revising and tinkering seems natural to writing but less so to reading. Yet just as you tinker and wrestle with your own writing, you should do the same with what you read. You should scribble, underline, question, challenge. Reading in this way, reading critically with pen or pencil in hand, will give you a fuller appreciation of what you read and a better understanding of how to write.

7   If you're not used to reading in this manner, it may seem foreign to you. After all, what's printed on the page should be easy enough to understand. But because words only stand for things and are not the things themselves, different readers find different meanings. If, for instance, your only memory of a beach was of nearly drowning in the Atlantic Ocean, then you would have to suspend that association when you read an essay that praises

beach walking. And if your skin turns bright red at the mere mention of the sun, that adds one more obstacle to understanding why others enjoy the seashore. How then can a reader comprehend all that an author is saying? More specifically, how can a reader go about reading an essay critically?

8   It helps to know what different kinds of writing have in common. Whether business letter, lab report, journal entry, news story, poem, or essay, all writing must focus on a subject, address a reader, and have a point. All have a purpose and a style; they are written for specific reasons and in certain ways. These shared elements are perhaps more familiar as questions used to spark ideas for writing, the familiar journalistic *who? what? where? when? how? why?*

9   These questions can be equally useful for reading. To whom is an essay addressed? What is the writer's main point? How is the piece organized? Why is it structured that way? Where and when does the action take place? Many, many more inquiries can be spun off those seemingly simple questions, and they are useful tools for exploring an essay. The kind of analysis they lead to not only contributes to the pleasure you derive from an essay, but also makes you more aware of how to address similar concerns in your own writing. No one ever learned to write only by reading, but good writers are also good readers.

Purpose and Audience

10   In writing, as in speech, your purpose determines the relationship among your subject, yourself, and your reader. Most of the writing you will be doing in college, for instance, is intended to inform. For that reason, most of the essays included in this book are expository; their primary purpose is to explain a subject, to inform the reader. In most of your other courses, you will find that your reading fits into this category, one occupied by stacks of textbooks. As for your writing, when you write a lab or book report, a précis, or an essay exam, you focus on your subject so that you explain it to your readers.

11   Though explaining may be your primary purpose, secondary aims enter in as well. In an essay exam, you are also trying to convince your reader that you know what you are writing about. Or think about the sort of manual that comes with a computer or

VCR. The central aim is to explain, but the attempts to be "user-friendly" are persuasive, as though to say "Operating this machine isn't as hard as you think it is, and the results will be terrific."

12   If you do find yourself immediately responding to the writer's personal reaction to a subject, you are probably reading a journal or diary entry, a personal letter, an opinion piece in the newspaper, or a meditative essay. In this kind of writing, the focus is on the writer. If, for example, your teacher asks you to keep a journal in which you respond to what you read, your responses may range from fury over an opinion you disagree with to mild musings on what you think about the author's subject. What is important is what you feel, and your writing expresses those feelings by communicating them clearly to your reader. You, not the subject, are center stage.

13   Conveying what you feel about a subject and persuading your reader to share your opinion, however, are two different aims. Consider the difference between a letter to the editor and an editorial, both on the "three strikes and you're out" policy of a mandatory sentence of life imprisonment for those convicted of a third felony. The letter writer rages on about the number of violent crimes and says that life imprisonment is too good for "knife-wielding career felons." While the writer of the letter may feel better for having let off some steam, few minds, if any, will have been changed; probably the only readers who finished that letter were those who agreed to begin with. The letter both appeals to the emotions (the universal fear of crime) and uses emotions to express ideas (name-calling). An editorial, however, leans on reason for its appeal. An editorial may point out that the definition of what is or is not a felony differs from state to state, that many more prisons would have to be built and maintained, that judges weigh the severity of the offense and the punishment it deserves, that the "three strikes" policy creates more problems than it solves. The editorial writer is careful to address a range of readers who agree, disagree, or have no opinion. The writer's intent is to make the reader think, and ideally, to change opinions, so the argument's appeal rests primarily on reason, not emotion.

14   That is also your goal when you are given a writing assignment that asks you to take a stand and defend it. You must know your audience and rely on evidence, on reason, and to a lesser extent on emotion to win over those readers. Blatant persuasion hawks

products on television commercials, sells political candidates, and begs you to support various causes; the more subtle variety appears in college catalogs, public debates, and the editorial pages. All ask you to consider a certain stand, adopt a given opinion, or take an action: the writer focuses primarily on the reader.

15   Recognizing valid evidence, separating emotional appeals from appeals to reason, and spotting logical fallacies can protect you in a world of contradictory claims and high-powered propaganda. In the newspapers, on the television set, in the halls of Congress, and in your living room, issues are debated and opinions voiced. Sorting through them takes the kind of concentrated thought that reading and writing argumentative essays requires.

16   Whether the argument is blatant or subtle, being able to recognize the techniques at work, the purpose, and the intended audience helps you evaluate assertions and illuminate their validity, whether debating a point in class or at home or reading or writing an essay for a course. Sometimes, however, the reader, like the writer, will have to work at determining the primary purpose behind a piece. An effective description of an unusual scene such as a giant feedlot, for example, will not only explain what it looks, smells, and sounds like but also convey how the author feels about it and perhaps imply a need for change. While basically expository, such an essay also incorporates self-expression and persuasion.

17   And other, less obvious motives and audiences may be driving a piece. A student, for instance, may write a paper for the simple reason that it is assigned or to get a good grade; but successful essays go beyond those immediate goals to change both reader and writer. The writer learns from the act of writing because of being forced to examine the subject closely, to explore it, and to communicate something of interest about it. So, too, the reader learns from a good essay, perhaps finding a fresh perspective on a familiar topic or discovering information about an unfamiliar one. Both reader and writer work to create meaning out of what is on the page. The result is not just sweat and knowledge, but pleasure. Good prose delights.

Detecting the Thesis

18   In much of the reading we do, we are looking for information. The election coverage reported in the newspaper, the syllabus for a course, and a set of directions all exemplify this kind of reading,

but reading for information and reading for comprehension are as different as a vitamin pill and a five-course dinner. To understand not only what a writer is saying but also its implications and why that writer might have chosen to say it that way isn't easy.

19   The title of an essay is a good place to start, for most titles tip you off not only to the subject of the piece but also to the author's stand. You don't need to turn to the essay titled "Sweatin' for Nothin'" to figure out that it may be about exercising and that the author doesn't see much point to fitness fads. Other titles, such as "Left Sink," just imply a subject and raise your curiosity. What about a left sink? What does it mean? Still others tip you off to the author's tone, the writer's attitude toward the subject: if an essay were called "Tube E or Not Tube E," the play on the familiar line from *Hamlet* would suggest a humorous discussion of a chemistry lab course. Some titles, however, may state the thesis, such as an editorial headlined "Your Vote Counts." Others focus clearly on their subject, as in "Living with Cancer."

20   Knowing, or at least having a hint about, the subject is the first step to discovering an essay's thesis, the assertion the author is making about the subject. The first paragraph or set of paragraphs that act as an introduction will also help you form a tentative thesis. Sometimes the writer will place the thesis in the first paragraph or introduction. In this essay, for example, the thesis appears in the last sentence of paragraph 6: "reading critically with pen or pencil in hand, will give you a fuller appreciation of what you read and a better understanding of how to write." But sometimes a bare-bones version of the thesis will appear in the title. If you see it, you should mark it. If you don't spot a thesis, you should still jot down a tentative version of your own so that you have a focus for what is to follow, an idea that you can test other ideas against.

21   The obvious comparison here is your own writing. Many writers start with a general idea that then gets refined into a thesis as they write. Once that thesis is clear, then the writer must decide where to place it for the greatest effect. Some opt for the introduction, others choose the conclusion, and still others decide on a more subtle solution by weaving bits and pieces of the thesis into the essay as a whole.

22   If you are reading the essay, this last choice can present a challenge. You must create the thesis by identifying key sentences and then mentally composing a statement that covers those ideas, a process that often takes more than one reading but is made easier

if you underline the important sentences. Even then, you may well find that someone else who reads the essay comes up with a different thesis statement. And you both may be right. What's happening here? If you think about how slippery words are and the different experiences that different readers bring to an essay, you can begin to see why there can be more than one "correct" thesis. If you were to give the same essay to ten critical readers, you might find that their versions of the thesis differ but overlap. Their readings would probably cluster around two or three central ideas. If an eleventh person read the essay and came up with a thesis that contradicted the other ten, that version would probably be off base. Perhaps that was the reader who almost drowned and can't take the sun.

23   Sometimes writers set traps, making it easy to mistake a fact for a thesis. If you keep in mind that a thesis is both a sentence and an assertion—a value judgment—you can avoid those traps. "The average American watches a lot of TV" states a fact most readers would shrug off with a "So what?" On the other hand, "Television rots the minds of its viewers" takes a stand that will probably raise hackles and a "Hey, wait a minute!"

Recognizing Patterns of Development

24   Once you've nailed down a thesis, go a step further to examine how that thesis is developed. Writers depend on various patterns of thought that are almost innate. To tell a joke is to narrate; to convey what a party was like is to describe and to use examples; to jot down a grocery list is to divide and classify; to figure out which car to buy is to compare and contrast (and if you think of your old car as a peach or a lemon, you are drawing an analogy); to give directions is to use process; to consider how to improve your tennis game is to weigh cause and effect; to explain how you feel is to define. Narration, description, example, division and classification, comparison and contrast, analogy, process, cause and effect, and definition are the natural modes of thinking on which writers rely.

25   These modes provide the structure of the essay, the means by which the author conveys the major point—the thesis—and, more often than not, the writer draws on several patterns of development to support the thesis. Rarely does an essay rely solely on one

pattern of development. So far, for instance, the essay you are now reading has used definition (paragraph 5), cause and effect (paragraph 7), process (paragraph 4), and description (paragraph 5), and will use analogy (paragraph 28), and, most of all, example (virtually every paragraph). The other essays that you will read in this book also employ more than one mode, but each has been placed in a category according to the primary means of development. In fact, the whole textbook can be thought of as organized by division and classification: the essays are first divided into primary purpose—to explain or to argue—and then each one is classified according to the pattern of development it relies on the most.

26   When you are writing, these modes provide ways to think about your topic as well as ways to organize your essay. With practice, they become as much second nature as shifting gears in a manual-transmission car. At first you might be a bit tentative about knowing when to shift from first to second, but with time you don't even think about it. Similarly, at first you might wonder if your point is clear without an example; in time, you automatically supply it.

The Final Draft

27   Knowing what you want to write and having a fair idea of how it should be organized still does not necessarily help shape individual sentences so that they convey the desired tone. That requires draft after draft. Hemingway rewrote the last page of *A Farewell to Arms* 39 times, and Katherine Anne Porter spent 20 years writing and rewriting *Ship of Fools*. Writing nonfiction doesn't make the process any easier. Wayne Booth, a distinguished essayist and scholar, speaks for most writers: "I revise many, many times, as many times as deadlines allow for. And I always feel that I would have profited from further revision." Poet, novelist, essayist, journalist, student, or professional, all continue in the tradition expressed in the eighteenth century by a fellow writer, Samuel Johnson, who said, "What is written without effort is in general read without pleasure." Pleasurable reading derives from a pleasing writing style, and though some writers strive for elegance as well as clarity, most readers will happily settle for clarity.

28   Far from following a recipe, writing an essay is like driving a car while at the same time trying to impress the passengers, read a

road map, recognize occasional familiar landmarks, follow scrawled and muttered directions, and watch for and listen to all the quirks of the car. You know vaguely where you are going and how you want to get there, but the rest is risk and adventure. With work and a number of dry runs, you can smooth out the trip so that the passengers fully appreciate the pleasure of the drive and the satisfaction of reaching the destination. That is the challenge the writer faces, a challenge that demands critical reading as well as effective writing.

▨ POINTERS FOR READING

1. **Settle in.** Gather up a good dictionary and whatever you like to write with, and then find a comfortable place to read.
2. **Think about the title.** What sort of expectations do you have about what will follow? Can you identify the subject? A thesis? Can you tell anything about the writer's tone?
3. **Look for a specific focus.** Where is the essay going? What appears to be its thesis? At what point does the introduction end and the body of the essay begin? What questions do you have about the essay so far? Is the essay directed at you? If not, who is the intended audience?
4. **Look for a predominant pattern of organization.** What are the most important ideas in the body of the essay? Note the modes the writer uses to develop those ideas. Note those you disagree with or question.
5. **Identify the conclusion.** Where does the conclusion begin? How does it end the essay? What effect does it have on you?
6. **Evaluate the essay.** Did the essay answer the questions you had about it? How effective was the support for the main ideas? Did the writer's choice of words fit the audience? What effect did the essay have on you? Why?

▨ POINTERS FOR WRITING

1. **Settle in.** Get hold of whatever you find comfortable to write with—computer, pen, pencil, legal pad, note paper, notebook—and settle into wherever you like to write. Start by jotting down words that represent a general idea of your subject. As words cross your mind, write them down so that at this point you have a vague focus.
2. **Focus.** Try writing right away and quickly. Just get ideas down on paper without worrying about organization or punctuation or whether what

you write is right. If you run out of steam, pause and read over what you have written and then summarize it in one sentence. Then start up again, writing as quickly as you can. At some point you will have written your way into a tentative thesis that will help you focus as you revise what you have written.

3. **Reread.** Go over what you have written, looking for sentences that state an opinion. Mark them in some way (a highlighter is useful). These sentences can become topic sentences that lead off paragraphs and therefore help you organize your ideas.

4. **Organize what you have.** Go through what you have written, asking yourself questions. What would make a good introduction? A good conclusion? What order best suits what's in between? What examples do you have? Where would they work best?

5. **Think about your purpose.** As you reread what you've written, think about the effect you want to have on your readers. Are you explaining something to them? Arguing a cause? Telling them how you feel? Entertaining them? Some combination of purposes?

6. **Think about your readers.** What do they know about your subject? Your answer to this question may make you cut out some information; and what they don't know will guide you to what you need to include. Do they have a bias for or against what you have to say? Your answer here will tell you if you need to account for those biases and suggest how you might do that.

7. **Revise.** You've probably been revising all along, but at this point you can revise more thoroughly and deeply. You know your purpose, audience, and thesis—all of which will help you organize your paper more effectively.

8. **Proofread.** Now look for surface errors, checking for spelling and punctuation. If you're using a word-processing program, run your text through the spelling checker. As for punctuation, if you have access to a grammar checker on your word processor, try it. You may find it useful, but probably a handbook of grammar and usage will be much more helpful. When using a handbook, you can find answers to your questions quickly by looking up the key word in the index.

Description

Description turns up in various guises in all types of prose, for it is the basic device a writer uses to convey sense impressions. For that reason, it is as essential to **objective**[1] writing as it is to **subjective** prose, and of course to everything in between. A quick sketch of a family gathering that you might include in a letter to a friend draws on the same skills as a complex report on the effectiveness of a new product. Both rely on the ability to observe, to select the most important details, to create a coherent sequence for those details, and then to convey the result by appealing to the reader's senses. To describe something, then, is to recreate it in such a way that it becomes alive again, so that the reader can see and understand it. Prose that depends heavily on description invites the reader to share the writer's initial sense of vividness and perception.

The role description plays in writing will vary. Personal narratives depend heavily on description to bring scenes and actions to life, to depict an outdoor wedding, for instance, or to convey what it feels like to have a toothache. Other types of expository essays use description in a less obvious role, perhaps to clarify a step in a process or make an example vivid. And persuasion often gets its punch from description, for it enables the reader to see the prisoner on death row or the crime that led to the death sentence. While no essay relies solely on description, each of the essays that follow uses description as its primary pattern of organization. The essays' general subjects are familiar—a place, a per-

---

[1]Words printed in boldface are defined under "Useful Terms" at the end of each introductory section.

son, a frog—but by selecting details, each author tailors description uniquely.

AUDIENCE AND PURPOSE   Most writers start with a general sense of purpose and audience. Perhaps you want to explain an event or how something works or what you think about a particular place, person, or idea, in which case your purpose is expository and what you write is **exposition.** You focus on your subject so that you can explain it clearly to your reader. That's not as dull as it sounds. Odds are that if you wrote a description of your neighborhood in such a way that your readers felt as though they could see it, you'd have an interesting expository essay. Sure, it represents your opinion, how you see your neighborhood, but the focus is clearly on the subject; you are in the position of narrator, telling your readers about your subject, explaining it to them.

But imagine that as you begin to think about your neighborhood your thoughts turn to ways in which your life there could be improved. Perhaps the garbage could be picked up more frequently, the sidewalks could be repaired, or the property taxes lowered. All of a sudden you're off on an argumentative tear, one that can take a number of different forms—essay, letter to the editor, letter to your city or state representative. But no matter who you write for, you're engaging in **persuasion** and your focus is on the reader, the person whose mind you want to change.

Writers who aim their work at a definite audience, say the readers of a particular magazine, have a head start by knowing the readership. One of the essays in this chapter comes from *Sierra*, the journal of the Sierra Club, an organization devoted to the preservation of American wildlife and nature. Writing for that audience, the author can assume a definite interest in animal life of almost any variety, so the only problem that remains is how to make the particular creature real and interesting.

If your audience is a more general one, say the readers of a newspaper or your classmates, the situation is quite different. The assumptions you can make must be more general. For a newspaper it's safe to assume, for instance, that most of the readers are educated and fall into a general age group ranging from young adult to middle-aged. Knowing that can help you estimate the distance between your subject and the audience. If your subject is old age, you will know that your readers are generally knowledgeable about the topic but that their experience is indirect. That means you must fill in the gap with descriptive details so that their experience becomes more direct, so that the readers can see and feel what it's like to be old. If you were to keep old age as your subject but change the audience from newspaper readers to your classmates, the gap between subject and audience would become wider, so your description would have to be more full.

In addition to having a firm sense of what your audience does and does not know, it helps to know how your readers may feel about your subject and how you want them to feel. How you want them to feel is a matter of **tone,** your attitude toward the subject and the audience. Many readers, for example, are understandably squeamish about the subject of war, and that creates a problem for the writer, particularly one who wants to describe a scene realistically and at the same time elicit sympathy. One solution is to pretty it up, but that does a disservice to reality; yet too realistic a description can be so revolting that no one would read it. Nor would anyone read a dry, objective account. Rudyard Kipling, who most of us know through his *Jungle Stories,* faced this problem when he wrote *The Irish Guards in the Great War,* a history of a military unit in World War I. At one point, he describes the German positions before the British attack on the Somme and solves the problem of tone by finding a middle, yet realistic, ground:

> Here the enemy had sat for two years, looking down upon France and daily strengthening himself. His trebled and quadrupled lines of defense, worked for him by his prisoners, ran below and along the flanks and on the tops of ranges of five-hundred-foot downs. Some of these were studded with close woods, deadlier even than the fortified villages between them; some cut with narrowing valleys that drew machine-gun fire as chimneys draw draughts; some opening into broad, seemingly smooth slopes, whose every haunch and hollow covered sunk forts, carefully placed mine-fields, machine-gun pits, gigantic quarries, enlarged in the chalk, connecting with systems of catacomb-like dug-outs and subterranean works at all depths, in which brigades could lie till the fitting moment. Belt upon belt of fifty-yard-deep wire protected these points, either directly or at such angles as should herd and hold up attacking infantry to the fire of veiled guns. Nothing in the entire system had been neglected or unforeseen, except knowledge of the nature of the men who, in due time, should wear their red way through every yard of it.[2]

Compare that description with the same scene described objectively and with most of the details removed to create an intentionally flat, dull tone:

---

[2]Quoted in Paul Fussell's *The Great War and Modern Memory* (New York: Oxford UP, 1977) 171.

The Germans had been strengthening their defenses for two years. It was a defense in depth, exploiting the smooth slopes ascending to their high ground. They fortified forests and villages and dug deep underground shelters in the chalky soil. They protected their positions with copious wire, often arranged to force attackers into the fire of machine guns. (Fussell 172)

Kipling's description is essentially an explanation, but note the argumentative twist he puts in his last sentence, his reference to the men of the Irish Guards and their valiant attack and huge losses, the blood of their "red way." There's no question about whose side Kipling is on. And there's no question about how he wants his readers to feel.

DETAILS   No matter what the purpose or audience, descriptive essays are characterized by their use of detail. Note how many details are in the paragraph by Kipling, most of which are **concrete words.** The German defenses had not just been strengthened but "trebled and quadrupled." Nor is Kipling satisfied with **abstract words.** He tells us the quarries were "gigantic," an abstract word that has different meanings to different people, so he gives us a concrete sense of just how large those quarries are—they could hide whole brigades. We get a visual idea of their size. Visual detail also helps us see the wire defenses. Because Kipling's book, from which the passage was taken, was published in 1923, shortly after the end of World War I, a time when tanks, missiles, and bombers as we know them were unheard of, the general particulars of trench warfare were still fresh in his readers' minds; they would know, for example, that the wire he refers to is barbed wire, but Kipling makes his audience (both then and now) see it by saying that it was "belt upon belt" of wire, "fifty-yard-deep" wire.

Visual details make us see what a writer is describing, but appealing to the other senses also brings prose to life. Once you start thinking about it, you'll find images that draw in other senses. For auditory appeal, for instance, you might think of a time when you walked in very cold weather and heard the small squeal your footsteps make when the snow is so dry that a snowball turns to powder; and if your climate goes to the other extreme, you might remember a blistering night and the chirps, bleeps, squeaks, and rasps put forth by a chorus of summer bugs.

COMPARISON   Take any object and try to describe what it looks, feels, smells, sounds, and tastes like, and you'll quickly find yourself shifting over to comparisons. Comparisons enrich description in that they can produce an arresting image, explain the unfamiliar, make a connection with the reader's own experience, or reinforce the major point in the essay. Comparing the unfamiliar to the familiar makes what is being described more real. Even the computer illiterate among us get the idea embedded in the term *world wide web*, immediately imagining an electronic spider web that encompasses the globe. The image is a metaphor, and often comparisons take the form of **metaphor, simile,** or **allusion.**

Simile and *metaphor* both draw a comparison between dissimilar things; the terms differ in that a simile uses a comparative word such as *like* or *as.* As a result, metaphor is often the more arresting because it is a direct equation. If you were writing and got stuck to the point where nothing worked—the classic writer's block—you might describe your state as "impaled by words like a butterfly on a pin." Then when you broke through and started writing again, you might think of it as being able to "open the locked door." Or you might think the process of writing is like the labors of Hercules, an allusion to the hero of Greek myths and his difficult and superhuman feats.

Unfortunately, the first comparisons that often come to mind can be overworked ones known as **clichés:** *green as grass, hot as hell, mad as a hornet, red as a rose,* and the like. While you can guard against them by being suspicious of any metaphor or simile that sounds familiar, clichés can sneak into your writing in less obvious ways. Watch out for descriptive words that come readily to mind—waves that pound or crash, clouds that are fluffy, bells that tinkle.

Analogy is another form of comparison. Think of it as a metaphor that is extended beyond a phrase into several sentences or a paragraph. You can follow how that can happen if you think of a metaphor for the way you write. Some may imagine a roller coaster; others might think of having to manage a busy switchboard; and for some it may be trying to build a house without having any blueprints or knowing what materials are needed. No matter which image you choose, you can tell that it will take more than a sentence or two to develop the metaphor into an analogy.

DICTION   The words a writer chooses determine whether the description is more objective or subjective, whether its tone is factual or impressionistic. Although total objectivity is impossible, description that leans toward the objective is called for when the writer wants to focus on subject as opposed to emotional effect, on what something is rather than how it felt. Read the paragraph below by J. Merrill-Foster in which she describes an 85-year-old woman.

> She is frightened and distressed by letters from retired military men. They write that unless she sends $35 by return mail, the Russians will land in Oregon and take over America. The arrival of the daily mail looms large in her day. Once, every few weeks, it contains a personal letter. The rest is appeals and ads. She reads every item. (34)

That passage comes from the first part of Merrill-Foster's essay, which ends with this paragraph:

> I watch the woman—my mother—walking carefully down the frozen, snow-filled driveway to the mail box. She is a photograph in black and white, which only loving memory tints with stippled life and color. (36)

The first description reports the unnamed woman's feelings and the facts that give rise to them, and then generalizes on the importance of the daily mail, noting what it contains and the attention the woman gives it. The second description uses first person and identifies the woman as the author's mother, the words *I* and *mother* forming an emotional bond between reader and writer, overlaying with feeling the picture of the woman walking to the mailbox. On finishing the first passage, the reader understands the role an everyday event—the arrival of the mail—plays in the life of an old woman; on finishing the second, the reader knows and feels how old age has diminished a once vital person.

THESIS AND ORGANIZATION   All the details, all the comparisons are presented according to a pattern so that they add up to a single dominant impression. In descriptive essays, this single dominant impression may be implicit or explicit, and it stands as the **thesis.** An explicit thesis jumps off the page at you and is usually stated openly in one or two easily identifiable sentences. An implicit thesis, however, is more subtle. As reader, you come to understand what the thesis is even though you can't identify any sentence that states it. If that process of deduction seems mysterious, think of reading a description of the ultimate pizza, a description that alluringly recounts its aroma, taste, texture. After reading about that pizza you would probably think, Wow, that's a really good pizza. And that's an implied thesis.

Whether implicit or explicit, the thesis is what the writer builds the essay on. It's the main point. The writer must select the most important details, create sentences and paragraphs .around them, and then sequence the paragraphs so that everything not only contributes to but also helps create the thesis. In description, paragraphs can be arranged by **patterns of organization,** such as process and definition, and according to spatial, temporal, or dramatic relationships. The writer can describe a scene so that the reader moves from one place to another, from one point in time to another, or according to a dramatic order. If this last idea seems vague, think of how a film or novel builds to a high point, one that usually occurs just before the end.

The building block for that high point and for the essay itself is the paragraph. And just as the essay has a controlling idea, an assertion that is its thesis, so, too, does the paragraph, usually in the form of a **topic sentence.** Like the thesis, the topic sentence can be explicit or implied, and it can be found in one sentence or deduced from the statements made in several. A topic sentence often covers more than one paragraph, for paragraphs frequently cluster around a central idea, particularly in a longer essay, one over 600 words or so.

There's no magic number for how many words make up a paragraph and no magic number for how many paragraphs make up an essay. But it is safe to say that all essays have a beginning, middle, and end. The same is true of a paragraph or group of paragraphs that function under one topic sentence. As you read, ask yourself why a given paragraph ends where it does and what links it to the one that follows. You may discover that sometimes paragraph breaks are not set in cement, that they could occur in several different places and still be "right."

USEFUL TERMS

Abstract words Words that stand for something that cannot be easily visualized and therefore may hold different meanings for different people. A box of cereal labeled "large" may be your idea of "small."

Allusion An indirect reference to a real or fictitious person, place, or thing.

Analogy A point-by-point comparison to something seemingly unlike but more commonplace and less complex than the subject. An analogy is also an extended metaphor.

Cliché A comparison, direct or indirect, that has been used so often that it has worn out its novelty, such as *cool as a cucumber* or *ice cold.*

Concrete words Words that stand for something that can be easily visualized and have fixed meaning. If you replaced the "large" on the cereal box with "8 ounces" or "two servings for moderately hungry people," you would be replacing the abstract with more definite, concrete details.

Exposition Writing that explains; also called expository writing.

Metaphor An implied but direct comparison in which the primary term is made more vivid by associating it with a quite dissimilar term. "Life is a roller coaster" is a metaphor.

Objective prose Writing that is impersonal.

Patterns of organization Paragraphs and essays are usually organized according to the patterns illustrated in this book: description, narration, example, division and classification, comparison, process, cause and effect, and definition. Although more than one pattern may exist in a paragraph or essay, usually one predominates.

Persuasion Writing that argues a point, that attempts to convince the reader to adopt the writer's stand.

Simile A comparison in which the primary term is linked to a dissimilar one by *like* or *as* to create a vivid image. "Life is like a roller coaster" is a simile. Remove the linking word and you have a metaphor.

Subjective prose Writing that is personal.

Thesis A one-sentence statement or summary of the basic arguable point of the essay.

Tone A writer's attitude toward the subject and the audience.

Topic sentence A statement of the topic of a paragraph containing an arguable point that is supported by the rest of the paragraph.

▩ POINTERS FOR USING DESCRIPTION

Exploring the Topic

1. **What distinguishes your topic?** What characteristics, features, or actions stand out about your subject? Which are most important? Least important?
2. **What senses can you appeal to?** What can you emphasize about your subject that would appeal to sight? Smell? Touch? Taste? Motion?

3. **What concrete details can you use?** What abstract words do you associate with each of the features or events you want to emphasize? How can you make those abstractions concrete?
4. **How can you vary your narrative?** Where might you use quotations? Where might you use dialogue?
5. **What can your audience identify with?** What comparisons can you use? What similes, metaphors, or allusions come to mind?
6. **What order should you use?** Is your description best sequenced by Time? Place? Dramatic order?
7. **What is your tentative thesis?** What is the dominant impression you want to create? Do you want it to be implicit? Explicit?
8. **What is your relationship to your subject?** Given your tentative thesis, how objective or subjective should you be? Do you want to be part of the action or removed? What personal pronoun should you use?

Drafting the Paper

1. **Know your reader.** If you are writing about a familiar subject, ask yourself what your reader might not know about it. If you are writing about an unfamiliar subject, ask yourself what your reader does know that you can use for comparison.
2. **Know your purpose.** If you are writing to inform, make sure you are presenting new information and in enough detail to bring your subject to life. If you are writing to persuade, make sure your details add up so that the reader is moved to adopt your conviction. Keep in mind that your reader may not share your values and indeed may even hold opposite ones.
3. **Vary sensory details.** Emphasize important details by appealing to more than just one sense.
4. **Show, don't tell.** Avoid abstract terms such as "funny" or "beautiful." Instead, use concrete details, quotations, and dialogue. Don't settle for vague adjectives such as "tall"; replace them with sharper details such as "6 feet 7 inches."
5. **Use comparisons.** Make your description vivid with an occasional metaphor or simile. If you are writing about something quite unfamiliar, use literal comparison to make your description clear.
6. **Arrange your details to create a single dominant impression.** If you are writing descriptive paragraphs, check the order of your sentences to make sure they follow each other logically and support the impression you wish to create. If you are writing an essay that relies heavily on description, check for the same points from one paragraph to another. Is your topic sentence or thesis implicit or explicit? Reexamine your first paragraph. Does it establish The scene? The tone?

The Mute Sense

Diane Ackerman

As an undergraduate at Boston University and then Pennsylvania State University, Diane Ackerman studied both science and literature, twin interests she would pursue as a writer. A staff writer for The New Yorker, *Ackerman often writes on nature and its inhabitants.* The Moon by Whale Light, *a collection of her essays, was published in 1991; it is subtitled and* Other Adventures among Bats, Penguins, Crocodiles, and Whales. *Her most recent nonfiction book,* A Slender Thread *(1997), grew out of her volunteer work as a counselor at a suicide prevention and crisis center. The essay below comes from Ackerman's* The Natural History of the Senses, *which was published in 1990 and has since been translated into many languages. Ackerman is also a well-respected poet, and in "The Mute Sense" she manages to combine the vivid detail and compression characteristic of poetry with the precise detail and keen observation associated with science.*

WHAT TO LOOK FOR   *Good writers have a way of listening to words so that the words talk back, one word suggesting another or a whole image that can lead both writer and reader into the prose. They use strong verbs that suggest action, not forms of the verb* be. *Try to tune your own ear so that you pick up the comparisons implicit in your verbs. That's what might have happened when Ackerman chose* detonate *toward the end of her first paragraph, a verb from which she spins a metaphor. Notice, too, how often she uses comparisons and allusions, piling on examples so that if a reader misses one, another is sure to hit home.*

1   Nothing is more memorable than a smell. One scent can be unexpected, momentary, and fleeting, yet conjure up a childhood summer beside a lake in the Poconos, when wild blueberry bushes teemed with succulent fruit and the opposite sex was as mysterious as space travel; another, hours of passion on a moonlit beach in Florida, while the night-blooming cereus drenched the air with thick curds of perfume and high sphinx moths visited the cereus in a loud purr of wings; a third, a family dinner of pot roast, noodle pudding, and sweet potatoes, during a myrtle-mad August in a midwestern town, when both of one's parents were alive. Smells

21

detonate softly in our memory like poignant land mines, hidden under the weedy mass of many years and experiences. Hit a trip-wire of smell, and memories explode all at once. A complex vision leaps out of the undergrowth.

2   People of all cultures have always been obsessed with smell, sometimes applying perfumes in Niagaras of extravagance. The Silk Road opened up the Orient to the western world, but the scent road opened up the heart of Nature. Our early ancestors strolled among the fruits of the earth with noses vigilant and precise, following the seasons smell by smell, at home in their brimming larder. We can detect over ten thousand different odors, so many, in fact, that our memories would fail us if we tried to jot down everything they represent. In "The Hound of the Baskervilles," Sherlock Holmes identifies a woman by the smell of her notepaper, pointing out that "There are seventy-five per-fumes, which it is very necessary that a criminal expert should be able to distinguish from each other." A low number, surely. After all, anyone "with a nose for" crime should be able to sniff out culprits from their tweed, Indian ink, talcum powder, Italian leather shoes, and countless other scented paraphenalia. Not to mention the odors, radiant and nameless, which we decipher without even knowing it. The brain is a good stagehand. It gets on with its work while we're busy acting out our scenes. Though most people will swear they couldn't possibly do such a thing, studies show that both children and adults, just by smelling, are able to determine whether a piece of clothing was worn by a male or a female.

3   Our sense of smell can be extraordinarily precise, yet it's almost impossible to describe how something smells to someone who hasn't smelled it. The smell of the glossy pages of a new book, for example, or the first solvent-damp sheets from a mimeograph ma-chine, or a dead body, or the subtle differences in odors given off by flowers like bee balm, dogwood, or lilac. Smell is the mute sense, the one without words. Lacking a vocabulary, we are left tongue-tied, groping for words in a sea of inarticulate pleasure and exaltation. We see only when there is light enough, taste only when we put things into our mouths, touch only when we make contact with someone or something, hear only sounds that are loud enough. But we smell always and with every breath. Cover your eyes and you will stop seeing, cover your ears and you will

stop hearing, but if you cover your nose and try to stop smelling, you will die. Etymologically speaking, a breath is not neutral or bland—it's *cooked air;* we live in a constant simmering. There is a furnace in our cells, and when we breathe we pass the world through our bodies, brew it lightly, and turn it loose again, gently altered for having known us.

Thesis and Organization

1. Ideally, a first paragraph can do many jobs: introduce the topic, suggest or state the thesis, snag the reader's interest, set the tone of the essay. Rereading Ackerman's first paragraph, you can understand more fully how it functions in relation to the rest of the essay. Explain what you have discovered and give examples to support your ideas.
2. Does paragraph 2 have a topic sentence? If so, what is it? If not, what topic sentence would you supply?
3. Try out paragraph 3 as the introductory paragraph. Explain why it doesn't work well in that position.
4. To what extent is the last paragraph a satisfactory ending for the essay?
5. In your own words, without looking at the essay, state what you find to be its thesis. Then look at the essay. What sentence, if any, comes closest to your statement?

Technique and Style

1. Take a highlighter and mark all the active verbs you find in one paragraph. Choose one and explain how it is or is not effective.
2. Ackerman's essay alludes to both people and places: "a lake in the Poconos," "a moonlit beach in Florida," "a midwestern town," "Niagaras," "The Silk Road," Sherlock Holmes, and "The Hound of the Baskervilles." Explain how these allusions relate to Ackerman's sense of her audience.
3. Do you think the tone of Ackerman's essay is more objective than subjective or the other way around? Explain your answer by citing examples from the text.
4. When you write an essay that uses a central term, you risk ineffective repetition. Reread Ackerman's essay, keeping track of the number of times she uses the word *smell.* In what ways do you find the repetition effective or ineffective?
5. Poets rely on sound as well as sense to carry meaning, and Ackerman is well aware of the sound of her language. Look, for example, at the *s*

sounds in Ackerman's second sentence. Try this device in your own writing by taking one of your longer sentences and revising it in such a way that you emphasize its sound.

Suggestions For Writing

Journal

1. Try out Ackerman's idea that "Nothing is more memorable than a smell" by describing a particular smell you have experienced and its associations for you.
2. Think of a smell that would be familiar to almost everyone in the class, one that has neutral to pleasant associations, and describe it without naming it. You may want to try out your description on the class to see if anyone recognizes your subject.

Essay

With the word choice *conjure up* in Ackerman's second sentence, she implies that the sense of smell has an almost magical effect on memory. Assuming she is correct, think of a smell that triggered (or triggers) your memory of a place, person, or event. Once you have a topic, write down as many details as you can, then examine your list to find out what order would be best to present them in. Consider your readers' general attitude toward your subject; if it is neutral or hostile, try to counter it. Suggestions:

the indoor smell of cut flowers
the smell of leather, bread baking, or brakes burning
the smell of a parents' or relatives' aftershave or perfume
the smell of a particular hospital, school, or church

A Confederacy of Friends

Kristy Guarino

The title of the essay is an allusion to A Confederacy of Dunces, *a novel by John Kennedy Toole set in New Orleans. New Orleans is also where tourists flock to the French Quarter—also known as the "Vieux Carré" or old square, formed by streets named Decatur, Canal, Rampart, and Esplanade—wander around Jackson Square, and drink hurricanes at Pat O'Brien's bar. The Quarter is also the setting for Kristy Guarino's description of a well-known local character. As you might suspect from reading the essay, Kristy Guarino is a native New Orleanian who knows the French Quarter well. She is also a former "drop-in drop-out" student going for a record two-years straight enrollment at the University of New Orleans. She is currently a junior, as she puts it, "majoring in majoring."*

WHAT TO LOOK FOR   *You'll find that the essay reads as though the writer is talking to you, an effect achieved at the expense of a few rules of formal written English. The principle that allows a writer to break rules is one of appropriateness. A formal essay that described this person would be more of a case history than a portrait of a person. Be on the lookout for fragments, slang, and unusual punctuation.*

1   "Get off my sidewalk," she mutters, as someone passes her, slouched curbside against a stop sign on Bourbon and Dumaine. Her head hangs as though she hasn't the strength or need to lift it. Hidden beneath a dingy pile of polyester, she drags her fingertips across the leather of her face, which she shifts slowly, side-to-side, as her lips scrunch roundabout as if she's talking to someone. But no one is there.

2   She gets up, staggering. Then stands—and stands tall (though she barely measures five feet in height). Better move, . . . or she'll move you.

3   I should know. Pushed me clear off a bar stool once. Cursed me too. I was sitting in the Alibi Lounge on Iberville, drinking with some friends. Wasn't the usual food and beverage crowd; too early in the evening, I guess. Mostly college frats—spread out wall-to-wall, wearing tee-shirts advertising TKE's Carnival Cruise Night,

ATO's Beach Blanket Bonsai Bash (whatever that might be). A rowdy bunch; chanting fight songs between funnelling beers and shooting vodka slammers; slapping high-fives for any reason whatsoever; paying no mind to the hunched-over pile of polyester lurking in the back of the club. But they managed to get her riled up as well. While forcing her way to the bar, she stumbled over, jabbed me in the side with her elbow, and told me to get the hell away. I did. No problem. I didn't mind standing. Anyway, my friends got a laugh out of it, saying, "That's Ruthie for ya'."

4   They were right. That is Ruthie.

5   But no one in the French Quarter remembers when she first appeared, and yet no one can imagine the streets and bars of the Vieux Carré without her. Like a doctor on rounds, Ruthie, "The Duck Lady," routinely curses and knocks her way about—somehow capturing the hearts of many locals, making herself as much a landmark as Jackson Square and Pat O'Brien's.

6   Rumors make up Ruthie's past. Tales of wealth and eccentricity spread throughout the Quarter. How she comes from money; how her family owned prime real estate on Bourbon Street, right across from Lafitte's Blacksmith Shop. Supposedly, when her parents died and the property was sold, Ruthie inherited a fortune, and now she parades about the streets doing whatever she pleases.

7   And parade she does. All over. From Esplanade to Canal. From Decatur to Rampart. Aimlessly going to who-knows-where or why. These outings only fuel up rumors of mental illness, leading some people to believe she's sick and disoriented. Warren, a bartender at Lafitte's, remembers Ruthie having a "half-wit" brother, but says "It's anybody's guess. Even though everyone may know of Ruthie, no one person knows too much about her."

8   And some prefer not to. Like Warren. "I don't know if she's rich, mental, or what. And I could care less. To me, she's just a disgusting old drunkard."

9   Others dismiss the rumors entirely. One local guy doesn't even worry about it; he enjoys believing she has just "sprung out the concrete." Although Ruthie's past remains a mystery, everyone does know how she earned her trademark name.

10   For years, Ruthie would dress in a battered wedding gown and floppy hat and go roller skating along the streets of the Quarter with a duck trailing her. Locals joke that "wherever Ruthie went,

that duck was sure to go." And go it did—everywhere from mass at St. Louis Cathedral to the corner grocery. The clerk at Grandad's General Store remembers Ruthie coming in—especially when the duck would "squirt all over the place." Wasn't one particular duck, though. Seems Ruthie had a number of them over time; and often, when one died, she'd skate around with it cradled in her arms. People must have complained, because the police finally forced her to get rid of them. That didn't stop her. She still carries a duck—a stuffed one. But a duck no less.

11   Now, Ruthie, "The Duck Lady," celebrates celebrity status. *Gambit* and WGNO television featured her in articles and specials centering on New Orleans. Her image, captured on film, canvas, and postcards, represents the French Quarter.

12   Which is sometimes hard to understand—considering how much she likes her Budweiser. But, like a celebrity, Ruthie gets catered to, watched over, and even forgiven. Merchants and vendors sneak food out to her, bartenders and waiters hand over spare change. She rarely pays for a thing. Paul, manager of Lafitte's, believes that "if we lose Ruthie, we lose the Quarter. She's the cornerstone." And he watches out for her. When she's had too much to drink (which is most of the time), he'll get someone to walk her home. She lives only a few blocks from Lafitte's, right off Esplanade, on Dauphine. But he won't chance her safety. "Means too much to us. If anybody would try to hurt her, the whole Quarter would come out of the woodwork."

13   Except Warren. Unlike Paul, he won't let her in the bar. "No way." But if Paul is tending bar, he doesn't mind. He can handle her. "She was in here the other day, kicking some tourists. I just raised my voice, told her to sit her ass down and behave. She listens. I think I'm the only bartender here she hasn't slugged." The majority of locals, like Paul, put up with her. "No one wants to break her spirit," Paul says. "That's just Ruthie."

14   And he's right. That is Ruthie—at least sometimes.

15   I should know. Saw it with my own eyes. I was sitting in Port of Call, drinking with some friends. Was the usual local crowd, with a few tourists sipping on monsoons, paying no mind to the lady sitting at the bar. Why should they mind? Nothing strange about her. Dressed neatly in a black lace gown that draped to the ground, she was covered by a red, tapered peacoat with a shiny, red floppy hat. Pinned at the flap with a black carnation.

16   "It can't be her." I kept repeating. My friends got a laugh out of it, saying, "Well, it is Sunday."

17   I didn't buy it. *"Can't be her—her clothes match."* And she just sat, drinking her Budweiser, bothering no one.

18   I kept watching her. I was amazed and confused at the same time. Then, from the back of the bar, a loud voice started singing along with the jukebox: "I'm just a gigolo, and everywhere I go. . . ."

19   The lady at the bar just lowered her head as the voice grew louder and more off-key with every note being sung.

20   "Miss Ruthie," the voice hollered, as a man swayed over to the lady. Placing his arm around her, he asked, "What's the matter? You like my singin', don't you?"

21   Eagerly, I watched. It was Ruthie. I just knew she was gonna sock him in the jaw. But she didn't.

22   Instead, she looked at the bartender, flashing a grin so hard and wide her rosy cheeks almost slammed her eyes shut. That's when I saw her. For the first time, I was really seeing Ruthie; seeing the sparkle in her eyes; seeing her as many locals must—like a child. A kid at heart and at play. Both mischievous and innocent at the same time. That's Ruthie.

23   Before I left Port of Call, I sent her down a Budweiser. She didn't acknowledge me. I didn't expect her to, and I didn't care. I just wanted to join in on the confederacy of friends she has here in the Quarter.

Thesis and Organization

1. What information is supplied by the introduction, paragraphs 1–4?
2. What connects paragraphs 5–8? 9–14? 15–22?
3. Which details most effectively create the picture of Ruthie?
4. Summarize the framing device Guarino uses to begin and end her essay.
5. Like many essays that describe people, this one shows rather than tells. One example of that technique is Guarino's use of an implied thesis. State that thesis in your own words.

Technique and Style

1. What does the author's interaction with Ruthie lend to the essay?
2. Paragraphs 3, 7–10, 12, 13, and 17–20 use dialogue. How many different people are quoted? What reasons can you think of for using that many?

3. The pace and tone of the essay are affected by the intentional use of fragments. Choose one and convert it into a full sentence. What is gained or lost?

4. What reasons can you think of for delaying the information about Ruthie's nickname?

5. Guarino depends heavily on details of the local setting. How necessary do you find the references to street names, people, and places? In what ways do they add to or detract from the essay?

Suggestions for Writing

Journal

1. Is Ruthie someone you would like to meet? Why or why not? Looking over Guarino's essay again, use some of the details to support your ideas as you record them in your journal.

2. Many people have a favorite item of clothing, worn nearly to the point of disintegration but so revered that it is impossible to throw it out. If you have something that fits this description, use your journal to jot down what it looks like and why you are so attached to it. Later you may want to turn this entry into an essay.

Essay

1. Almost every neighborhood, family, school, or business has at least one "character." Think of one you know and write down what that person looks like as well as any distinctive dress, statements, and behavior. Think, too, of the setting the person is in and how it contrasts or serves as a backdrop. Also note how other people react to the person, and try to record a range of responses. When you write your draft, consider how conversational you want to be and whether or not dialogue would add to the essay.

2. If you prefer to write a descriptive essay about yourself, think of what a setting or object or choice of clothing implies about you. If you were to empty your pocketbook or wallet, for instance, you would probably turn up a number of objects, old and new, that relate to you in different ways. The same may well be true of your room, apartment, or house, or even your car. Select a setting or object, noting the details, and then use those details as the basis for an essay that reveals something about your character.

l Hoyo

Mario Suarez

When Mario Suarez returned from four years in the navy, he enrolled at the University of Arizona and found himself taking freshman English. The essay that follows was written for that class and so impressed his teacher, Ruth Keenan, that she not only encouraged him to take other writing courses but also to submit "El Hoyo" to The Arizona Quarterly, *where it was published. That was a long time ago (1947), but it started Suarez on a successful writing career; it is a rare anthology of Chicano literature that doesn't include at least one of Suarez's works.*

WHAT TO LOOK FOR *Like many writers, Suarez faces the problem of explaining the unfamiliar, but for Suarez the problem is compounded. Many of his readers do not know the meaning of* bar-rio, *nor are they familiar with Latino culture. Those who do know the terms may have negative associations with them. As you read his essay, note the techniques he uses to combat these problems. Also note how Suarez uses repetition effectively to lend emphasis to his description. Read Suarez's second paragraph out loud so you can hear the repetition more clearly.*

1   From the center of downtown Tucson the ground slopes gently away to Main Street, drops a few feet, and then rolls to the banks of the Santa Cruz River. Here lies the section of the city known as El Hoyo. Why it is called El Hoyo is not very clear. In no sense is it a hole as its name would imply; it is simply the river's immediate valley. Its inhabitants are chicanos who raise hell on Saturday night and listen to Padre Estanislao on Sunday morning. While the term chicano is the short way of saying Mexicano, it is not restricted to the paisanos who came from old Mexico with the territory or the last famine to work for the railroad, labor, sing, and go on relief. Chicano is the easy way of referring to everybody. Pablo Gutiérrez married the Chinese grocer's daughter and now runs a meat department; his sons are chicanos. So are the sons of Killer Jones who threw a fight in Harlem and fled to El Hoyo to marry Cristina Mendez. And so are all of them. However, it is doubtful that all these spiritual sons of Mexico live in El Hoyo because they love each other—many fight and bicker constantly. It is doubtful

they live in El Hoyo because of its scenic beauty—it is everything but beautiful. Its houses are simple affairs of unplastered adobe, wood, and abandoned car parts. Its narrow streets are mostly clearings which have, in time, acquired names. Except for some tall trees which nobody has ever cared to identify, nurse, or destroy, the main things known to grow in the general area are weeds, garbage piles, dark-eyed chavalos, and dogs. And it is doubtful that the chicanos live in El Hoyo because it is safe—many times the Santa Cruz has risen and inundated the area.

2   In other respects living in El Hoyo has its advantages. If one is born with weakness for acquiring bills, El Hoyo is where the collectors are less likely to find you. If one has acquired the habit of listening to Octavio Perea's Mexican Hour in the wee hours of the morning with the radio on at full blast, El Hoyo is where you are less likely to be reported to the authorities. Besides, Perea is very popular and sooner or later to everyone "Smoke in the Eyes" is dedicated between the pinto beans and white flour commercials. If one, for any reason whatever, comes on an extended period of hard times, where, if not in El Hoyo, are the neighbors more willing to offer solace? When Teofila Malacara's house burned to the ground with all her belongings and two children, a benevolent gentleman carried through the gesture that made tolerable her burden. He made a list of 500 names and solicited from each a dollar. At the end of a month he turned over to the tearful but grateful señora $100 in cold cash and then accompanied her on a short vacation. When the new manager of a local store decided that no more chicanas were to work behind the counters, it was the chicanos of El Hoyo who, on taking their individually small but collectively great buying power elsewhere, drove the manager out and the girls returned to their jobs. When the Mexican Army was en route to Baja California and the chicanos found out that the enlisted men ate only at infrequent intervals, it was El Hoyo's chicanos who crusaded across town with pots of beans and trays of tortillas to meet the train. When someone gets married, celebrating is not restricted to the immediate friends of the couple. Everybody is invited. Anything calls for a celebration and a celebration calls for anything. On Memorial Day there are no less than half a dozen good fights at the Riverside Dance Hall. On Mexican Independence Day more than one flag is sworn allegiance to amid cheers for the queen.

3   And El Hoyo is something more. It is this something more
which brought Felipe Suarez back from the wars after having
killed a score of Vietnamese with his body resembling a patch-
work quilt to marry Julia Armijo. It brought Joe Zepeda, a gunner,
. . . back to compose boleros. He has a metal plate for a skull. Perhaps El Hoyo is proof that those people exist, and perhaps exist
best, who have as yet failed to observe the more popular modes of
human conduct. Perhaps the humble appearance of El Hoyo justi-
fies the indifferent shrug of those made aware of its existence. Perhaps El Hoyo's simplicity motivates an occasional chicano to move
away from its narrow streets, babbling comadres and shrieking
children to deny the bloodwell from which he springs and to claim
the blood of a conquistador while his hair is straight and his face
beardless. Yet El Hoyo is not an outpost of a few families against
the world. It fights for no causes except those which soothe its immediate angers. It laughs and cries with the same amount of passion in times of plenty and of want.

4   Perhaps El Hoyo, its inhabitants, and its essence can best be explained by telling a bit about a dish called capirotada. Its origin is
uncertain. But, according to the time and the circumstance, it is
made of old, new or hard bread. It is softened with water and then
cooked with peanuts, raisins, onions, cheese, and panocha. It is
fired with sherry wine. Then it is served hot, cold, or just "on the
weather" as they say in El Hoyo. The Sermeños like it one way,
the Garcias another, and the Ortegas still another. While it might
differ greatly from one home to another, nevertheless it is still
capirotada. And so it is with El Hoyo's chicanos. While being divided from within and from without, like the capirotada, they remain chicanos.

Thesis and Organization

1. Examine the essay using the standard journalistic questions. Which paragraph describes *where* El Hoyo is? What paragraphs describe *who* lives
there? What paragraph or paragraphs describe *how* they live? *Why* they
live there?
2. All of the questions above lead to a larger one: *What* is El Hoyo? Given
the people and place, and how and why they live there, what statement
is the author making about El Hoyo?
3. The essay ends with an analogy, and toward the end of paragraph 4,
Suarez spells out some details of the analogy. What other characteristics

of capirotada correspond to those of chicanos? Where in the essay do you find evidence for your opinion?

4. How would you describe the movement in the essay? Does it move from the general to the particular? From the particular to the general? What reasons can you give for the author's choice of direction?
5. In one sentence, state Suarez's opinion of El Hoyo.

Technique and Style

1. The introductory paragraph achieves coherence and cohesion through the author's use of subtle unifying phrases. Trace Suarez's use of "it is doubtful." How often does the phrase occur? Rewrite the sentences to avoid using the phrase. What is lost? Gained?
2. What key words are repeated in paragraph 2? Why does he repeat them?
3. Paragraph 2 gives many examples of the advantages of living in El Hoyo. List the examples in the order in which they appear. The first two can be grouped together under the idea of El Hoyo as a sanctuary, a place where people aren't bothered. What other groupings does the list of examples suggest? What principle appears to have guided the ordering of the examples?
4. Why might the author have chosen not to use either first or second person? What is gained by using "one"?

Suggestions for Writing

Journal

1. Write a journal entry explaining why you would or would not like to live in El Hoyo. Use examples from the essay to flesh out your reasons.
2. Suarez compares the dish capirotada to El Hoyo, developing it as a metaphor. Think of a metaphor that would work for your neighborhood or for one of your classes. Write a paragraph or two developing your comparison and you will probably discover that using metaphor may also make you see the familiar in a new way.

Essay

If you live in an ethnic neighborhood, you can use the essay as a close model. If you do not, you can still use the essay as a general model by choosing a topic that combines people and place. Suggestions:

    family ritual at Christmas or Hanukkah
    family ritual at Thanksgiving
    dinner at a neighborhood restaurant
    busy time at the university student center

F rightened by Loss

J. Merrill-Foster

By combining the objective with the subjective, the particular with the general, and the past with the present, the author presents a compelling picture of old age. The essay was published in the New York Times *in 1988.*

WHAT TO LOOK FOR *When you use description in your essays, you may find yourself in the position of a narrator who stands outside of the scene. If you find that this position becomes tiresome and gives more of an impression of distance from your subject than you want, you might try two of the techniques Merrill-Foster uses— dialogue and metaphor. By quoting a person you are describing, you bring the reader into the scene directly, as Merrill-Foster does when she lists a string of statements made by the old woman she depicts. Note that the dialogue doesn't have to be a continuous chunk; a few pertinent, though not consecutive, sentences will do the job. Metaphor also changes the pace of an essay, slowing the reader slightly by presenting a vivid image; that vividness also brings the reader closer to the subject.*

1   Her walk is slow, hesitant, leaning slightly forward from the waist. Her hands, swollen and misshapen with arthritis, have traceries of blue veins across the back. They are never still.

2   She often interrupts to ask what we are talking about. The telephone seems to confuse her; she thinks the ringing is on the television. She calls us to report that she has lost her Christmas card list. It turns up on her desk, hidden under a pile of appeals. She is on every mailing list there is, and is constantly importuned to "Save the whales" and "Stop the Japanese slaughter of dolphins."

3   She is frightened and distressed by letters from retired military men. They write that unless she sends $35 by return mail, the Russians will land in Oregon and take over America. The arrival of the daily mail looms large in her day. Once, every few weeks, it contains a personal letter. The rest is appeals and ads. She reads every item.

4   Her checkbook is a constant puzzle of missing entries and double deposits of retirement checks. She goes out to do an errand and cannot find the place—a place she's frequented for years. She telephones to say the furnace door has exploded open; the kindly repair man arrives at 10 P.M. to check and assure her that all is well. She tells you about it, not because there is anything needing to be done. She tells you in order to make you understand that life is out of control—that there is a conspiracy of inanimate objects afoot.

5   Often, if you suggest this or that solution, she is annoyed. She wasn't asking for a solution. She was merely reporting disaster. She sits down to read and falls asleep.

6   America's life style prepares us well for our first day at school, for adolescence, for college, for matrimony, for parenthood, for middle age, for retirement. But it prepares us not at all for old age. Busy and active until her seventy-eighth year, the woman, now 85, is frightened by her own loss of power.

7   "Why am I so tired all the time?" she asks.

8   "I couldn't figure out how to turn on the dashboard lights."

9   "I look at the snow and wonder how I'll live through the winter."

10   "I think I must light the wood stove. I'm so cold."

11   I do not see the woman as she is today. I look at her familiar face and see her on a stage, floating up a flight of stairs in *Arsenic and Old Lace,* with that skilled power in her knees that made her seem to glide from one step to another. I hear her speak and remember her light but lovely contralto singing Katisha in *The Mikado.*

12   I watch her sleeping in her chair, her head on her chest, and remember her pacing up and down an English classroom, reading aloud from Beowulf, bringing to life the monster Grendel for a class of 16-year-olds. I remember late winter afternoons, fortified with hot cocoa, sitting on the floor at her feet, listening to "The Ballad of the White Horse," *Don Quixote* and *King Lear.*

13   I remember her as a young widow, coming home from school and pulling three children through the snow on a sled. I remember always the summer jobs when school was let out, selling life insurance or encyclopedias, or studying remedial reading at New York University. I remember her as a bride the second time, and the second time a widow. Hers was the home the family came to, a place of books, a big, old house where civility was spoken.

14   There is some rage in aging—a disbelief that one's life has rounded its last curve and this stretch of road leads to death. She has always been a woman of strong faith, and it seems that faith at last has failed her. She quotes Claudius in *Hamlet:*

15   "My words fly up, my thoughts remain below;
16   Words without thoughts never to heaven go."
17   Widowed, alone, children and grandchildren flung wide from California to New England, she fills her days with little things. Socializing fatigues her. She withdraws from the intense conversational jousting that used to delight her.

18   I watch the woman—my mother—walking carefully down the frozen, snow-filled driveway to the mail box. She is a photograph in black and white, which only loving memory tints with stippled life and color.

Thesis and Organization

1. Paragraph 1 describes the woman physically, and paragraphs 2–5 describe her psychologically, both leading up to the concluding sentence of paragraph 6. What details in paragraphs 1–5 relate to the idea of being "frightened by her own loss of power"?

2. Test the assertions in the first two sentences of paragraph 6. To what extent do they hold true in the experience of you and your family? Are the assertions valid?

3. Paragraphs 7–10 use quotations from the present to illustrate the generalization that ends paragraph 6 and to set up the shift to the past that takes place in paragraphs 11–13, while paragraphs 14–18 return to the present. Do you find the essay's chronology effective or ineffective? How so?

4. How would you characterize the author's feelings for the old woman? What evidence can you cite to support your ideas?

5. Where in the essay do you find the author generalizing on old age? What generalization is being made about the author's mother? About old age? Putting the two generalizations together, how would you express the thesis of the essay?

Technique and Style

1. The author alludes to a play and an operetta (paragraph 11) and to an epic, a poem, a novel, and a play (paragraph 12). What do these allusions imply about the author's mother? What do they contribute to her characterization—the person she was then and the person she is now?

2. In a standard dictionary, look up *pity* and *empathy*. Which does the author feel for the old woman? Which does the writer evoke in you? Cite examples to support your opinion.
3. Throughout the essay the author never refers to the old woman by name. What is the effect of using a pronoun instead? What effect is achieved by holding off identifying her as "my mother"?
4. Examine paragraph 13 for details. What do they imply about the author's mother? How do those characteristics compare with those you can deduce from paragraphs 7–10? What does this contrast achieve?
5. The essay concludes with a metaphor. Rephrase the metaphor in your own words and explain how that statement supports the thesis of the essay.

Suggestions for Writing

Journal

1. Merrill-Foster says "There is some rage in aging—a disbelief that one's life has rounded its last curve and this stretch of road leads to death." Does that statement hold up to what you have observed in your experience? If so, describe a person to whom it applies; if not, describe a person who refutes the idea.
2. Write a journal entry that describes someone performing an everyday repetitive action such as walking, reading, or eating. It's easiest to write such a description if you do it as you observe the person. That way you note each movement. You may want to use some of this description in the essay assignment that follows.

Essay

Think of someone you know who would make a good subject for a character sketch, a short essay in which you describe a person so that you report the qualities that make up the individual. Like Merrill-Foster, you may also want to generalize about the larger category that the person represents. Rely on quotation as well as description to create the overall impression you wish to make. That impression, implicit or explicit, is your thesis. For subjects to write about, think of someone who typifies a certain

   manner
   age
   occupation

eft Sink

Ellery Akers

Ellery Akers is a writer, naturalist, and poet who lives near San Francisco. Knocking on the Earth, *her first book of poems, was published in 1989 by* Wesleyan University Press. *As you read the essay, you'll discover that her prose reflects a number of characteristics of poetry—imagery, concise language, and an acute eye for detail. You'll also see that the line between description and narration is a fine one. The essay won the 1990 Sierra Club Award for nature writing and was published the same year in* Sierra. *While the essay is longer than most in this book, you'll find its length is deceptive. You'll read it quickly.*

WHAT TO LOOK FOR   *Writers who deal with familiar subjects face the challenge of making the familiar new or unusual, and to do that they rely on concrete detail. Ellery Akers knows her readers are familiar with bathrooms and frogs, but she goes on to individualize this particular bathroom and the frog she names Left Sink. Some writers might be content to state "The frog was small." Akers, however, takes the word* small *and gives it substance, "no bigger than a penny, and his round, salmon-colored toes stuck out like tiny soupspoons." Remember as you write that one person's idea of a general term, such as "small," may not be the same as another's, so it's best to use concrete details to show just what you mean.*

1   The first time I saw Left Sink, I was brushing my teeth and almost spit on him by mistake. I wasn't expecting to find a frog in a Park Service bathroom, but there he was, hopping out of the drain and squatting on the porcelain as casually as if he were sitting beside a pond.

2   He was a small green tree frog, no bigger than a penny, and his round, salmon-colored toes stuck out like tiny soupspoons. For a few minutes I stared into his gold eyes, each pupil floating in the middle like a dark seed.

3   I was so close I could see his throat pulse, but I was probably too close, for he looked at me fearfully and leaped onto the silver "C" of the cold-water faucet.

4   Then he must have thought better of it, for he jumped down again, and sat, hunched over, by the soap. He kept making ner-

vous little hops toward the safety of the drain, but my looming face was obviously in the way, so I ducked below the basin for a moment, and when I looked again he was descending into the hole, head first.

5 Feeling I'd disturbed his evening hunt, I decided to make amends. I grubbed around the floor for a dead moth, found one (though it was a little dried up), and offered it to the hole. The wing slanted into the drain, but nothing happened. I thought perhaps he'd hopped back down into the pipe. Trying to find something a little more appealing, I picked around the window sills until I discovered a really decent-looking moth, pushed it up to the drain, and waited. After a few minutes, I got discouraged and walked away. When I turned back to sneak one last look, I found both moths had vanished.

6 The next day was so hot I forgot Left Sink completely. It is always hot in the California chaparral in September, especially in the Gabilan Mountains. I spent the afternoon in the shade, lying on the cool pebbles of a dry wash and looking over my field notes. I had been camping for weeks, studying birds, and by now I had gotten used to the feeling of expectation in the landscape.

7 Everything seemed to be waiting for rain. The streambeds were dry, the fields were dry, and when the buckeye leaves hissed in the wind they sounded like rattlesnakes. Ravens flew overhead, croaking, their wings flapping loudly in the air, and the rocks baked. Once in a while a few thirsty finches fluttered up to a seep in a cliff and sipped from a damp clump of algae.

8 I leaned against the cool flank of a boulder and fanned myself with my hat. From far away I could hear the staccato drill of a Nuttall's woodpecker.

9 All the animals had some way of coping with the heat. The wrentits could last for several weeks without drinking. The deer found beds of shade and waited patiently until evening. Even the trees adapted. Though I couldn't see it, I knew that somewhere beneath my boots, 100 feet down, the root of a digger pine was twisting along a crevice in the bedrock, reaching far below the surface to tap into the permanent water.

10 And the frogs—the normal ones—were sleeping away the summer and fall, huddled in some moist spot in the ground in a kind of hot-weather hibernation.

11   That night, when I went back to the bathroom, I discovered Left
      Sink had a neighbor. Even before I turned on the water in the
      right-hand basin, I noticed a second frog, and when I stepped
      back to look at both of them in their respective sinks, I started to
      laugh: They reminded me of a couple of sober, philosophical old
      monks peering out of their cells.

12   Overhead was a third frog, puffy and well-fed, squatting on top
      of the fluorescent lights, surrounded by tattered moths. Light Bud-
      dha, I would call him.

13   In the world of the bathroom the light shelf was a delicatessen
      of the highest order. Light Buddha sat there night after glorious
      night, lazily snapping up moths as they fluttered past. The other
      two frogs seemed content to stake out the sinks, which weren't
      quite as dependable a food source, though they weren't bad. Al-
      most every night I found a damp moth thrashing around in one of
      the basins, one little flopping death after another, leaving a trail of
      scales behind.

14   Right Sink was extremely shy, and spent most of his time
      crouched far back in the pipe. Usually I saw his gold eyes shining in
      the darkness, but that was all. Left Sink was more of an adventurer,
      and explored the whole bathroom, darting behind the mirror, splat-
      ting onto the porcelain, hopping on the window sills, leaping on the
      toilet, and climbing the slippery painted walls toe pad by toe pad.

15   From time to time I was tempted to pick him up as he was
      climbing. But I didn't think it would be fair; I knew this geometri-
      cal universe, and he didn't. Besides, there was no place for him to
      hide on those smooth, painted bricks, so I let him be.

16   I was amazed at how few people noticed Left Sink, even when
      he was sitting on top of the faucet. Kids saw him right away,
      though, and I worried sometimes that one night a little girl would
      pop him into a jar and take him home to some confining terrarium.

17   Also, he stood out. Even though tree frogs can change color in
      ten minutes, there was nothing in Left Sink's repertoire that could
      possibly match white paint; the best he could do was a sickly pink.

18   I could always tell if he had just emerged from the drain be-
      cause he would still be a murky gray-green. As the evening wore
      on he got paler and paler. Once I couldn't find him for half an
      hour. Finally I caught sight of him over my head. Plopped on a
      narrow ledge, he looked like a pale pebble in all that metal and
      paint. I climbed onto the toilet for a better look. To my horror he

began hopping along the ledge, which was no wider than half an inch. It was a ten-foot fall to the floor—for a frog that small, an abyss. He bounded past me, his grainy throat quivering.

19 He headed toward a swarm of moths and flies that circled the fluorescent lights. A fly drifted down from the glare; Left Sink, his pink mouth flashing, snapped it up.

20 I was never quite sure just how skittish he really was. Sometimes he tolerated my watching him, sometimes he didn't. I got in the habit of sidling up to the plumbing, bent over so as not to be seen, and I must have looked pretty peculiar. One night a woman came into the bathroom and caught me hunched over like Quasimodo, staring intently at the drains, my hands full of dead moths.

21 "Left Sink! Right Sink!" I was saying. "Got a little treat for you guys!"

22 The woman bolted out the door.

23 For the next few weeks I checked on the frogs every morning and evening. Sometimes when I saw Left Sink skidding down a length of plastic, unable to hold on in spite of his adhesive toe pads, I worried. I couldn't help thinking there was something unnatural about a frog in a bathroom.

24 Of course, I knew there were a few oddballs that *had* managed to live with us in our artificial world, but they were mostly insects. One year in school I had learned about the larvae of petroleum flies: They lived in the gunk of oil fields, so numerous at times that, according to my textbook, they imparted "a shimmering effect to the surface of the oil." Their world was oil; if you deprived them of it, took them out and cleaned them off, they'd curl up and die in less than a day.

25 In that same class I'd learned that furniture beetles live in our table legs, and occasionally, in wooden spoons; drugstore beetles float happily in bottles of belladonna, mating, pupating, dying. We have cheese mites in our cheese, and flour mites in our flour.

26 As far as I knew no one had ever done any research on frogs and plumbing. Luckily, I always carried a trunkful of books and field guides in my car, and one night I flipped through every book I had to see if I could find any instances where humans and animals—wild ones—had actually gotten along. Arthur Cleveland Bent said that wrens nested in old clothes in barns, and swallows on moving trains. Edwin Way Teale said he had once read about a pigeon using rubber bands and paper clips in her nest on a window ledge off Times Square. One year, he wrote, a thrush spent

the entire winter in a florist's shop on Madison Avenue, flitted about between the iced gladiolas and roses, and flew away in spring.

27 But no one mentioned anything about frogs.

28 Actually, considering the drought, Left Sink had a pretty good set-up. It was already October and still no rain. Once in a while a few drops would plop into the dirt and gravel, and I would catch a whiff of wet dust, soaked cheat grass, and buckwheat. But that was all.

29 All the other frogs were holed up in the dirt, huddled in a moist crack or an abandoned gopher hole, waiting for the first rains of winter to wake them up. There were probably a few hiding in the field next to Left Sink's bathroom, their eyelids closed, their toes pulled under them to conserve moisture, unmoving, barely breathing, their heartbeats almost completely stilled. If I dug them up they would look like small stones.

30 One night just before I was about to leave, I had a nightmare. It was a dream I had had many times, a dream of a city so polluted the air rose in black plumes above the granite and cement. I was at the entrance of a tunnel. Inside I could hear a whoosh of air: Millions of butterflies were flashing in the dark, thousands of ducks, eagles, sparrows, their wings making a vast rustling as they flew off and vanished.

31 I heard a low shuffling. After a while I realized it was the sound of feet: the slow trudge of bears, the pad of badgers, the pattering of foxes, the rasp of a hundred million beetles, rabbits, ants, mice. I looked around, panicked, to see if any animals were left. There were still cockroaches scuttling over the window sills. There were pigeons, flies, starlings. I named them over and over in a kind of chant: the adaptable, the drab, the ones who could live with us, who had always lived with us.

32 A fox coughed close to my camp in the middle of the nightmare and woke me up. I unzipped the tent and looked out at the stars: Rigel, Algol, clear, cold, and changeless. A golden-crowned sparrow chirped from a nearby branch, then sputtered off into silence. For a while I tried to stay awake, but soon drifted off.

33 The next morning huge bluish clouds rolled across the sky. A couple of ravens sailed past the cliff in front of me. One of them jackknifed its wings, plummeted straight down, and then, at the last minute, unfolded them and flapped away. It was still early, but when I reached the bathroom it had already been cleaned. It reeked of ammonia, and a mop and bucket leaned against the door.

34   I rinsed off my face, brushed my hair, and looked sleepily into the drains. As usual, Right Sink was huddled far back into the dark pipe; he retreated still further when I bent over.

35   Left Sink, however, was gone. I wondered if he had slipped behind the mirror, or had come up in the world and was squatting above with Light Buddha. The shelf was empty. I looked on the window sill—not there either.

36   It was not until I opened the door to the toilet that I found him. There, in the center of the ammonia-filled bowl, his green bloated body turning gray, was Left Sink, splayed out in the milky liquid, dead. Floating in front of him was a dead damselfly. I suppose he must have jumped in after his prey, convinced he was at the edge of a strange-looking pond, his toe pads gripping the cold, perfectly smooth surface of the porcelain.

37   His skin looked curdled, and it occurred to me he might have been there all morning waiting to die. Then I remembered that frogs breathe through their skin; it must have been a hard, stinging death, but a quick one.

38   I flushed him down, wishing I could think of something to say as he made his way through the pipes and rolled out to the septic tank, some acknowledgment of the link between my kind and his, but I couldn't think of anything except that I would miss him, which was true.

39   When I opened the door, a couple of nervous towhees blundered into the bushes. It was beginning to rain.

Thesis and Organization

1. The story of Left Sink unfolds slowly. Which paragraphs provide the introduction? What reasons can you give for your choice?
2. An essay of this length tends to group paragraphs around a topic sentence or main idea rather than have a topic sentence for each paragraph. What groupings can you identify? What ideas tie those paragraphs together?
3. Paragraphs 30 and 31 stand out because they strike a very different note from the rest of the essay. What function do they serve?
4. Akers says "there was something unnatural about a frog in a bathroom" (paragraph 23). What does she imply in that paragraph and elsewhere about the relationship between humans and nature?
5. Many essays have an explicit thesis, one that you can spot in a complete sentence. Others, however, have an implied thesis, one that the writer

suggests and the reader must deduce. That is the case with Akers' essay. What do you find to be its thesis?

Technique and Style

1. What does Akers think and feel about Left Sink? What details can you find to support your opinion?
2. What details can you find that lead to the conclusion that Akers is a naturalist?
3. Unlike many more formal essays, Akers uses lots of short paragraphs. Look up types of paragraphs in your handbook. What justification can you find for short paragraphs?
4. Akers' choice of verbs helps create the fast pace of the essay and its readability. Find a sentence that uses unusual verbs and rewrite it, substituting other verbs. What is gained? lost?
5. At various places in the essay, Akers refers to rain or the lack of it. What does that contribute to the essay?

Suggestions for Writing

Journal

1. The tone of an essay can be tricky, particularly if it appeals to emotion. To pinpoint Akers' tone, explain how you feel about the frog at the start of the essay, in the middle, and at the end.
2. Take a moment to jot down all the words you associate with the word *frog*. Looking at your list, mark the associations according to whether they are positive, negative, or neutral. Then make another list of the adjectives you think Akers would use for Left Sink. What differences do you find between your list and Akers'?

Essay

Day-to-day life is apt to be full of contrasts, though not usually so striking as a frog in a bathroom. See how many contrasts you can spot in the course of a day when you're looking for them. Jot down what you see and then choose from your notes to work the contrast into a descriptive essay. Like Akers' essay, yours should have a thesis, either implied or explicit. Suggestions:

at a beach, look for a fully dressed person
in a library, look for someone who is nervous or loud
at a film, look for someone who has brought a baby
in a cafeteria, look for someone who is studying

Narration

Whether prompted by the child's "Tell me a story" or the adult's "What happened?" **narration** supplies much of our entertainment and information. But anyone who has asked "What happened?" only to be overwhelmed with every detail knows that telling everything can blunt the point and bore the listener. Effective narration takes more than telling a story; it calls for compressing and reshaping experience so that the listener or reader relives it with you and is left with a particular point. Shaping narrative draws on some of the same skills used in description: keen observation, careful selection of details, and coherent sequencing. But with a narrative you must go a step further: you must present a conflict and its resolution. A story with no point is indeed pointless; one with no conflict is no kind of story at all.

Often the narrative and the subject are the same: if you are writing about what happened to you when lightning struck your house, what happened is the subject of your narrative. Frequently, however, a writer chooses narrative to introduce or to conclude an essay or perhaps to do both, thus building a narrative framework. Or perhaps you would opt for narrative to emphasize a particular point. An essay that explains the dangers of toxic waste may be made more effective if it starts with a brief narrative of what happens at a place where pollution threatens the area and its residents; an essay on Los Angeles and its smog, for example, might begin with the story of an asthma attack. A paper on the same subject that argues for stricter federal and state controls may end by predicting what might happen without tougher regulation. The essays in this chapter, however, rely on narration for their primary structure. All present conflicts, build to a point, and spring from personal experience—from the something that happened.

AUDIENCE AND PURPOSE   No one tells a story for the sake of telling a story, at least no one who wants to be listened to. Most of us will use a narrative to explain something, or to argue a point, or perhaps to entertain. If you think of a journal, the concepts of narration, audience, and purpose may become clearer. If you've ever kept a journal, then you realize that even though *you* are the audience, much of what you write may not make much sense later. It does, of course, right after you finish the journal entry, but two months or two years down the line, you can no longer supply the details from your memory. "Had a terrible argument," you might write, but unless you explain what the argument was about, you may be mystified when you reread that entry. And had you told the whole story behind the quarrel, you might have found that you could muster even more ammunition to support your side than you did in the heat of battle. In that case, you would not only have written about an argument, you would also have written one.

Much of what people write in journals, however, has explanation and entertainment as the goals. Writing in a journal helps many of us think through problems or events. Essentially, we are reliving the incident or situation so that we may examine and comprehend it more clearly: we retell our stories to understand them. A seemingly simple question—"Why did I feel so _____?"—calls for a narrative that provides the context. Often, however, we record an event simply because it gave us pleasure, pleasure that we want to be able to relive, once as it is written and again and again as you reread it.

The need for details increases as the distance between the reader and the subject grows. Yet there are always general experiences held in common. Say, for example, you are writing an essay based on something that happened to you in high school. And say you went to a small, all-male Catholic high school in Chicago. You might well wonder how you can make your narrative speak to a general readership, people who attended public, private, or religious schools (some single sex but most coed), schools large and small, rural and urban. Big differences, yes, but when you start thinking about details, you may find yourself turning to description to tap into shared experience—the blurred hum and jangle of students gathered together before a bell rings, the stale, dusty smell of chalk, the squeal of rubber-soled shoes on a waxed floor. Emotion also speaks across differences. Anyone who has ever been to school knows the panic of being called on by a teacher when you don't even know the question, much less the answer. Moments of praise are equally memorable, whether it be for a point scored on a test or on a basketball court. Joy, despair, fear, elation, anguish, frustration, boredom, laughter, embarrassment—all these and an almost infinite number of other emotions are interwoven in narratives, no matter what the topic, making the topic more interesting because the reader has experienced the same feeling.

WHO, WHAT, WHERE, WHEN, HOW, WHY   These are the standard questions used in journalism, and they are important in narrative essays as well. *What happened?* That's the essential question for narrative, and you'll probably find that the greater part of your essay supplies the answer. *How* and *why* will probably figure in as well, and *who* is obviously essential. But it's easy to neglect *where* and *when*.

If you think of both *where* and *when* as the **setting,** as ways to set the scene, you can remember them more easily and perhaps put them to good use. An essay that relates the tale of a job interview that began as a disaster and ended as a success, for example, might begin by describing the writer as a night person, barely human before 11 a.m. The time of the interview? Nine o'clock. Sharp. The office is impersonal to the point of being cell-like, and the interviewer is so buttoned into his three-piece suit that it looks like armor. Add to those descriptions so that the reader gets the impression that the interview itself will make the Spanish Inquisition look like Woodstock, and the writer will have set the tone for the essay as well as built up the readers' interest in what will happen next, the meat of the essay.

CONFLICT   Narratives are structured around a **conflict**. In its simplest form, conflict is *x* versus *y*, Superman versus the Penguin, the Roadrunner versus Wily Coyote. But rarely does conflict exist in such a clear-cut way. Put real people in place of any of those terms, and you begin to understand that what seemed so simple is not; the defense versus the prosecution, a Republican candidate versus a Democrat—these conflicts are complex. The issues become even more complex when you substitute ideas, such as reality versus illusion, a distinction that even a postcard can blur (how many of us have been disappointed when a scene didn't live up to its photograph?). Even distinguishing good from evil isn't always clear, as the debates over capital punishment and abortion constantly remind us. When a writer explores the complexity involved in a conflict, the essay gains depth and substance, making the reader think. That exploration can be direct, such as naming the opposing forces, or indirect, implying them.

The conflict that occurs in narrative essays is of two kinds and many layers. If, for instance, you were to write about leaving home for the first time—whether you were headed off to college, to the army, or just off—your initial conflict might have been **internal**: Should you go or should you stay? But it might have been **external** as well—what your parents wanted you to do versus what *you* wanted to do. And the conflict was probably also one of ideas—of freedom versus constraints, independence versus dependence.

POINT OF VIEW   A not-so-obvious question about any narrative you're about to write is "Who tells it?" This question pinpoints the **point of view,** the perspective from which the narrative is related. Probably the first pronoun that comes to mind is *I*, first-person singular, and that's a good choice if you want your readers to identify with you and your angle on the narrative you're relating. When a reader sees first person, an automatic psychological identification takes place, one that allows the reader to look through the writer's eyes. That sort of identification is strongest if you, as narrator, are part of the action. Obviously, there's a huge difference between "I was there" and "I heard about it."

At some point in some classroom, you have probably been warned off *I*. There are at least three reasons: it's easy to overuse the pronoun; it can modify your purpose in a way you hadn't intended; and it can lead to an overly informal tone. If you were to take a look at your first draft for an essay you wrote using *I*, odds are you used it too frequently. The result is apt to be short, choppy sentences that are similar in structure—subject (*I*) followed by a verb and its complement (the word or words that complete the sense of the verb). That's fine for a first draft, and you can revise your way out of the problem. You *need* to revise because too many *I*'s can shift the aim of your essay away from exposition or argument to self-expression; what becomes important is you, not your subject. Your tone may also change, becoming more informal than the assignment calls for, which is why you don't see many research papers that use first person.

Choosing to relate the narrative from the position of *he* or *she* (rarely *they*) puts more distance between the subject and the reader. Think of the difference between "I fell out of the window" and "He fell out of the window." With the latter, the reader's sympathies are at one remove. That's not the case with the second person, *you*. *You* is direct and that's what makes it a somewhat slippery choice. If you're going to use a second-person point of view, make sure the reader understands exactly who is meant by *you*. Many a teacher has been stopped short when reading an essay that has a sentence such as "When you graduate, you'll start looking for a job that can turn into a career"; if that sentence occurred in an essay on surviving an important job interview, its author had too narrow an audience in mind, one composed only of classmates and ignoring everyone else interested in the topic—including the teacher. One way around that problem is to specify the audience in your paper. "All of us who are now in college worry about jobs" tells the reader just who the audience is, and the teacher then reads the essay from the perspective of a college student.

THESIS AND ORGANIZATION Narratives often begin with the setting, which is the context for the conflict, then establish the nature of the conflict and move toward its resolution. Setting, conflict, and resolution all reinforce the essay's thesis, one that can be explicit or implicit. If the thesis is explicit, it's apt to occur in the introduction; sometimes, however, the writer will reserve it for the conclusion. That kind of placement puts an extra burden on the writer, in that everything in the essay must build to the conclusion. If the organization isn't tight, the reader wonders where the story is going; with a delayed thesis, the reader needs to have the feeling that the story is going somewhere, even though the final destination isn't apparent till the very end.

With narrative essays, as with short stories, the thesis is often implied and the reader must deduce it. If you opt for an implied thesis, make sure that the reader can easily identify your subject and then, without too much effort, move on to infer your thesis. The question that reader needs to ask is "What is the writer saying about the subject?" The answer, phrased as a complete sentence, is the thesis.

One way to control what the reader infers is to work with the narrative's chronology. The sequence of events can be shaped to emphasize different elements. It may help to list the most important incidents in the narrative on a scrap of paper; then you can review them to check that each one is essential and to figure out the best order in which to present them. Writers often disrupt exact chronology, opting for dramatic placement over actual time sequence. The **flashback** is a technique that allows the writer to drop from the present into the past and bring in an event that occurred prior to the narrative's action. You may be most familiar with this device from seeing it in films, the moment when the camera fades out on a scene and then fades into a past event.

You can also reinforce your thesis, implicit or explicit, by underscoring the relationship between what happens and where it happens. If the two are incongruous, for example, then the resulting irony will probably emphasize your main point. A narrative of the job interview that began badly but ended well, for example, may use the turn from bad to good to imply that "all's well that ends well."

USEFUL TERMS

Conflict   An element essential to narrative. Conflict involves pitting one force, a force that may be represented by a person or a physical object or abstract concept, against another.

External conflict   Conflict that is outside of a person in the narrative though it may involve that person, as in St. George versus the Dragon.

Internal conflict   Conflict that takes place within a person, as in "Should I or should I not."

Flashback   A break in the narrative that takes the reader to a scene or event that occurred earlier.

Narration   Narration tells a story, emphasizing what happened.

Point of view   In essays, point of view usually refers to the writer's use of personal pronouns. These pronouns control the perspective flow from which the work if written. For example, if the writer uses *I* or *we* (first-person pronouns), the essay will have a somewhat subjective tone because the reader will tend to identify with the writer. If the writer depends primarily on *he, she, it,* or *they* (third-person pronouns), the essay will have a somewhat objective tone because the reader will be distanced from the writer. Opting for *you* (second person) can be a bit tricky in that *you* can mean you the reader, quite particular, or you a member of a larger group, fairly general. In both cases, *you* brings the reader into the text.

Setting   The *where* and *when* in the narrative, its physical context.

▓ **POINTERS FOR USING NARRATION**

Exploring the Topic

1. **What point do you want to make?** What is the subject of your narrative? What assertion do you want your narrative to make about the subject? Is your primary purpose to inform, to persuade, or to entertain?
2. **What happened?** What are the events involved in the narrative? When does the action start? stop? Which events are crucial?
3. **Why and how did it happen?** What caused the events? How did it cause them?
4. **Who or what was involved?** What does the reader need to know about the characters? What do the characters look like? talk like? How do they think? How do others respond to them?
5. **What is the setting for your story?** What does the reader need to know about the setting? What features are particularly noteworthy? How can they best be described?
6. **When did the story occur?** What tense will be most effective in relating the narrative?
7. **What was the sequence of events?** What happened when? Within that chronology, what is most important: time, place, attitude?
8. **What conflicts were involved?** What levels of conflict exist? Is there any internal conflict?
9. **What is the relationship between the narrator and the action?** Is the narrator a participant or an observer? What is the attitude of the narrator toward the story? What feelings should the narrator evoke from the reader? What should be the attitude of the reader toward the narrative? What can be gained by using first person? second person? Third person?

Drafting the Paper

1. **Know your reader.** Try to second-guess your reader's initial attitude toward your narrative so that if it is not what you want it to be, you can choose your details to elicit the desired reaction. A reader can be easily bored, so keep your details to the point and your action moving. Play on similar experiences your reader may have had or on information you can assume is widely known.
2. **Know your purpose.** If you are writing to inform, make sure you provide enough information to carry your point. If you are writing to persuade, work on how you present yourself and your thesis so that the reader will be favorably inclined to adopt your viewpoint. If you are

writing to entertain, keep your tone in mind. A humorous piece, for in-stance, can and probably will vary from chuckle to guffaw to belly laugh. Make sure you're getting the right kind of laugh in the right place.

3. **Establish the setting and time of the action.** Use descriptive details to make the setting vivid and concrete. Keep in mind the reaction you want to get from your reader, and choose your details accordingly. If, for in-stance, you are writing a narrative that depicts your first experience with fear, describe the setting in such a way that you prepare the reader for that emotion. If the time the story took place is important, bring it out early.

4. **Set out the characters.** When you introduce a character, immediately identify the person with a short phrase such as "Anne, my sister." If a character doesn't enter the narrative until midpoint or so, make sure the reader is prepared for the entrance so that the person doesn't appear to be merely plopped in. If characterization is important to the narrative, use a variety of techniques to portray the character, but make sure what-ever you use is consistent with the impression you want to create. You can depict a person directly—through appearance, dialogue and ac-tions—as well as indirectly—through what others say and think and how they act toward the person.

5. **Clarify the action.** Narration is set within strict time limits. Make sure the time frame of your story is set out clearly. Within that time limit, much more action occurred than you will want to use in your narrative. Pick only the high points so that every action directly supports your the-sis. Feel free to tinker with the action, sacrificing a bit of reality for the sake of your point.

6. **Sharpen the plot.** Conflict is essential to narration, so be sure your lines of conflict are clearly drawn. Keeping conflict in mind, review the action you have decided to include so that the plot and action support each other.

7. **Determine the principle behind the sequence of events.** Given the action and plot you have worked out, determine what principle should guide the reader through the events. Perhaps time is the element you want to stress, perhaps place, perhaps gradual change. No matter what you choose, make sure that the sequence has dramatic tension so that it builds to the point you want to make.

8. **Choose an appropriate point of view.** Your choice of grammatical point of view will depend on what attitude you wish to take toward your narrative and your audience. If you can make your point more effectively by distancing yourself from the story, you will want to use *he, she,* or *they.* On the other hand, if you can make your point most effectively by being in the story, use first person and then decide whether you want to be *I* the narrator only or *I* the narrator who is also directly involved in the story.

9. **Make a point.** The action of the narrative should lead to a conclusion, an implicit or explicit point that serves as the thesis of the piece. If explicit, the thesis can appear in a single sentence or it can be inferred from several sentences, either in the introduction or conclusion of the essay. Ask yourself if everything in the narrative ties into the thesis.

The Night of Oranges

Flavius Stan

Flavius Stan was seventeen years old when this piece was published on Christmas Eve day, 1995, in the New York Times. *At the time, he was an exchange student at the Fieldston School in the Bronx, one of New York City's five boroughs. The time and place he writes about, however, is Christmas Eve in the city of Timisoara in the Romania of 1989, when the country was emerging from Communist rule. It had been an incredible December. On December 16, government forces opened fire on antigovernment demonstrators in Timisoara, killing hundreds. The President, Nicolae Ceausescu, immediately declared a state of emergency, but that did not stop antigovernment protests in other cities. Finally, on December 22, army units also rebelled, the President was overthrown, and civil war raged. The new government quickly won out, and Ceausescu was tried and found guilty of genocide. He was executed on December 25.*

WHAT TO LOOK FOR   *Few of us reading this essay have had firsthand experience of a revolution, nor have many of us lived under Communism or a dictatorship, much less a government whose leader was not only overthrown, but also executed. But all of us know oranges. What is familiar to us was strange to Stan, and what is strange to us was his everyday world. The resulting gap between Stan's society and ours is huge, yet in this essay he is able to bring his readers into the cold, postrevolution world of a city in Romania and make us see our familiar orange in a new way. Read the essay once for pleasure and then read it again, looking for the ways in which he makes the unfamiliar familiar and vice versa.*

1   It is Christmas Eve in 1989 in Timisoara and the ice is still dirty from the boots of the Romanian revolution. The dictator Nicolae Ceausescu had been deposed a few days before, and on Christmas Day he would be executed by firing squad. I am in the center of the city with my friends, empty now of the crowds that prayed outside the cathedral during the worst of the fighting. My friends and I still hear shots here and there. Our cold hands are gray like the sky above us, and we want to see a movie.

2   There is a rumor that there will be oranges for sale tonight. Hundreds of people are already waiting in line. We were used to

such lines under the former Communist Government—lines for bread, lines for meat, lines for everything. Families would wait much of the day for rationed items. As children, we would take turns for an hour or more, holding our family's place in line.

3   But this line is different. There are children in Romania who don't know what an orange looks like. It is a special treat. Having the chance to eat a single orange will keep a child happy for a week. It will also make him a hero in the eyes of his friends. For the first time, someone is selling oranges by the kilo.

4   Suddenly I want to do something important: I want to give my brother a big surprise. He is only 8 years old, and I want him to celebrate Christmas with lots of oranges at the table. I also want my parents to be proud of me.

5   So I call home and tell my parents that I'm going to be late. I forget about going to the movie, leave my friends and join the line.

6   People aren't silent, upset, frustrated, as they were before the revolution; they are talking to one another about life, politics and the new sitiuation in the country.

7   The oranges are sold out of the back doorway of a food shop. The clerk has gone from anonymity to unexpected importance. As he handles the oranges, he acts like a movie star in front of his fans.

8   He moves his arms in an exaggerated manner as he tells the other workers where to go and what to do. All I can do is stare at the stack of cardboard boxes, piled higher than me. I have never seen so many oranges in my life.

9   Finally, it is my turn. It is 8 o'clock, and I have been waiting for six hours. It doesn't seem like a long time because my mind has been flying from the oranges in front of me to my brother and then back to the oranges. I hand over the money I was going to spend on the movie and watch each orange being thrown into my bag. I try to count them, but I lose their number.

10   I am drunk with the idea of oranges. I put the bag inside my coat as if I want to absorb their warmth. They aren't heavy at all, and I feel that is going to be the best Christmas of my life. I begin thinking of how I am going to present my gift.

11   I get home and my father opens the door. He is amazed when he sees the oranges, and we decide to hide them until dinner. At dessert that night, I gave my brother the present. Everyone is silent. They can't believe it.

12   My brother doesn't touch them. He is afraid even to look at them. Maybe they aren't real. Maybe they are an illusion, like

everything else these days. We have to tell him he can eat them
before he has the courage to touch one of the oranges.

13   I stare at my brother eating the oranges. They are my oranges.
My parents are proud of me.

Thesis and Organization

1. Paragraphs 1–3 introduce the essay. Explain how they do or do not fit the journalistic questions establishing *who, what, where, why, when, how.*
2. The central part of the essay takes the reader from the time Stan decides to buy the oranges to his presenting them to his brother. What is the effect of presenting the narrative chronologically?
3. The last paragraph functions as the essay's one-paragraph conclusion, a conclusion presented in three short sentences. Explain whether you find the ending effective.
4. On the surface, Stan's essay has a simple thesis—that finding the rare and perfect gift for his brother fills him with pride, pride also reflected by his family. If you dig a bit, however, you may also discover other less obvious theses. What, for instance, might Stan be implying about Christmas? About Romania's future?
5. How would you characterize the conflict or conflicts in this essay?

Technique and Style

1. Although the essay was written in 1995, it is set at an earlier time, 1989. Many writers would therefore opt for the past tense, but Stan relates his narrative in the present. What does he gain by this choice?
2. Trace the number of contrasts Stan has in his essay. What do you discover? How do they relate to the thesis?
3. Paragraphs 7 and 8 describe the clerk in charge of selling the oranges in some detail. What does this description add to the essay?
4. Why is it important that the money Stan spends on the oranges is the money he was going to spend on the movies?
5. Reread the first paragraph, one that sets not only the scene, but also the atmosphere, the emotional impression arising from the scene. In your own words, describe that atmosphere.

Suggestions for Writing

Journal

1. Choose a common object and describe it as though you were seeing it for the first time.
2. In a sense, Stan's essay is written from the perspective of an eleven-year-old, the age he was at the time of the narrative. Leaf through your journal

to find a short narrative and then try rewriting it from the perspective of a much younger person.

Essay

Sift through your memory to find several times when you felt proud. Choose one to turn into a narrative essay. Perhaps, like Stan, you may want to retell the event in the present tense, placing yourself in the position of reliving it. If you do, check your draft to see if you have an implied thesis that is larger than the apparent one, for you want your essay to have some depth to it. For ideas of what might have made you feel proud, consider something you

    did

    didn't do

    saw

    owned

    said

T he Pie

Gary Soto

Gary Soto grew up in the San Joaquin Valley, and as he describes it, "We had our own culture which was more like the culture of poverty." Thinking he couldn't get into the University of California system, he applied to California State University, Fresno, where he soon changed his major from geography to English after being particularly struck by a poem by Edward Field, "Unwanted," that depicted the alienation Soto himself felt. Since then, he has earned an MFA at the University of California, Irvine, and taught at a number of universities, including Berkeley. Now, he devotes himself full-time to writing. The results are apparent in Books in Print, *where you will find that Soto has a very long list indeed. In 1996 alone, three of his books were published, all children's fiction. Soto is also well known for his poetry, as numerous awards attest. The essay that follows was first published in his collection* A Summer Life *(1990). Though the essay is hardly "poetic" in the stereotypical sense, you'll find he uses a number of techniques that also characterize his poetry: precise diction, strong verbs, and imagery that appeals to the senses.*

WHAT TO LOOK FOR   *To make writing memorable, the first draft of an essay will frequently depend more on adverbs and adjectives than on verbs, yet it is verbs that have muscle and can best get the job done—but not just any verb. All too often that same first draft is sprinkled with various forms of the verb* be, *usually in its most simple form* is. *Soto shows you how to avoid that trap by using action verbs that convey far more precisely exactly what he is feeling.*

1   I knew enough about hell to stop me from stealing. I was holy in almost every bone. Some days I recognized the shadows of angels flopping on the backyard grass, and other days I heard faraway messages in the plumbing that howled underneath the house when I crawled there looking for something to do.

2   But boredom made me sin. Once, at the German Market, I stood before a rack of pies, my sweet tooth gleaming and the juice of guilt wetting my underarms. I gazed at the nine kinds of pie, pecan and apple being my favorites, although cherry looked good, and my dear, fat-faced chocolate was always a good bet. I nearly wept trying to decide which to steal and, forgetting the flowery

dust priests give off, the shadow of angels and the proximity of God howling in the plumbing underneath the house, sneaked a pie behind my coffee-lid frisbee and walked to the door, grinning to the bald grocer whose forehead shone with a window of light.

3   "No one saw," I muttered to myself, the pie like a discus in my hand, and hurried across the street, where I sat on someone's lawn. The sun wavered between the branches of a yellowish sycamore. A squirrel nailed itself high on the trunk, where it forked into two large bark-scabbed limbs. Just as I was going to work my cleanest finger into the pie, a neighbor came out to the porch for his mail. He looked at me, and I got up and headed for home. I raced on skinny legs to my block, but slowed to a quick walk when I couldn't wait any longer. I held the pie to my nose and breathed in its sweetness. I licked some of the crust and closed my eyes as I took a small bite.

4   In my front yard, I leaned against a car fender and panicked about stealing the apple pie. I knew an apple got Eve in deep trouble with snakes because Sister Marie had shown us a film about Adam and Eve being cast into the desert, and what scared me more than falling from grace was being thirsty for the rest of my life. But even that didn't stop me from clawing a chunk from the pie tin and pushing it into the cavern of my mouth. The slop was sweet and gold-colored in the afternoon sun. I laid more pieces on my tongue, wet finger-dripping pieces, until I was finished and felt like crying because it was about the best thing I had ever tasted. I realized right there and then, in my sixth year, in my tiny body of two hundred bones and three or four sins, that the best things in life came stolen. I wiped my sticky fingers on the grass and rolled my tongue over the corners of my mouth. A burp perfumed the air.

5   I felt bad not sharing with Cross-Eyed Johnny, a neighbor kid. He stood over my shoulder and asked, "Can I have some?" Crust fell from my mouth, and my teeth were bathed with the jam-like filling. Tears blurred my eyes as I remembered the grocer's forehead. I remembered the other pies on the rack, the warm air of the fan above the door and the car that honked as I crossed the street without looking.

6   "Get away," I had answered Cross-Eyed Johnny. He watched my fingers greedily push big chunks of pie down my throat. He swallowed and said in a whisper, "Your hands are dirty," then returned home to climb his roof and sit watching me eat the pie by

myself. After a while, he jumped off and hobbled away because the fall had hurt him.

7   I sat on the curb. The pie tin glared at me and rolled away when the wind picked up. My face was sticky with guilt. A car honked, and the driver knew. Mrs. Hancock stood on her lawn, hands on hip, and she knew. My mom, peeling a mountain of potatoes at the Redi-Spud factory, knew. I got to my feet, stomach taut, mouth tired of chewing, and flung my frisbee across the street, its shadow like the shadow of an angel fleeing bad deeds. I retrieved it, jogging slowly. I flung it again until I was bored and thirsty.

8   I returned home to drink water and help my sister glue bottle caps onto cardboard, a project for summer school. But the bottle caps bored me, and the water soon filled me up more than the pie. With the kitchen stifling with heat and lunatic flies, I decided to crawl underneath our house and lie in the cool shadows listening to the howling sound of plumbing. Was it God? Was it Father, speaking from death, or Uncle with his last shiny dime? I listened, ear pressed to a cold pipe, and heard a howl like the sea. I lay until I was cold and then crawled back to the light, rising from one knee, then another, to dust off my pants and squint in the harsh light. I looked and saw the glare of a pie tin on a hot day. I knew sin was what you take and didn't give back.

Thesis and Organization

1. What does the first paragraph lead you to expect in the rest of the essay?
2. The time sequence traces Soto's guilt. What stages can you identify?
3. How would you describe the nature of the conflict in the essay?
4. What emotions does Soto feel in the course of his narrative?
5. What does Soto learn?

Technique and Style

1. Soto relates his narrative from the perspective of his six-year-old self. What is the first clue about his age?
2. Reread paragraph 4. What images appeal to what senses?
3. Paragraphs 5 and 6 bring in Cross-Eyed Johnny. What does that incident add to the narrative?
4. What other titles can you think of for the essay? What is gained? Lost?

5. Choose two sentences from paragraph 3 and rewrite them, using different verbs. Which versions do you prefer and why?

Suggestions for Writing

Journal

1. Place yourself in the position of Cross-Eyed Johnny and retell the scene (paragraphs 5 and 6) from his perspective.
2. The area under the house and its howling plumbing holds special significance for Soto. Think of a place that holds similar significance for you and describe it. Like Soto, you may want to use that place to frame a narrative.

Essay

Soto's experience probably reminds you of a similar one of your own or of a friend's. Recall a time when, directly or indirectly, you lived though such an event and use your memory of it as the basis of a narrative. Like Soto, you will want to describe not only what you or your friend did, but also how it made you feel. Suggestions:

    being embarrassed

    feeling guilty

    getting caught

    getting away with "it"

My Inner Shrimp

Garry Trudeau

Garry Trudeau needs no introduction to anyone who attended Yale University when he was there earning his BA and MFA, for the comic strip he wrote then became the one all of us know now, "Doonesbury." Recognizing the writer behind the strip, however, is a bit difficult. Certainly the strip shows imagination and humor, often of a rather zany nature, but it also reveals Trudeau to be a master satirist of the political scene, so much so that "Doonesbury" appears on the editorial page of a number of newspapers. His excellence as a political cartoonist has earned him a Pulitzer Prize.

This piece, however, appeared in the New York Times Magazine *in 1996 in "Lives," a regular feature devoted to personal essays.*

WHAT TO LOOK FOR   *Anyone reading the title and author's name would expect a humorous tone, perhaps laced with some poisonous political comments, and perhaps a narrative about a Doonesbury-like character. But the character in this essay is Trudeau, and his essay shows how it's possible to set out two narratives to illustrate a general point. In the original printing of the essay, that point is made explicitly in a headline, placed just below the title, that reads "No matter how much you grow, once you've been looked down on, you'll never walk tall." In newspapers, the headlines are written by someone other than the writer of the piece; fortunately, the person who wrote this headline picked up on the kind of humor and wordplay that characterize Trudeau's essay. Be on the lookout for puns, allusions, and metaphors.*

1   For the rest of my days, I shall be a recovering short person. Even from my lofty perch of something over six feet (as if I don't know within a micron), I have the soul of a shrimp. I feel the pain of the diminutive, irrespective of whether they feel it themselves, because my visit to the planet of the teen-age midgets was harrowing, humiliating and extended. I even perceive my last-minute escape to have been flukish, somehow unearned—as if the Commissioner of Growth Spurts had been an old classmate of my father.

2   My most recent reminder of all this came the afternoon I went hunting for a new office. I had noticed a building under construction in my neighborhood—a brick warren of duplexes, with wide,

westerly-facing windows, promising ideal light for a working studio. When I was ushered into the model unit, my pulse quickened; the soaring, 22-foot living room walls were gloriously aglow with the remains of the day. I bonded immediately.

3   Almost as an afterthought, I ascended the staircase to inspect the loft, ducking as I entered the bedroom. To my great surprise, I stayed ducked; the room was a little more than six feet in height. While my head technically cleared the ceiling, the effect was excruciatingly oppressive. This certainly wasn't a space I wanted to spend any time in, much less take out a mortgage on.

4   Puzzled, I wandered down to the sales office and asked if there were any other units to look at. No, replied a resolutely unpleasant receptionist, it was the last one. Besides, they were all exactly alike.

5   "Are you aware of how low the bedroom ceilings are?" I asked.

6   She shot me an evil look. "Of course we are," she snapped. "There were some problems with the building codes. The architect knows all about the ceilings.

7   "He's not an idiot, you know," she added, perfectly anticipating my next question.

8   She abruptly turned away, but it was too late. She'd just confirmed that a major New York developer, working with a fully licensed architect, had knowingly created an entire 12-story apartment building virtually uninhabitable by anyone of even average height. It was an exclusive high-rise for shorties.

9   Once I knew that, of course, I couldn't stay away. For days thereafter, as I walked to work, some perverse, unreasoning force would draw me back to the building. But it wasn't just the absurdity, the stone silliness of its design that had me in its grip; it was something far more compelling. Like some haunted veteran come again to an ancient battlefield, I was revisiting my perilous past.

10   When I was 14, I was the third-smallest in a high school class of 100 boys, routinely mistaken for a sixth grader. My first week of school, I was drafted into a contingent of students ignominiously dubbed the "Midgets," so grouped by taller boys presumably so they could taunt us with more perfect efficiency. Inexplicably, some of my fellow Midgets refused to be diminished by the experience, but I retreated into self-pity. I sent away for a book on how to grow tall, and committed to memory its tips on overcoming one's genetic destiny—or at least making the most of a regrettable situation. The book cited historical figures who had gone the latter

route—Alexander the Great, Caesar, Napoleon (the mind involuntarily added Hitler). Strategies for stretching the limbs were suggested—hanging from door frames, sleeping on your back, doing assorted floor exercises—all of which I incorporated into my daily routine (get up, brush teeth, hang from door frame). I also learned the importance of meeting girls early in the day, when, the book assured me, my rested spine rendered me perceptibly taller.

11   For six years, my condition persisted; I grew, but at nowhere near the rate of my peers. I perceived other problems as ancillary, and loaded up the stature issue with freight shipped in daily from every corner of my life. Lack of athletic success, the absence of a social life, the inevitable run-ins with bullies—all could be attributed to the missing inches. The night I found myself sobbing in my father's arms was the low point; we both knew it was one problem he couldn't fix.

12   Of course what we couldn't have known was that he and my mother already had. They had given me a delayed developmental timetable. In my 17th year, I miraculously shot up six inches, just in time for graduation and a fresh start. I was, in the space of a few months, reborn—and I made the most of it. Which is to say that thereafter, all of life's disappointments, reversals and calamities still arrived on schedule—but blissfully free of subtext.

13   Once you stop being the butt, of course, any problem recedes, if only to give way to a new one. And yet the impact of being literally looked down on, of being *made* to feel small, is forever. It teaches you how to stretch, how to survive the scorn of others for things that are beyond your control. Not growing forces you to grow up fast.

14   Sometimes I think I'd like to return to a high-school reunion to surprise my classmates. Not that they didn't know me when I finally started catching up. They did, but I doubt they'd remember. Adolescent hierarchies have a way of enduring; I'm sure I am still recalled as the Midget I myself have never really left behind.

15   Of course, if I'm going to show up, it'll have to be soon. I'm starting to shrink.

Thesis and Organization

1. Paragraph 1 serves as the introduction. What does it tell you about Trudeau's thesis? His tone?

2. The first narrative begins in paragraph 2 and runs through paragraph 8. How does it set out the conflict?

3. Draw a straight line to represent the essay's time sequence, the left margin representing the past and the right the future. Reread the essay, marking what tenses Trudeau uses where. Place what occurs when at the appropriate spots on the line you have drawn, and the result is an outline of the essay's chronology. How does it compare with the way Trudeau sequences the events in the essay?
4. Identifying the beginning of the second narrative is easy enough, but where would you say it ends? Explain the reasons behind your choice.
5. List as many conflicts as you can find in Trudeau's essay. Which is the primary one? What do the multiple conflicts contribute to the essay?

Technique and Style

1. Based on what you know from the essay, how would you characterize Trudeau? How would you describe his attitude toward this subject? Your answers will help pinpoint Trudeau's *persona*, the character a writer assumes in order to engage the intended audience.
2. The essay is written primarily in first person, but Trudeau uses other pronouns as well. The "we" in paragraph 12, for instance, stands for Trudeau and his father, but who is the *you* in paragraph 13?
3. *Wordplay* is a term used to describe a subtle or clever use of language. What examples can you find in Trudeau's essay? What do they add?
4. You may never have used a paragraph for dramatic effect, but that is what Trudeau does with two sentences in paragraph 15. Explain how that paragraph ties into the rest of the essay and whether you find it effective.
5. Trudeau uses dialogue in paragraphs 4–7. Explain how the effect on the reader would have differed if the same information had been presented indirectly, by summary instead of dialogue.

Suggestions for Writing

Journal

1. Write a journal entry explaining why you would or would not like to meet Garry Trudeau. Draw your reasons from the impression of Trudeau you receive from his essay, or from "Doonesbury," or both.
2. Think of a time when your classmates in high school singled you out. Recount an incident that gives the essence of how you felt.

Essay

If you chose the second option above, you have the makings of a narrative essay. Like Trudeau, you may want to include how you feel about that incident now, in which case you may also want to break up the chronology in somewhat the same way that Trudeau does. If you're not starting from a journal entry, think of some of the emotions you have felt as the result of events or incidents. Write down the emotions and then choose one as the center of your narrative. Be a little cautious about selecting a very dramatic event, as your tone can easily slip toward the sentimental. Suggested contexts:

school (including elementary)
work
family gatherings
parties

I Have a Gun

Tania Nyman

Sometimes being able to defend yourself can be as frightening as being defenseless, a paradox sharply felt by Tania Nyman, who wrote this essay her sophomore year at the University of New Orleans. At the time, 1989, New Orleans was fast becoming the murder capital of the United States, a fact that the editors of the local newspaper, the Times-Picayune, *were well aware of. Urban violence makes many people feel the way Tania Nyman does, which is one reason the* Times-Picayune *published her essay as an opinion piece.*

WHAT TO LOOK FOR   *Pace, the speed at which the story unfolds, is crucial to the impact of a narrative, and one way to quicken the pace is to use present tense. Notice how Nyman relies on the present tense to make her story immediate. Note, too, how she uses flashbacks to interrupt her narrative but still maintains its pace and supports her thesis.*

1   I have a gun, a .38 caliber that holds five bullets. It is black with a brown handle and it stays by my bed.

2   I don't want a gun. I don't even like guns. But it seems I need one.

3   I've always believed in gun control, and the funny thing is I still do. But my gun is loaded next to my bed.

4   It wasn't ignorance of crime statistics that previously kept me from owning a gun. Nor was it the belief that I was immune to violence.

5   I thought that because I didn't believe in violence, that because I wasn't violent, I wouldn't be touched by violence. I believed that my belief in the best of human nature could make it real.

6   I want to believe in a world where people do not need to protect themselves from one another. But I have a gun, and it stays by my bed.

7   I should carry the gun from my house to my car, but I don't. What the gun is capable of, what the gun is for, still frightens me more than what it is supposed to prevent.

67

8   If I carry my gun and I am attacked, I must use it. I cannot shoot to injure. I must shoot to kill.

9   I have confronted an attacker not in reality but in my imagination. The man is walking down the street. To prove I am not paranoid, I lock my car and walk to my door with my house key ready.

10   Before I reach the steps, I think I hear a voice. "Money." Before I open the door I hear a voice. "Money." I turn to see the man with the gun.

11   He is frightened. I am frightened. I am frightened that I will scare him and he will shoot. I am frightened that I will give him my money and he will shoot.

12   I am frightened, but I am angry. I am angry because there is a gun pointed at me by someone I've never met and never hurt.

13   There is something that bothers me about this robbery I have created in my head. It is something that makes me uncomfortable with myself. It is something I don't want to admit, something I almost intentionally omitted because I am ashamed.

14   I guess I understand why I imagine being robbed by a man. They're physically more intimidating and I've never heard of anyone being robbed by a woman, though I'm sure it happens. But I'm being robbed by a man.

15   But why is he a black man? Why is he a black man with a worn T-shirt and glassy eyes? Why do I not imagine being robbed by a white man?

16   I am standing in a gas station on Claiborne and Jackson waiting to pay the cashier when a black man walks up behind me. I do not turn around. I stare in front of me waiting to pay. I try not to admit that I am nervous because a black man has walked up behind me in a gas station in a bad neighborhood and he does not have a car.

17   There is another scenario I imagine. I am walking to my door with my gun in my hand and I hear the voice. The man mustn't have seen my gun. I get angry because I am threatened, because someone is endangering my life for the money in my pocket.

18   I turn and without really thinking, angry and frightened, I shoot. I kill a man for $50. Or it could be $100. It does not matter that he was trying to rob me. A man has died for money. Not my money or his money, just money. Who put the price on his life, he or I?

19   I remember driving one night with my friend in her parents' car. We stop at a red light at Carollton and Tulane and a black man is

crossing the street in front of us. My friend quickly but nonchalantly locks the doors with the power lock.

20   I am disgusted that she sees the man as a reminder to lock her doors. I wonder if he noticed the two girls nonchalantly lock their doors. I wonder how it feels to have people lock their doors at the sight of you.

21   I imagine again a confrontation in front of my house. I have my gun when the man asks for money. I am angry and scared, but I do not use the gun. I am afraid of what may happen to me if I don't use it, but I am more afraid of killing another human being, more afraid of trying to live with the guilt of murdering another person. I bet my life that he will take my money and leave, and I hope I win.

22   I am in a gas station on St. Charles and South Carollton near my house and there is a black man waiting to pay the cashier. I walk up behind him to wait in line and he jumps and turns around.

23   When he sees me, he relaxes and says I scared him because of the way things have gotten in this neighborhood.

24   "Sorry," I say and smile. I realize I am not the only one who is frightened.

Thesis and Organization

1. As in the Merrill-Foster essay, the paragraphs here conform to newspaper columns. If you were reparagraphing for a regular page, what paragraphs would you use to make up an introduction? What reasons do you have for your decision?
2. List the three imaginary incidents. What do they have in common? How are they different?
3. List the real incidents. What do they have in common? How are they different?
4. What is the point of the last narrative?
5. What is the author's attitude toward violence? Toward having a gun? Toward race? Combine your answers into a thesis statement.

Technique and Style

1. How would you describe the *I* in this essay? Is this the kind of person you would like to know? Why or why not?
2. The author uses repetition intentionally. Find an example and describe its effect.

3. What effects are achieved by mixing real and imagined situations?
4. How would you describe the various conflicts in the narrative? Which is the most important and why?
5. The author depends heavily on the first-person singular, *I.* Explain whether she overuses the pronoun.

Suggestions for Writing

Journal

1. Turn to a blank page and get set to do a timed entry, say five minutes or so. Think of the word *gun* and write down all the associations that come to mind. The result will be a list that may make sense only to you, but if you select one of your associations, you can probably build a narrative around it if you want to turn your ideas into an essay.
2. These days, it's almost impossible that a person has not been confronted by violence. Write a journal entry that briefly relates a violent incident and your response to it. You may want to return to this entry later and use it in an essay.

Essay

Think of a time when your action or actions contradicted your values. What were your values? What situation or action conflicted with those values? Perhaps you will want to develop how the conflict made you feel, how it affected others, and how you either resolved the conflict or learned to live with it. To come up with ideas for a topic, you might try to remember times when you

were forced to lie to protect a friend
kept silent when you should have spoken
spoke when you should have kept quiet
were pressured to do something you knew you shouldn't do

A ngels on a Pin

Alexander Calandra

"Angels on a Pin" was first published in the Saturday Review *in 1968 in the wake of the United States' push to surpass Russia's strides in scientific technology, strides that led to Sputnik, the first artificial earth satellite. Sputnik was launched in 1957. Now, some 40 years later, we no longer have "Sputnik-panicked classrooms," but we are still trying to come to terms with our educational system.*

WHAT TO LOOK FOR   *More often than not when you write a narrative, you find yourself at the center of it. But you may not want to be. Calandra, for example, could have told the story of the student from the teacher's point of view. Instead, he tells it from his own perspective, that of an impartial observer. When you write a narrative, ask yourself what point of view would be most effective, and if you choose first person, then also ask yourself about your stance in relation to the narrative: do you want to be an observer or a participant?*

1   Some time ago, I received a call from a colleague who asked if I would be the referee on the grading of an examination question. He was about to give a student a zero for his answer to a physics question, while the student claimed he should receive a perfect score and would if the system were not set up against the student. The instructor and the student agreed to submit this to an impartial arbiter, and I was selected.

2   I went to my colleague's office and read the examination question: "Show how it is possible to determine the height of a tall building with the aid of a barometer."

3   The student had answered: "Take the barometer to the top of the building, attach a long rope to it, lower the barometer to the street, and then bring it up, measuring the length of the rope. The length of the rope is the height of the building."

4   I pointed out that the student really had a strong case for full credit, since he had answered the question completely and correctly. On the other hand, if full credit were given, it could well contribute to a high grade for the student in his physics course. A

high grade is supposed to certify competence in physics, but the answer did not confirm this. I suggested that the student have another try at answering the question. I was not surprised that my colleague agreed, but I was surprised that the student did.

5   I gave the student six minutes to answer the question, with the warning that his answer should show some knowledge of physics. At the end of five minutes, he had not written anything. I asked if he wished to give up, but he said no. He had many answers to this problem; he was just thinking of the best one. I excused myself for interrupting him, and asked him to please go on. In the next minute, he dashed off his answer which read:

6   "Take the barometer to the top of the building and lean over the edge of the roof. Drop the barometer, timing its fall with a stopwatch. Then, using the formula $S = 1/2at^2$, calculate the height of the building."

7   At this point, I asked my colleague if *he* would give up. He conceded, and I gave the student almost full credit.

8   In leaving my colleague's office, I recalled that the student had said he had other answers to the problem, so I asked him what they were. "Oh, yes," said the student. "There are many ways of getting the height of a tall building with the aid of a barometer. For example, you could take the barometer out on a sunny day and measure the height of the barometer, the length of its shadow, and the length of the shadow of the building, and by the use of a simple proportion, determine the height of the building."

9   "Fine," I said. "And the others?"

10   "Yes," said the student. "There is a very basic measurement method that you will like. In this method, you take the barometer and begin to walk up the stairs. As you climb the stairs, you mark off the length of the barometer along the wall. You then count the number of marks, and this will give you the height of the building in barometer units. A very direct method.

11   "Of course, if you want a more sophisticated method, you can tie the barometer to the end of a string, swing it as a pendulum, and determine the value of *g* at the street level and at the top of the building. From the difference between the two values of *g,* the height of the building can, in principle, be calculated."

12   Finally he concluded, there are many other ways of solving the problem. "Probably the best," he said, "is to take the barometer to the basement and knock on the superintendent's door. When the

superintendent answers, you speak to him as follows: 'Mr. Superintendent, here I have a fine barometer. If you will tell me the height of this building, I will give you this barometer.'"

13   At this point, I asked the student if he really did not know the conventional answer to this question. He admitted that he did, but said that he was fed up with high school and college instructors trying to teach him how to think, to use the "scientific method," and to explore the deep inner logic of the subject in a pedantic way, as is often done in the new mathematics, rather than teaching him the structure of the subject. With this in mind, he decided to revive scholasticism as an academic lark to challenge the Sputnik-panicked classrooms of America.

Thesis and Organization

1. In a narrow sense, the essay focuses on the question, "What is the correct answer to the examination question?" But paragraphs 8–13 take up a broader point, and there the essay concentrates on the question, "What is the purpose of education?" How do the three participants answer this question?

2. At first, the conflict arises between the instructor and the student. What larger conflict is involved in their dispute? What paragraph serves as a transition between the smaller and larger conflicts?

3. Does the author intend the essay primarily to inform, persuade, or entertain? Cite evidence to support your view.

4. The subject of the essay is education. What statement is the author making about education? Where in the essay does he put forth his assertion? Is the essay's thesis expressed in one of Calandra's sentences? Which one? Or do you find that the thesis is composed of several ideas? Where are they expressed?

5. What principle guides the order in which the paragraphs are presented? What words or phrases does the author use to bring out that principle?

Technique and Style

1. To show how "to determine the height of a tall building with the aid of a barometer," the student depends on process analysis. How many processes does he provide in answer to the examination question? Why might the student have saved his "best" answer for last?

2. In every example the student gives, the barometer plays a role that belies its most important function. What roles does it play? How do these roles subvert the instructor's questions?

3. What is the relationship of the narrator to the story? What is the narrator's point of view? Given the information in paragraph 4, what impression of the narrator is conveyed to the reader? Does the narrator take sides? What evidence can you find to support your opinion?

4. Use your library to find out about *scholasticism* (paragraph 13) and the allusion to "angels on a pin." How does the author's choice of title relate to his thesis?

Suggestions for Writing

Journal

1. The student in Calandra's essay has his own reasons for what he did (see paragraph 12), but his explanation isn't a very full one. Make up your own version, substituting your reasons for his.

2. In a way, the student's examination is a practical joke. Think back to some of the practical jokes you have done or that have been done to you, choose one, and then relate it in your journal.

Essay

No matter how positive your experience with education may be, you spend so many years in schools that it's impossible to avoid some negative episodes. Think of a time when you were the victim of education and turn that incident into a narrative essay. For ideas, try to remember a specific occasion when, perhaps, you

were falsely accused of cheating or plagiarism or receiving help on a
    paper
did something to embarrass the teacher or vice versa
were not allowed to make up a test when you had a legitimate reason
    for missing it
received a zero because the teacher lost your paper
intended a joke but were taken seriously

Example

Any time you encounter *for instance, such as,* or *for example,* you know what will follow: an **example** that explains and supports the generalization. Used with general statements, examples fill in the gaps. If you are writing on the subject of violent crime and want to show that the facts contradict what many people believe, you might write "Many people believe most crime is violent and that crime is increasing." Then you might continue by citing statistics as examples that show the rate of crime peaked in the seventies but then ceased to rise in the eighties and actually fell in the nineties. You would have supported the idea that crime rates have fallen, but you would still need to provide evidence for the idea that many people believe the opposite. Readers also need to know what evidence supports your claim that crime, to many people, means violent crime. That evidence is apt to come in the form of an example, an illustration that clarifies or develops a point. The most basic building block of all, examples pin down generalizations, supporting them with specifics.

To use examples well, you first need to know when to use them, then which ones to select, and finally, how to incorporate them. If you read actively, responding to the words on the page as you would to a person talking to you, odds are you will spot where examples are needed. On reading the sentence above about crime, you might think to yourself, "Hey, wait a minute! How about that violent crime statement?" Often it helps to read your own work belligerently, ready to shoot down any generalization with a "Says who?" The response to "Says who" will vary according to your audience. A sociology paper will call for statistics; a personal narrative will draw on your own experience. Other good sources are the experiences of others and those of authorities whose work you can quote. The skill here is to match the example not only to the generalization it supports, but also to the readers to whom it is addressed. After you have found good examples, you need to sequence them logically, while at the same time you avoid overusing terms such as "for example." Where you use multiple examples, you can use **transitions** that signal addition (*and, also, again, besides, moreover, next, finally,* etc.); where you use examples that compare, opt for transitions that indicate a turn (*but, yet, however, instead, in contrast,* etc.). Occasionally you may find yourself introducing an example that serves as a concession, calling for *of course, certainly,* or *granted.* Other times you may want a transition that indicates result—*therefore, thus, as a result, so.* More obvious are transitions setting up a summary, as in *finally, in conclusion, hence,* or *in brief.* Less obvious, and therefore apt to be more effective, are transitions that don't call attention to themselves, such as the repetition of a key word from the previous sentence or the use of a personal or demonstrative pronoun. If you use pronouns, however, make sure that what they refer to is clear. The demonstrative pronoun *this,* for instance, should usually be followed by a noun, as in *this sentence* or *this idea.* A *this* standing by itself may force your reader to go back to the previous sentence to understand exactly what it refers to.

AUDIENCE AND PURPOSE   In general, the less familiar your audience is with your subject, the more important it is to have examples, and lots of them. If you find yourself writing about a sport, for instance, you would do well to think about what your audience may or may not know about it. If the sport is ice hockey and your readers are your classmates most of whom live in New Mexico, you'll know that most of your readers won't know much about your topic, so you will have to use lots of examples. And if you are arguing that ice hockey is an underrated sport, you can draw on your readers' experience with more familiar games such as basketball. You might use the example of the pace of a basketball game to make the point that ice hockey is even faster, so fast that at times the crowd can't even see the puck.

If your readers are relatively familiar with your topic, then your job is to make that familiarity come to life and shape it to your purpose. If you are writing an essay that explores the various levels of anxiety experienced by a first-year college student, you will probably cite a num-

Example   77

ber of instances. You might start with the example of registering by telephone and the mild concern that the machine on the other end of the line will send your course requests to electronic heaven, then the fear of not finding the right classroom and turning up, if at all, late for class; next the uneasiness that occurs with the first look at the course syllabus, followed by the apprehension over the speed of a lecture; and then you might end with the sheer terror of the first test. If you provide enough examples, at least one is bound to remind a reader of a similar response.

The examples get harder to come by if your subject is a controversial or sensitive one. On familiar topics such as abortion, capital punishment, and prayer in public schools, your readers are not only apt to have opinions but very set ones, so set that you might do well to steer clear of the topic. Even less touchy subjects are difficult to write about because you have to be sensitive to views that differ from yours so that you don't alienate those readers. When dealing with a topic on which there has been much debate, it often helps to list the opposing arguments so you can find examples to support your points and to defeat the opposite ones.

Now and then, you may also find yourself writing an essay that tackles a subject that isn't controversial but still requires some caution on your part. You might, for example, want to write about what you find to be our culture's "throwaway" mentality and how it is adversely affecting the environment. When you start listing the more obvious throwaway items you can think of, you find you have fast-food wrappings and boxes, ballpoint pens, paper napkins and towels, and plastic coverings for CDs, all items your readers probably use and throw away without thinking. Your problem then becomes one of educating your readers without insulting or blaming them, which isn't easy. Recognizing the problem, however, is halfway to solving it, and you'll read essays in this chapter that do just that.

TYPES OF EXAMPLES   Examples generally fall into two categories, extended and multiple. An essay that rests its assertion on only one example is relatively rare, but you will run across one now and then. When you do, the example often takes the form of a narrative in support of the author's thesis. To show that a minimum-wage job can be a fulfilling one (or a demeaning one—take your pick), you might support your thesis by telling about a typical day on the job. While you are relying on only one example, you will have developed it in considerable depth, and you probably will have included a sentence or two to indicate that other experiences may contradict yours, so your readers will accept your extended example as valid. Far more frequent, however, are multiple examples. They add clarity, support, and emphasis, and save you from having to make the kind of disclaimer mentioned above. Sometimes the examples will be drawn from your own experience and the experiences of others, but often you will find you want more generalized sources, so you consult books, magazines, interviews, reports, and so on. You may well find that examples drawn from outside sources give your essay a more objective, reasoned **tone**. If you think of that term as similar to tone of voice, you will realize that it means the writer's attitude toward the subject and audience. Examples drawn from personal experience are apt to create an informal, conversational tone; those drawn from outside sources often provide a cooler, more formal tone. No matter where you find your examples, however, you can present them with some variety, summarizing some, quoting others.

Examples not only illustrate generalizations, they expand and develop them. After you have written a draft of an essay, you may find it useful to double-check each of your examples by asking several questions: How does the example support the generalization? Is the source of the example clear? How does it connect to the readers' experiences? If the example is an extended one, is it sufficiently developed so that it can support the thesis by itself? Then you might think about the examples as a whole: Do they draw on a variety of sources? Do they incorporate both summary and quotation?

DETAILS   In presenting an example, the writer uses many of the same techniques that come into play in description. Descriptive details can come from unlikely places, such as the song titles Molly Ivins cites as examples to support her claim that

> women in country music are either saints or sluts, but they're mostly sluts. She's either a "good-hearted woman" or a "honky-tonk angel." There are more hard-hearted women in country music ("I Gave Her a Ring, She Gave Me the Finger"), despicable bimbos ("Ruuuby, Don't Take Your Love to Town"), and heartless gold diggers ("Satin Sheets to Lie On, Satin Pillow to Cry On") than scholars can count. (84)

But Molly Ivins can count, and does.

Example   **79**

As with description, details are used to make the abstract concrete. If you were writing about an abstract principle such as freedom, for example, you might find yourself writing about one kind of freedom that you particularly value, the freedom that your parents allowed you to make mistakes. You would probably provide a number of examples, and each one might be in the form of a short narrative, but the effectiveness of those narratives will lie in the details you use. Your parents might not have wanted you to go out with a particular person, for instance, but merely stated their reasons and left the decision up to you. You decided not to take their advice, and the result was a "disaster." Spell out the details so that the reader concludes it was a disaster, and you will have made your point effectively.

THESIS AND ORGANIZATION   Whether an essay is developed by multiple examples or a single extended example, it has a major assertion. In your first draft, you may want to state your thesis in one sentence and in an obvious place, such as the end of your introduction. When you revise, however, you may want to play with the placement of the thesis, delaying it until the conclusion. If that's where you decide you want it, check to make sure that everything that precedes the conclusion leads up to it and that the reader has a clear focus on your subject all the way.

You might also try weaving your thesis into the introduction in a subtle way, taking the thesis apart so that it is in bits and pieces, each in its own sentence. If you try that idea, check to make sure that someone reading your introduction will come up with a thesis that closely matches the one-sentence assertion you had in your first draft.

Delaying your thesis or weaving it into your introduction are subtle ways of treating your major assertion. If you are worried that they are so subtle that the reader may miss your point, consider getting some mileage out of a title. An imaginative title can serve several purposes: arouse the reader's curiosity, set the tone, highlight the subject, reveal the essay's organization, or pave the way for the thesis. Good titles serve more than one purpose.

When examples are used as the primary mode for an essay, they are usually arranged in chronological or dramatic order, moving from what came first and ending with what came last or beginning with the least dramatic and finishing with the most. To decide which example is the most dramatic, all you need to do is ask some obvious questions: Which is the most important? Which is most likely to affect the reader? Which carries the most impact? Odds are you'll come up with the same answer for each question. That's the example you should use to cap your essay, the one that all the others should lead up to.

Although all the essays in this chapter have a thesis developed by examples, the examples themselves often cross over into other categories. You will discover that is also the case with your own writing. You may well find yourself using an example that is also a narrative, or, to put it more precisely, a narrative that functions as an example. Other patterns of organization such as a description, an analysis of causal relationships, a comparison, a definition, or an analysis of a process can also serve as examples. The function—to support and develop an assertion—is more important than the label.

USEFUL TERMS

Example   An illustration that supports a generalization, usually an assertion, by providing evidence that develops or clarifies it.

Transition   A word, phrase, sentence, or paragraph that carries the reader smoothly from point A to point B. Some transitions, such as time markers (*first, next,* and the like) are obvious; others are more subtle, such as a repeated word or phrase or a synonym for a key term.

Tone   A writer's attitude toward the subject and the audience. An author's tone can be contemplative, intense, tongue-in-cheek, aloof, matter of fact—as many kinds as there are tones of voice.

▧ POINTERS FOR USING EXAMPLE

Exploring the Topic

1. **What examples can you think of to illustrate your topic?** Are all of them from your own experience? What examples can you find from other sources?
2. **Check to see that your examples are both pertinent and representative.** Do they fit? Do they illustrate?
3. **Which examples lend themselves to extended treatment?** Which are relatively unimportant?
4. **How familiar is your audience with each of your examples?**
5. **Which examples best lend themselves to your topic?** In what order would they best be presented?
6. **What point do you want to make?** Do your examples all support that point? Do they lead the reader to your major assertion?

Example   **81**

7. **What is your purpose behind your point?** Is your primary aim to express your own feelings, to inform, to persuade, or to entertain?

Drafting the Paper

1. **Know your reader.** Figure out where your reader may stand in relation to your topic and thesis. It may be that your audience knows little about your subject or that the reader simply hasn't thought much about it; on the other hand, maybe the reader knows a great deal and holds a definite opinion. Once you have made an informed guess about your audience's attitude toward your topic and thesis, reexamine your examples in light of that information. Some may have to be explained in greater detail than others, and the more familiar ones will need to be presented in a new or different light. Use the techniques you would employ in writing descriptive papers.

2. **Know your purpose.** Self-expressive papers are often difficult to write because you are so close to being your own audience. If you are writing with this aim in mind, try making yourself conscious of the personality you project as a writer. Jot down the characteristics you wish to convey about yourself and refer to this list as you revise your paper. While this is a highly self-conscious way to revise, when it is done well, the result appears natural. You will also need to double-check your examples, making sure that you present them in sufficient detail to communicate fully to your audience. That warning serves as well for informative and persuasive papers. Again, use description to make your examples hit the mark: use sensory detail, compare the unfamiliar to the familiar, be concrete. If you are writing a persuasive paper, use these techniques to develop your emotional appeal.

3. **Consider extended example.** If an essay rests on one example, you must choose and develop that illustration with great care. Make sure your example is representative of its class and that you provide all relevant information. Make as many unobtrusive connections as you can between your example and the class it represents. During revision, you may want to eliminate some of these references, but at first it's best to have too many. If you are writing a persuasive paper, you don't want to be found guilty of a lapse in logic.

4. **Consider multiple examples.** Most essays rely on multiple examples to support their points; nevertheless, some examples will be more developed than others. Figure out which examples are particularly striking and develop them, reserving the others for mere mention. Show how your examples fit your point and stress what is noteworthy about them. To lend breadth and credibility to your point, consider citing statistics, quotations, authorities, and the experience of others as well as your own.

Comment on what you take from other sources in order to make it more your own.

5. **Arrange your examples effectively.** The most frequent pattern of organization moves from the less dramatic, less important to the most, but examples can also be arranged chronologically or in terms of frequency (from the least to the most frequent). Like the essay itself, each paragraph should be developed around a central assertion, either stated or implied. In longer papers, groups of paragraphs will form a section in support of a unifying statement. These statements guide the reader through your examples and prevent the paper from turning into a mere list.

6. **Make a point.** Examples so obviously need to lead up to something that it's not hard to make a point in this kind of paper. The only real pitfall is that your point may not be an assertion. Test your thesis by asking whether your point carries any information. If it does, it's an assertion. Say you come up with, "We live in a world of time-saving technology." You can think of lots of examples and even narrow down the "we" to "anyone who cooks today." The setting is obviously the kitchen, but is the revised thesis an assertion? Given the information test, it fails. Your audience already knows what you are supposed informing them about. But if you revise and come up with "Electronic gizmos have turned the kitchen into a laboratory," you've given the topic a fresher look, one that does contain information.

H onky Tonking

Molly Ivins

Molly Ivins isn't ashamed to admit she loves country music, and she isn't ashamed to write about it in her typical style, a cross between Deep Texan and Standard American English. A confessed member of what she terms the "arthur bidness," she is a regular contributor to several newspapers and various magazines such as Atlantic, Texas Monthly, *the* Washington Journalism Review, Mother Jones, *and the* Progressive. *This essay was first published in* Ms. *in September, 1988, and then reprinted in her first collection of essays,* Molly Ivins Can't Say That, Can She?, *published in 1991. Molly Ivins continues to be outrageous, and country music continues to attract more fans and more amazing song titles.*

WHAT TO LOOK FOR *Not many writers can match Molly Ivins for range of diction, so as you read the essay, be aware of the different types of diction she uses—colloquial, slang, conversational, formal, academic. Also be on the lookout for the range of allusions she draws on. Not many writers would think of putting Earl Scruggs and Ludwig van Beethoven in the same sentence.*

1   I can remember being embarrassed about liking country-western music, but I can't remember when I quit. It was a long time before they put Willie Nelson on the cover of *Newsweek*. Since there's a country song about everything important in life, there's one about this too—"I Was Country, When Country Wasn't Cool."

2   Being hopelessly uncool is the least of the sins of country music. Back when I went to college, listening to Dave Brubeck and Edith Piaf was a fundamental prerequisite for sophistication, on a par with losing your virginity. Knowing a lot of Ernest Tubb songs didn't do squat for the reputation of the aspiring cosmopolite.

3   Country music was also politically incorrect. The folkies were on the right side of issues: Bob Dylan and Joan Baez sang at civil rights rallies; it seemed more than likely that Bull Connor listened to country.

4   The Beatles, Janis Joplin, the Jefferson Airplane, the Doors—
everybody anybody listened to in the 1960s was against the Vietnam War. From the country side, Merle Haggard contributed "I'm
Proud to Be an Okie from Muskogee." (Hippies quickly turned
"Okie" into a longhair anthem and Kinky Friedman contributed a
version entitled "I Am Just an Asshole from El Paso.")

5   And to be a feminist country music fan is an exercise in cultural
masochism. There you are trying to uphold the personhood of the
female sex, while listening to "She Got the Gold Mine, I Got the
Shaft" or "Don't the Girls All Get Prettier at Closing Time." Women
in country music are either saints or sluts, but they're mostly sluts.
She's either a "good-hearted woman" or a "honky-tonk angel."
There are more hard-hearted women in country music ("I Gave
Her a Ring, She Gave Me the Finger"), despicable bimbos ("Ruu-
uby, Don't Take Your Love to Town"), and heartless gold diggers
("Satin Sheets to Lie On, Satin Pillow to Cry On") than the scholars
can count. Even the great women country singers aren't much
help. The immortal Patsy Cline was mostly lovesick for some
worthless heel ("I Fall to Pieces") and Tammy Wynette's greatest
contribution was to advise us "Stand by Your Man." (Tammy has
stood by several of them.)

6   Not until the great Loretta Lynn, who is also musically lovelorn
with great frequency but shows more spunk about it, did we hear
some country songs that can be considered feminist. "Don't Come
Home A-Drinkin' with Lovin' on Your Mind" is one of Loretta's
better ass-kickin' anthems. The high-spirited spoof "Put Another
Log on the Fire" is a classic parody of sexism: "Now, don't I let you
wash the car on Sunday?/Don't I warn you when you're gettin'
fat?/Ain't I gonna take you fishin' with me someday?/Well, a man
can't love a woman more than that." Evidence of the impact of the
Women's Movement on country music can be found in the hit
song "If I Said You Had a Beautiful Body, Would You Hold It
Against Me?"

7   But this is fairly limited evidence of redeeming social value in
the genre. So what do we see in it? For one thing, how can you
not love a tradition that produces such songs as "You Done
Stompt on my Heart, an' Squished That Sucker Flat"? (Featuring the
refrain "Sweetheart, you just sorta/stompt on my aorta.") Or
"Everything You Touch Turns to Dirt." Many cultures have popular

song forms that reflect the people's concerns. In Latin cultures the *corridos,* written by immortal poets such as Garcia Lorca, give voice to the yearnings of the voiceless. In our culture, "Take This Job and Shove It" serves much the same function.

8   If you want to take the pulse of the people in this country, listen to country-western music. I first knew a mighty religious wave was gathering when I heard ditties like "Drop-kick Me, Jesus, Through the Goalposts of Life." I also knew the Moral Majority was past its prime and Pat Robertson would go nowhere when I heard "I Wrote a Hot Check to Jesus" on country radio, followed by "Would Jesus Wear a Rolex on His Television Show?"

9   Contrary to popular opinion, it is not easy to write country songs: many try and fail. One guy who never made it is Robin Dorsey from Matador, Texas. He went to Tech and had a girlfriend from Muleshoe about whom he wrote the love song "Her Teeth Was Stained but Her Heart Was Pure." She took offense and quit him over it, which caused him to write the tragedy-love song "I Don't Know Whether to Commit Suicide Tonight or Go Bowlin'."

10   Country music is easily parodied and much despised by intellectuals, but like soap operas, it is much more like real life than your elitists will admit. What do most people truly care about? International arms control? Monetary policy? Deconstructive criticism? Hell, no. What they care about most is love ("We Used to Kiss Each Other on the Lips, but Now It's All Over"). Betrayal ("Your Cheatin' Heart"). Revenge ("I'm Gonna Hire a Wino to Decorate Our Home"; "Who's Sorry Now?"). Death ("Wreck on the Highway"). Booze ("Four on the Floor and a Fifth under the Seat"; "She's Actin' Single, I'm Drinkin' Doubles"). Money ("If You've Got the Money, Honey, I've Got the Time"). Loneliness ("Hello, Walls"). Tragedy-love songs ("She Used My Tears to Wash Her Socks"; "My Bride's Wedding Dress Was Wash-and-Wear").

11   Now here we're talking major themes. In a song called "You Never Even Called Me by My Name," which author Steve Goodman labeled "the perfect country-western song," momma, trucks, trains, and prison are also suggested as mandatory country-western themes.

12   In this country we waste an enormous amount of time and energy disapproving of one another in three categories where only personal taste matters: hair, sports, and music. We need not review the family trauma, high dudgeon, tsk-tsking, and lawsuits

caused over the years by hair and how people wear it. Consider the equally futile expenditure of energy in condemning other people's sports. And in music, good Lord, the zeal put into denouncing rock, sneering at opera, finding classical a bore, jazz passé, bluegrass fit only for snuff-dippers—why, it's stupefying. It's incomprehensible.

13   I am open to the argument that Ludwig van Beethoven has contributed more great music to the world than has Earl Scruggs. But there is a tiresome neoconservative argument these days that holds relativism responsible for all the evil in the modern world. These folks denounce the abandonment of absolute standards in everything—morality, taste, the postal service. As though the fact that people enjoy reading *The Three Musketeers* were a menace to Dante. I have felt the sting of their snotty scorn, the lash of their haughty sneers, and what I have to say is "You Are Just Another Sticky Wheel on the Grocery Cart of Life."

Thesis and Organization

1. What idea about country music does Ivins set out in her introduction, paragraphs 1 and 2?
2. Paragraphs 3–5 group together to support the idea that country music is "politically incorrect," an idea that Ivins develops using multiple examples. Choose one of those examples that you are familiar with and explain in greater detail how it does or does not support her assertion.
3. Ivins maintains that "If you want to take the pulse of the people in this country, listen to country-western music." She then uses paragraphs 8–11 to support that idea. What other examples can you think of?
4. The essay is a bit more subtle than it may first appear in that it covers a number of subjects: why Molly Ivins likes country music, attitudes toward country music, and snobbism are a few of those subjects. What else does she touch on? What is her main subject? What reasons do you have for your choice?
5. Given Ivins' point in her introduction, her assertions in paragraphs 3 and 8, and her conclusion in paragraphs 12 and 13, what is her thesis? Summarize your idea in one sentence.

Technique and Style

1. Using the WHAT TO LOOK FOR as a starting point, see how many types of diction you can find. Explain how that range of diction affects you as a reader.

2. At various points in the essay, Ivins is funny, scornful, serious, and annoyed. What other emotions come through? How would you characterize Ivins' tone?

3. Ivins begins with her personal experience, but by the end of the essay she has moved to more general statements about American culture and tastes. Explain how you would categorize the essay—as personal, general, or somewhere in between.

4. What reasons can you think of for including paragraph 9? What, if anything, does it add to the essay?

5. Think about the examples of country music singers, titles, and lyrics that Ivins cites. Given those examples, how would you define country music?

Suggestions for Writing

Journal

1. Use your journal to record the unusual or bizarre. Like Ivins, you might turn to music and the names of popular groups such as Smashing Pumpkins. Or record the more unusual bumper stickers or names of beauty salons or bars. At a later date, you may want to use what you find as examples in an essay.

2. Take a paragraph from the newspaper or a textbook and rewrite it, drawing on the same range of diction that Molly Ivins shows in her essay.

Essay

Consider another category of popular music—rap, rock 'n roll, blues, heavy metal, New Age, and the like. Choosing a type of music that you both like and know about, examine it as though it were a window into our culture. What do you see? What does it say about our concerns? Why do some people not like it? Use your notes to write an essay that illustrates its points through multiple examples. If music doesn't seem to be a worthwhile subject, then choose another topic that you can use as a way to examine popular culture. Suggestions:
television shows
films
books

Sweatin' for Nothin'

Michael Barlow

Unlike many students at the University of New Orleans, Michael Barlow went straight on to college after graduating from high school. As his essay implies, he is not a fitness freak, although he is engaged in a number of college activities. An education major concentrating in teaching English at the secondary level, he may soon turn up in the classroom on the other side of the desk. No matter what he does, he will try not to emulate Mimi.

WHAT TO LOOK FOR   *Starting and ending an essay are often the most difficult parts of writing. One technique that works well is the one Barlow uses. You'll see that he sets up a framework by first setting out the image of the hamster in the cage and then, in his conclusion, returning to it. The effect is a sense of closure. You can use the same technique by ending your essay with a reference to an idea you bring out in your introduction.*

1   During spring break, I visited my family in Fort Worth. It was a pleasant visit, but my, how things have changed. My mother has purchased a stairmaster and joined a fitness club. My father now jogs at 6:00 every morning, and my sister is contemplating aerobics as one of her first electives when she goes off to college this August. This was not the group of people I last saw in January. These were not the laid-back complacent folks I've known so well. This was not *my* family.

2   One night around 2 a.m., after partying with some friends from high school, I was lying in bed watching Mimi, my pet hamster, crank out revolutions on an exercise wheel. I should have gone to sleep but I was captivated. The creaking of the wheel made me think of the strenuous exercise that seems to have plagued everyone at 301 Lake Country Drive. What was it? What was going on? So I asked myself whether or not Mimi knew that sprinting in a metal cylinder wouldn't get her out of the cage. She probably didn't know—her brain is smaller than a kernel of corn.

3   But what about humans? What about my family? I see millions of Americans, like my family, in Spandex outfits and gel-cushioned shoes trying to get out of their cages. Something is wrong with the

fitness mania that has swept the Western World, and from watching Mimi I know what it is. Entropy.

4   Entropy is the measure of the amount of energy unavailable for useful work in a system—metaphorically speaking, it is a measure of waste. In our throwaway society, we waste energy at a maddening pace. Coal is lit to make a fire, which produces a lot of carbon dioxide, while heating a small amount of water to make steam, which produces electricity, which lights an incandescent bulb in a room in a house where nobody's home. Basic waste.

5   Exercise mania has crippled our culture. It is no coincidence that we are running out of cheap and available energy while at the same time polluting the air, land, and sea with our waste. According to the laws of physics, entropy diminishes in a closed system, meaning that eventually everything will be reduced to an amorphous, undifferentiated blob. The universe is a closed system. There are some parallels to a hamster cage, and Mimi creates entropy at a noisy rate.

6   What did we do for exercise in those past centuries when people did not act like captive hamsters? If a person chopped down wood or ran a long way, it was because he or she needed fuel or wanted to get somewhere. Now we do such things to fit into new pants or to develop our biceps. We have treadmills, rowing machines, stairmasters, stationary bikes, Nordic Tracks, butt busters, and wall climbers, and we labor at them while going nowhere. Absolutely nowhere! We do work that is beyond useless; we do work that takes energy and casts it to the wind like lint. And we don't even enjoy the work. Look at people in a health club. See anybody smiling?

7   There is nothing magical about fitness machines. We can get the exact same result by climbing up stairs in our homes or offices. Take a look at any set of stairs in any building. Anybody in Spandex headed up or down? No. People ride elevators all day, then drive to their fitness centers where they pay to walk up steps.

8   When I was looking at Mimi, I was thinking of Richard Simmons, the King of Entropy, who wants everybody to exercise all the time and has made insane amounts of money saying so. Simmons says that he has raised his metabolism so high that he can eat more without gaining weight. Working out to pig out—an entropy double whammy.

9   I have a solution for such gratuitous narcissism and I think Simmons might find a tearful video in it. Let people on the machines

create useable energy as they burn off their flabby thighs and excess baggage. Hook up engines and cams and drive shafts that will rotate turbines and generate electricity. Let exercisers light the health club itself. Let them air condition it. Let the clubs store excess energy and sell it to nearby shop owners at low rates.

10   Better yet, create health clubs whose sole purpose is the generation of energy. Pipe the energy into housing projects. Have energy nights where singles get together to pedal, chat, and swap phone numbers. Build a giant pony wheel that operates a flour mill, a rock crusher, a draw bridge, a BMW repair shop. Have the poles protrude from the wheel with spots for a couple hundred joggers to push the wheel around. Install magazine racks on the poles. Have calorie collections and wattage wars. Make it "cool" to sweat for the betterment of mankind, not just for yourself.

11   We cannot afford much more entropy. If we forget that, we might as well be rodents in cages, running into the night. Just like Mimi.

Thesis and Organization

1. The essay has a problem–solution structure. In your own words, what does Barlow describe as the problem?
2. Paragraphs 5–7 give examples of kinds of exercise. What distinctions does Barlow draw among them?
3. The solution appears in paragraphs 9–10 and is a humorous one. Summarize it.
4. In your own words, state the serious point made in the last paragraph.
5. What do you find to be the main subject of the essay? Exercise? Fads? Waste? Entropy? American culture? What reasons can you find for your choice?

Technique and Style

1. Look up *analogy* in an unabridged dictionary. What analogy does Barlow draw? What does the analogy contribute to the essay?
2. Paragraph 4 defines *entropy*. How necessary is that definition? What does it add to the essay?
3. What does the essay gain with the example of Richard Simmons?
4. Imagine you are one of the people filling up the fitness club. Would you be offended by this essay? Why or why not?

5. The person behind the words always comes through in an essay, sometimes more clearly than others. Explain why you would or would not want Michael Barlow as a classmate or friend.

Suggestions for Writing

Journal

1. Take a few minutes to write down what you think about the exercise craze or to record your reaction to a television commercial advertising an exercise product.
2. How does exercise make you feel? Write about why you do or do not enjoy exercising.

Essay

Try your own hand at a problem–solution essay, giving detailed examples of both the problem and the solution. Like Barlow, you may want your tone to be humorous, sugarcoating a serious point. As for the problem, you're apt to be surrounded with choices:
    getting enough hours into the day
    scraping tuition together
    keeping up with schoolwork
    deciding which pleasure to indulge
    sorting out family loyalties
Illustrate the problem by using examples. You may find examples for the solution harder to come by, in which case, like Barlow, you may want to propose something fantastic.

S top Ordering Me Around

Stacey Wilkins

*Like many students, Stacey Wilkins works in a restaurant waiting on
tables, a job that helps her pay off a student loan but one that also
extracts a price of its own, as her essay points out. The essay appeared in the January 4, 1993, issue of* Newsweek *in a regular feature, the "My Turn" column. A person who wants to be treated with
respect, Wilkins also apparently values her privacy, for the only identification that appears at the end of the essay is the note, "Wilkins
lives in Connecticut." Her forum, however, is a public one, and the
readers of* Newsweek *are her ideal audience in that as educated,
middle-class Americans, they are more likely to patronize the kind of
restaurant Wilkins works at than the local fast-food place.*

WHAT TO LOOK FOR   *The narrative that opens Wilkins' essay
serves as the primary example in the essay, and one that sets the
essay's tone as well. As you read the essay, try to hear it so that you
can identify her tone more exactly. At times, the tone may strike you
as angry, hurt, bitter, sarcastic, and any number of other variations.
How would you characterize it?*

1   I had just sat an extra hour and a half waiting for some country-
club tennis buddies to finish a pizza. They came in 15 minutes after the restaurant closed—they hadn't wanted to cut short their tennis match. The owner complied and agreed to turn the oven back
on and make them a pizza. The cook had long since gone home.

2   The customers had no problem demanding service after I explained that the restaurant had closed. They had no problem sitting there until well after 11 o'clock to recount the highlights of
their tennis game (the restaurant closed at 9:30 p.m.). And, most
important, they had no problem making me the brunt of their
cruel little post-tennis match. What fun it was to harass the pathetic
little waitress. "Oh, it's just so nice sitting here like this," one man
said. After getting no response, he continued: "Boy, I guess you
want us to leave." I was ready to explode in anger. "I am not going to respond to your comments," I said, and walked away.

3   He was geared up for a fight. The red flag had been waved. The
man approached me and asked about dessert. A regular customer,

he had never made a practice of ordering dessert before. You know, the '90s low-fat thing. But that night he enjoyed the power. He felt strong, I felt violated.

4   Three dollars and 20 cents later, I went home. Their tip was my payment for this emotional rape. As I drove, tears streamed down my face. Why was I crying? I had been harassed before. Ten years of waitressing should have inured me to this all-too-common situation. But this was a watershed: the culmination of a decade of abuse.

5   I am now at the breaking point. I can't take being the public's punching bag. People seem to think abuse is included in the price of an entree. All sense of decency and manners is checked with their coats at the door. They see themselves in a position far superior to mine. They are the kings. I am the peasant.

6   I would like them to be the peasants. I am a strong advocate of compulsory restaurant service in the United States. What a great comeuppance it would be for the oppressors to have to work a double shift—slinging drinks, cleaning up after kids and getting pissed off that a party of 10 tied up one of their tables for three hours and left a bad tip. Best of all, I would like to see that rude man with tomato sauce on his tennis shorts.

7   Eating in a restaurant is about more than eating food. It is an opportunity to take your frustrations out on the waiter. It is a chance to feel better than the person serving your food. People think there is nothing wrong with rudeness or sexual harassment if it is inflicted on a waiter.

8   Customers have no problem with ignoring the wait staff when they go to take an order. Or they won't answer when the waiter comes to the table laden with hot plates asking who gets what meal. My personal pet peeve is when they make a waiter take a separate trip for each item. "Oh, I'll take another Coke." The waiter asks, "Would anyone else like one?" No response. Inevitably when he comes back to the table someone will say, "I'll have a Coke, too." And so on and so on.

9   I find it odd because no matter what an insolent cad someone might be, they generally make an effort to cover it up in public. The majority of people practice common etiquette. Most individuals won't openly cut in line or talk throughout a movie. People are cognizant of acceptable behavior and adhere to the strictures it demands. That common code of decency does not apply while eating out.

10   Food-service positions are the last bastion of accepted prejudice. People go into a restaurant and openly torment the waiter, leave a small tip and don't think twice about it. Friends allow companions to be rude and don't say a word. The friends of this man did not once tell him to stop taunting me. They remained silent.

11   It doesn't cross their minds that someone has just been rotten to another human being. I have yet to hear someone stick up for the waitress, to insist a person stop being so cruel. This is because people don't think anything wrong has occurred.

12   However, if this man had shouted obscenities at another patron about her ethnicity, say, it would have rightly been deemed unacceptable. Why don't people understand that bad manners are just as unacceptable in a restaurant? Why do they think they have license to mistreat restaurant personnel?

13   I believe it is because food-service workers are relegated to such a low position on the social stratum. Customers have the power. Food-service employees have none. Thus we are easy targets for any angry person's pent-up frustrations. What better sparring partner than one who can't fight back? Most waiters won't respond for fear of losing their jobs. Consequently, we are the designated gripe-catchers of society, along with similar service workers.

14   If people stepped down from their spurious pedestals, they might see how wrong they are. We have dreams and aspirations just like everyone else. Our wages finance those dreams. Even an insulting 10 percent tip helps us to move toward a goal, pay the rent, feed the kids.

15   I'm using my earnings to pay off an encumbering graduate-school debt. Our bus girl is financing her education at the University of Pennsylvania. My manager is saving for her first baby. Another waitress is living on her earnings while she pursues an acting career. The dishwasher sends his pay back to his children in Ecuador.

16   Our dreams are no less valid than those of someone who holds a prestigious job at a large corporation. A restaurant's flexible working hours appeal to many people who dislike the regimen of a 9-to-5 day. Our employment doesn't give someone the right to treat us as nonentities. I deserve respect whether I remain a waitress or move on to a different career. And so do the thousands

of waiters and waitresses who make your dining experience a pleasant one.

Thesis and Organization

1. How does the opening narrative set the scene? Where else in the essay do you find references to that narrative? Do they unify the essay or distract you? Why?
2. At what point in the essay does the author move from the particular to the general? Which gets the most emphasis?
3. Reexamine the essay as one that poses a problem and a solution. What is the problem? The solution?
4. How successfully does Wilkins position her experience as representative of the experience of others?
5. Where do you find Wilkins' thesis? Explain whether you find that placement effective.

Technique and Style

1. How would you characterize the author's tone?
2. Does the opening narrative enlist your sympathies? Why or why not?
3. Some readers may find the essay's aim is more expressive than expository or persuasive, that the author is more concerned with venting her feelings than explaining the problem or persuading her readers to resolve it. Make a case for your interpretation of the author's aim.
4. In paragraph 2, Wilkins repeats variations on "they had no problem." Explain whether you find the repetition effective.
5. At various times in the essay, Wilkins uses words that suggest she is really writing about issues of power and class, as in her use of "peasant" (paragraphs 5 and 6) and "low position on the social stratum" (paragraph 13). What other examples can you find? Would the essay be stronger or weaker if these issues were discussed more openly?

Suggestions for Writing

Journal

1. We live in a service society, yet as Wilkins points out, sometimes we demand too much of those who provide the services. Record a few examples of rudeness that you have observed.
2. Write an entry recording your reaction to Wilkins' essay. Do you think her complaints are justified?

Essay

The odds are that you have or have had a job similar to Wilkins', if not waiting on tables then some other low-paying job that is also low on the totem pole of status. Like Wilkins, you may have found you were (or are) not treated with respect. On the other hand, your experience may be quite the opposite. Write an essay in which you use examples from your own experience or the experiences of others to explain how you were (or are) treated on your job. You will want to narrow your subject so that you can cover it thoroughly in three to five pages, so you might focus on a specific category of people:

    customers

    coworkers

    supervisor(s)

Another way to approach the topic would be to choose an example from each of those categories, but if you select that route, make sure your examples are representative.

When Only Monsters Are Real

Brent Staples

Now on the editorial staff of the New York Times, *Brent Staples has had a long and distinguished career in journalism. Throughout that career, he has been particularly sensitive to the relationship between the media and Afro-Americans, between the reporting of the black experience and its reality. The essay that follows appeared in the* New York Times *in November, 1993, where it was originally subtitled "'The Black Experience' and Kody Scott." Monsters are nothing new to Staples, a fact that runs through his autobiography* Parallel Time: Growing Up in Black and White *(1994), in which he examines the pain of shifting away from a predominantly black world and into a white one.*

WHAT TO LOOK FOR   *Odd as it may sound verbs have moods, and, as you might expect, their moods reveal the attitude of the writer. Most of the time when you write, you use the indicative mood, one that states a fact or asks a question—as in "I am reading this paragraph." Now and then, you'll use the subjunctive to state possibility, desire, contradiction, or uncertainty, as in a sentence built around* if: *"If I read the essay, I may enjoy it." The imperative mood—one that states a command or request—doesn't occur as often, but can be very useful. Consider (an imperative) how much mileage Staples gets out of it in his essay.*

1   Never forget Edmund Perry, the black Phillips Exeter graduate who seemed destined for Wall Street or Congress until he was shot to death trying to rob an undercover cop.

2   Edmund Perry did not come from the stereotypical underclass family. His mother was a teacher and president of the P.T.A. His older brother attended an Ivy League college. Growing up in Harlem, Edmund had been a bright Bible school student who quizzed the minister about God. But when he arrived at Exeter, Edmund shed his middle-classness and donned the mask of the angry urban thug. He played the role so well that other black students were encouraged to be like him. And playing tough ended his life.

3   Like many before and after him, Edmund succumbed to the American fascination with angry black men. The Cosby family notwithstanding, black prep school boys who study the classics and live within the law have found only marginal acceptance in American cultural reality. The culture's taste runs heavily to black Frankensteins. Lacking a visible alternative, black boys rush to the monster role. And when the news, entertainment and publishing industries embark on a "black story," they often focus, with a kind of perverse romanticism, on the swaggering urban criminal.

4   Consider the L.A. riots. When the press shifted its eye from the central characters, Rodney King and Reginald Denny, L.A.'s gangsters got more attention than people like Congresswoman Maxine Waters, or the prosperous blacks of Baldwin Hills. The most enduring figure to emerge was Monster Kody Scott, a murderous person and member of one of L.A.'s most brutal street gangs. Monster is now an inmate at Pelican Bay State Prison, a high-security fortress in northern California. He became a celebrity when interviewed on "60 Minutes."

5   Kody Scott's memoir, *Monster: The Autobiography of an L.A. Gang Member,* is the subject of an illuminating article in the December *Atlantic Monthly.* The book describes how Monster shot a dozen rivals and how one was dismembered with a machete. He has never been convicted of murder but has spent half his life in jail for assault and other crimes. Early publicity from the publisher, Grove/Atlantic, characterized Monster as "a primary voice of the black experience." After being denounced by Leonce Gaiter in *Buzz* magazine, Grove/Atlantic amended the phrase to "a primary voice coming out of the black underclass." But even that's too simple.

6   Kody—photographed in dark glasses, machine pistol in hand, his mammoth torso bare—presents himself as the inevitable product of the urban inferno. "To be in a gang in South Central when I joined," he writes, "is the equivalent of growing up in Grosse Pointe, Michigan, and going to college: everyone does it."

7   But Kody's criminalization was less inevitable than he lets on. The singer Ray Charles was his godfather. Kody's mother, though estranged from her husband, was a diligent homemaker and homeowner. Kody's brother Kevin is an actor living in Burbank. His brother Kim joined the Air Force. A third brother, Kerwin, works at the 32nd Street Market in South Central. His sister, Kendis, is studying data processing. Certainly the lure of the streets

was strong. But Kody Scott had choices. He chose to become Monster.

8   In *The Atlantic Monthly,* Mark Horowitz writes: "Apart from a few brief mentions Kevin, Kim, Kendis and Kerwin are nowhere to be found in *Monster.* There's no childhood, and very little about Kody's mother. They don't fit Monster's version."

9   In spirit, Monster's version of himself is pretty much the same as Richard Wright's portrayal of Bigger Thomas, the twisted, Frankenstinian character in the novel *Native Son.* Bigger rapes and murders, we're told, because he can't help it; abject poverty pushed him to it. Bigger—the soulless beast, empty of humanity—is the sort of person many Americans reflexively think of when they seek to define "the black experience." But there is no *one* black experience.

10   The black middle class is larger than ever, but the black prep school boy has yet to become a valid literary type. Morgan Entrekin, Grove/Atlantic's publisher, agrees that the bias is unfortunate. A book about the black middle class is scheduled for next year, but Grove/Atlantic worries that people will ignore it. Put me down for a dozen copies, Mr. Entrekin. Deliver me from Biggers and Monsters and Frankensteins.

Thesis and Organization

1. Staples opens his essay with the example of Edmund Perry, paragraphs 1–3. What is the point of that example?
2. The essay shifts from Edmund Perry to the Los Angeles riots, then to Kody Scott. What connection links these people and events?
3. Paragraph 5 discusses the publicity for Kody Scott's book. What does Staples object to?
4. Staples' essay touches on a number of subjects: America's "fascination" with "black Frankensteins" (paragraph 3), the media's "perverse romanticism" (paragraph 3), the media's coverage of blacks (paragraphs 3–5, 10), and the black middle class (paragraph 10). Which is his main subject? What reasons can you supply for your choice?
5. Given that subject, what is Staples' thesis?

Technique and Style

1. What connection can you discover between the introduction (paragraphs 1–3) and the conclusion (paragraph 10)?
2. Look up *irony* in an unabridged dictionary. What examples of it can you find in Staples' essay?

3. Paragraph 9 alludes to two literary figures, Bigger Thomas and Franken-stein. What do these allusions add to the essay?

4. Explain whether Staples' use of the imperative makes the essay more for-mal or more informal.

5. Staples uses Kody Scott as the extended example in the essay (para-graphs 4–9). In what ways does that example support the thesis?

Suggestions for Writing

Journal

1. Check out the validity of Staples' point by looking through a newspaper to see if you can find an example of the "American fascination with an-gry black men." Record the example and your response to it. If you don't find an example, write about whether you find Staples' point valid.

2. Watch the evening news on television, either the national news or the news segment of a local broadcast. Then write about your perception of the newscast and whether it focused on "monsters" and violence. If you use examples, you will find it easier to turn the entry into an essay at a later date.

Essay

The line between being an individual and being an outlaw is a fine one that's sometimes hard to draw. Think of a person you know or have read about who walks that line:

one of your high school classmates
a big name in music
a film star
a sports hero

Write an essay about that person, giving examples to prove your point. If you prefer, think of someone who projects a distinct "image," one you admire or despise. As you draft your essay, use examples to describe the image and explain what it means to you.

E lectronic Intimacies

Peter Steinhart

Audubon *is the magazine of the National Audubon Society, an organization devoted to protecting birds and their habitats, as well as other wildlife. In addition to publishing* Audubon *six times a year, the organization supports a number of nature reserves and education centers throughout the United States. Peter Steinhart writes frequently for the magazine about the pleasures of nature and the relation of the natural world to our human one. He has also written several books reflecting that interest, the most recent being* The Company of Wolves *(1995), which one reviewer cited as providing "both a scientific and a psychological exploration of the impact wolves have had on humans." In "Electronic Intimacies," Steinhart also examines an "impact," giving his readers numerous examples of the effect television's wildlife shows have had on their viewers. The essay is also a good illustration of how a writer uses various patterns of organization to support a thesis. Here, Steinhart puts example, description, and causal analysis to work.*

WHAT TO LOOK FOR   *Steinhart's essay is longer than most of the essays in this book, and longer essays force the writer to group ideas in larger clusters. A short essay may deal with a main point in one or two paragraphs, but a longer one will often take three or more paragraphs to develop an idea. Yet the same principle is at work, the principle of a generalization followed by supporting examples. As you read Steinhart's essay, mark the generalizations so that you are aware of the paragraph blocks that support them.*

1   In Yellowstone National Park a man trotted up to a lone buffalo. The buffalo didn't seem to be doing anything, so the man sought to improve its day by posing it for a picture. The buffalo became annoyed and bluff-charged. Undaunted, the man approached to within a few feet. The buffalo tossed him in the air and gored him.

2   A dozen visitors are injured by buffalo and a few more by bears or elk or moose every year in Yellowstone. Most of them are trying

to snuggle up for a photograph. These encounters suggest something about the way we view wild animals today: We expect them to be available, accessible, and capable of intimacies.

3   Little in our actual experience of wildlife supports that expectation. In real life, our view of most creatures is abrupt and flickering, shadowed and blurred. Much of the content of our encounters comes from imagination or convention. And, since most of the park adventurers who end up in bandages are city slickers, it seems quite likely that they have learned their conventions by viewing wildlife on television.

4   Television has become our chief means of seeing wild creatures. Our living rooms are livelier than any national park. Any day you can switch on *Nature* or the *National Geographic Specials* and watch monkeys cavorting in trees or lions slinking through the grass. Britain's Survival Anglia keeps twenty-two crews in the field around the world. One-third of the programming on The Discovery Channel is wildlife. It's the biggest single subject for nonfiction video.

5   Wildlife film has a relatively short history. In the first decade of this century, Cherry Kearton filmed birds in nests and showed the footage with lectures. Lenses and films were not fast enough to allow telephotos or shots in dim light, so the filmmakers were happy simply to get a shot of, say, a cheetah sauntering along the veldt several hundred yards away. Until the 1950s most wildlife film consisted of simple identification shots—a gazelle grazing in the distance, a zebra running the other way. Most were shown in lecture halls rather than movie theaters. "When color film came out," recalls Karl Maslowski, a filmmaker who for forty years toured on National Audubon's lecture circuit, "if you had a red bird, a yellow bird, and a sunset, people stood up and cheered."

6   In the 1950s Walt Disney changed the field forever. He sought to bring nature to the movie screen and hired cameramen with studio-quality equipment to film close-ups, sustained action, and whole sequences of behavior from several camera angles. Disney brought the animals closer, and his films were immensely popular. But they changed the nature of the animals. Movies dramatize. In a darkened theater, character is everything. In the Disney version, and virtually all the theater films that followed, wildlife was presented as distorted humanity, as bumbling bears, square-dancing

tarantulas, adolescent beavers running away from home, or the leering monsters of *Jaws* and *Grizzly*.

7   The big screen has seldom shown animals with what we might consider scientific integrity. Hollywood is a dream factory, and it values emotional intensity over factual accuracy. Modern wildlife filmmakers are quite critical of the Hollywood version. But Disney's popularization combined with increasingly faster films and lenses, lighter equipment, and cheap travel to remote areas to allow other filmmakers to go out into the wild for months on end and compile intimate biographies. Bill Burrud began filming wildlife in 1959, and Mutual of Omaha sent out crews in 1962. And they sold their films to television.

8   In the 1960s commercial television hadn't yet sought to displace Hollywood as our dream merchant. It still focused much on fact and event. So television's wildlife descended from the traveling wildlife lecture and the science films produced by the BBC's natural-history unit, whose programs explained how birds navigate or fish live in water. American television borrowed from the movies by weaving humans into the story, for example having Marlin Perkins help a scientist anesthetize a rhino. And there was much emphasis on action, on hunting and being hunted. The British tradition was much enriched when, in the 1960s, Survival Anglia sent crews to live in the field for two or three *years* at a time, to film great cradle-to-grave epics of wildebeest and caribou and elephant. That ushered in a golden age of wildlife film. Today we enjoy hour-long portraits, rich with insight and intimacy. The appetite for such films is enormous.

9   Despite the popularity of wildlife films, they have a way of seeming repetitious. In part, the repetition is real: Much of the stock footage produced by Bill Burrud in the 1960s is still being screened today. Old footage gets dated as better equipment and more skillful photographers raise the level of clarity and intimacy. And new films often recall what we have seen in the old ones. Christopher N. Palmer, executive producer of the *Audubon Television Specials,* cautions, "It takes an enormous amount of time and creativity to make them look fresh."

10   Cameramen are driven to find new species and places to film, and ways to get closer to the animals. Heinz Sielman cut away the side of a tree trunk and installed a window and a blind to film

nesting woodpeckers. Dieter Plage disguised a camera as a pelican and swam underwater to film waterfowl. The Oxford Scientific Films unit built a forty-foot-long indoor trout stream, with pumps to create currents and all the aquatic organisms needed to film a life history of trout.

11   Novelty doesn't come easy. Since the 1960s it has grown harder to make films overseas, because travel is now more expensive and many of the countries are politically unstable or simply hostile. There are fewer places in which animals survive, and so there is competition for the unobstructed view. Des and Jen Bartlett spent four years filming in Namibia's Etosha National Park in part because the wildlife in the more accessible parks of Kenya is always ringed with tour buses.

12   Filming is also more expensive. A complete portrait may take years in the field, and that time costs money. Belinda Wright and Stanley Breeden spent two years and $500,000 filming *Land of the Tiger*. That's more than television will pay for a wildlife film. To cut costs, some filmmakers use trained animals and staged shots.

13   Still, there is a sameness. A local newspaper columnist complains that every time he turns on PBS, he expects to see a show about insects.

14   The problem is not that we're seeing the same creatures over and over again, but that there is an orthodoxy to wildlife films. The organizing idea is almost invariably that a creature struggles to survive the hardships of nature and civilization. Says Bayer, "The typical life story of, say, the mountain lion is a story about survival, and it becomes repetitious."

15   The new orthodoxy is clearly not an interest in science, for the films show a marked preference for mammals and birds, for creatures that are warm-blooded and seemingly approachable, rather than for spiders, jellyfish, or lizards. Nor is the main interest conservation. The films seldom do a good job of explaining who is responsible for a species' decline or what a viewer can do about it. It's not because the filmmaker doesn't care. It's because he wants the film to last long enough to pay back its costs in video rentals and television syndication, so he does not delve into legal or regulatory issues which may be out of date by the time the film is edited and released, let alone rerun in syndication.

16   The focus on survival probably has more to do with television's growing envy of Hollywood than with wildlife's problems. Think-

ing about survival allows us to personify animals without seeming as anthropomorphic as Disney. And even the most exacting film-makers have doubts about science and survival as themes. Says James Murray, executive producer of *The Nature of Things:* "You're peering inside and looking at everything in detail, and you're miss-ing the emotional part of it." Photographer and filmmaker Jeff Foott says, "A lot of what's happening in wildlife films is terribly cerebral. I'd love to see films that let people just feel rather than learn."

17   Our real interest is empathy. Humans are designed to mytholo-gize. Give us acres of science and we'll still plant gardens of rhyme. We'll look for spirit anywhere it offers to blossom, and it seems to beckon from the eye shine of the tiger and the flight of the sparrow. We want honesty, but we don't want it to get in the way of vision. That's why, I suspect, the spine of many wildlife films is evolution. It is so abstract that, after a few repetitions, we can conveniently ignore it.

18   If we ignore the message and look for myths, the films may mis-lead us. For wildlife films suffer from the chief curse of television: They make experience seem accessible and well-organized when it fact it is not. Nature doesn't reveal itself in thirty minutes or an hour. To see wild creatures one needs to train one's senses, to ex-ercise imagination and temper it with effort and experience.

19   To film a red fox and her cubs, Karl Maslowski built a blind forty feet above a den in a black locust tree and then spent four or five days in the blind every spring for twelve years, waiting for a shot of the vixen and her pups. Only twice in those years did he get a shot. Filmmaker Wolfgang Bayer waited three days in a mine shaft, motionless behind a blind, for wild horses to come in to drink, and once waited three weeks for a coyote to come out of its den.

20   The patience and resourcefulness of the wildlife filmmaker are enormous. But they never appear on the screen. In the comfort of our living rooms we escape the cold feet, the mosquito bites, the uncertain glimpses that are part of our real relationship with the wild. And we miss the surges of impulse and imagination that flow out of these gaps in our vision. Still photographs elicit those surges because they usually leave the context of the shot unexplained and let the viewer imagine what has preceded and what follows the shot. But film organizes the experience, sets a context, a place, a meaning. There is at times too little for a viewer to do.

21   By taking the waiting out of watching, wildlife films also make wild creatures appear less modest and retiring than they really are. Animals become almost promiscuously available on television. We get lingering close-ups. The animals are fully revealed. There are no empty landscapes. That, I suspect, is why visitors to our national parks expect wildlife to be accessible. Says National Park Service naturalist Glen Kaye, "Whatever the hour of the day, the question is, 'Which meadow do I go to to see the deer or the elk or the bear *right now?*' There's no sense that the animals may not be available."

22   Films also make the animals seem confiding. Television's close-ups leap across centuries of evolution by taking us within the fight and flight distances that normally separate individuals. That probably explains why we assume a familiarity with movie stars and politicians that we wouldn't attempt with neighbors. We have been electronically intimate, close enough to hear them breathe and see their eyelids flutter. Among real people such things imply familiarity. So we'll barge in on them and demand autographs or recitations, though we are perfect strangers.

23   The same thing is true of wildlife. Filmmakers have taken us into the range of eye shine and body heat and personified the creature by telling us of its struggle. We're apt to feel the same cheap familiarity we feel with Tom Selleck or Oprah Winfrey. Says Mary Meagher, a Yellowstone biologist, "I don't think people have too much sense of flight distance in buffalo or bear, although humans have flight distances themselves. Even when I see that something dangerous is about to happen, if I explain to people that the animal is dangerous, I usually get the finger for my trouble. People can have all the warnings and disregard them."

24   Modern life seems tainted more and more with the expectation of gratification without effort, revelation without knowledge, feeling without understanding. Television is one of the culprits. Too often it absolves us of the responsibility to look for ourselves and sort the real from the perceived. Look at animals in the wild and you get an uncertain image, full of blur and shadow, which requires large measures of imagination and judgment. Look at them on film and you lose the responsibility to organize what you see.

25   Television brings wildlife into our hearts and minds. It makes us aware of humanity's aggrandizement of the Earth. But celluloid is not a substitute for experience. With or without television, we still

make much use of animals in our minds. We let them symbolize virtues and vices, carry thoughts and feelings. If wildlife films ever become our only access to wild animals, we may be the less intelligent, perceptive, and imaginative for it.

Thesis and Organization

1. Steinhart begins his essay with a narrative set in a national park. What point does he make later in the essay that most directly relates to that narrative?
2. What paragraphs make up the introduction to the essay? What evidence can you cite to support your opinion?
3. Steinhart includes a short history of wildlife films. What does that explanation contribute to the essay as a whole?
4. How would you summarize Steinhart's point about the effect of the wildlife films we now see on television?
5. Identify the major points in the essay. What paragraphs support those points?
6. What paragraphs provide the conclusion to the essay? How would you restate Steinhart's thesis?

Technique and Style

1. Steinhart's prose often provides a perfect example of the kind of paragraph that begins with a topic sentence and then supports it by examples. Select one paragraph that is organized this way and explain the relationship between the particular and the general.
2. It's probably safe to assume that most of Steinhart's readers watch television and occasionally enjoy wildlife programs, programs that Steinhart criticizes. What techniques does he use to avoid offending his readers?
3. Writers often use parallel phrases or clauses to emphasize ideas, as Steinhart does in the first sentence of paragraph 24. Do you find it effective? Why or why not?
4. In paragraphs 22 and 23 the author compares our attitudes toward celebrities and animals. What causal relationship does he draw? How valid does his point seem to be?
5. What sources does the author draw on for his examples? Does the variety seem sufficient?
6. What sense do you get of Steinhart as a person? If you were to describe him based only on what you know of him from this essay, what kind of person would you describe?

Suggestions for Writing

Journal

1. Take a few moments to record your impression of wildlife shows. Is there one you particularly remember? In general, do you like or dislike them, or does your response fall somewhere in between?

2. Steinhart states that "Modern life seems tainted more and more with the expectation of gratification without effort. . . ." Write an entry testing that statement against your own experience.

Essay

Think about the various categories of shows on television:
cartoons
soap operas
talk shows
dramas
situation comedies
You can probably add any number of others to the list. Like Steinhart, you will be writing an essay in which you analyze the difference between what the type of show presents as reality and reality itself. To make the topic more manageable, you might select one particular show and then use multiple examples from it. If you prefer, choose an advertisement from a magazine instead of a television show.

Definition

"When I use a word," said Humpty Dumpty, "it means just what I choose it to mean—neither more nor less." To that Alice replied, "The question is whether you can make words mean so many different things." Humpty Dumpty then pronounced, "The question is which is to be the master—that's all." Writers are the masters of their words, although not to the extent that Humpty Dumpty would like, and often a discussion or argument boils down to the meaning of a crucial word. *Liberty, justice, civil rights, freedom,* and other similar concepts, for example, are all abstractions until they are defined.

If you had to write a paper on what freedom means to you, you might be tempted first off to look up the word in a dictionary, but you will discover more to say if you put aside the dictionary and first think about some basic questions, such as "Whose freedom?" If it's your freedom you are writing about, who or what sets limits on your freedom? The law? the church? parents? family responsibilities? After you mull over questions such as these, you are in a better position to make use of a dictionary definition. The dictionary is the most obvious place to find what the word means, but what you find there is only explicit meaning, the word's **denotation**. Look up freedom in a collegiate dictionary and you'll see the different ways in which the word can be used, and also its etymology, but that won't convey the rich layers of meaning that the word has accumulated through the years.

What the dictionary does not reveal is the word's associative or emotional meanings, its **connotation**. One way to discover connotation is to ask yourself questions about the word, questions similar to those above that get at how the concept of freedom touches your life. The more specific your examples, the more concrete your definition can be, and the less the danger of slipping into clichés. Unless the word you are defining is quite unusual, most readers will be familiar with its dictionary definition; your own definition and your speculations on the word's connotation are of much greater interest.

A paper that defines a familiar word can hold just as much interest as one that examines an unfamiliar word or a word that is particularly powerful. "What does boredom mean?" "Why is synergism a useful concept?" "What does it mean to be called handicapped?" Questions such as these can be explored through almost any mode of thinking and writing. You can use those that you have already studied both to probe your subject as you think about it and to develop your ideas as you write.

Description   What details best describe it? What senses can you appeal to?

Narration   What story might best illustrate it? What kind of conflict might the word involve?

Example   What sorts of examples illustrate it? What different times and sources can you use to find examples?

And even though you may not have read essays that use the other modes discussed in this book, they are already familiar to you as ways to thinking and can therefore also be useful to you as you think and write about your central term.

Comparison and contrast   What is it similar to? What is it different from?

Analogy   What metaphor would make it vivid? What might the reader be familiar with that you can draw an analogy to?

Division and classification   How can it be divided? What types or categories can it be broken into?

Process   What steps or stages are involved in it? Which are crucial?

Cause and effect   What are the conditions that cause it? What effect does it have?

When questions such as these are tailored to the particular word or concept under scrutiny, they will help you develop your ideas.

AUDIENCE AND PURPOSE   Unless your subject is unusual, you can assume that your audience has a general understanding of the word or phrase to be defined. The nature of that general understanding, however differs. For instance, the word *spinster* most often raises an image of "little old lady," a picture possibly fleshed out with a cat or two and fussy furnishings. Short of those associations, a spinster is an unmarried woman of a certain age, but that age varies from one decade to another. Forty years ago, a single woman who was twenty-six might well have been considered a spinster. These days, the term—when used at all—would be applied to someone considerably older. Even so, the negative image remains, and those who use the word probably assume that the spinster leads a lonely, narrow life. Such an image, however, is a far cry from the likes of Katherine Hepburn, who never married but who, at the age of eighty plus, was still being asked about her long-term love affair with her married Hollywood costar, Spencer Tracy. Were you to write an essay arguing against the stereotype and focusing on the Katherine Hepburns of our time, you might introduce your subject by reminding your readers of the word's usual connotations.

Sometimes you not only want to change the reader's understanding but also want to make the reader aware of how the meaning of a word has changed, a change that has an effect on our society. In that case you may choose to argue for a redefinition of the word or go a step further and attack the effects of the term's changed meaning. Words such as *amateur, dilettante*, and *gay* have all undergone major shifts in meaning within a relatively short period of time, at least short in the linguistic sense. *Amateur* used to refer to someone engaged in an activity for pleasure, not pay, but it now has the common meaning of inexperienced, unskilled. *Dilettante* also had a positive connotation, someone who was a lover of the arts; now it is more likely associated with someone who dabbles at them. As for *gay*, today it is associated with the word *homosexual*, which puts a very different spin on the nineteenth century and its Gay Nineties.

Definition can also be used to explore what people know and don't know about a place. If you were to write an essay that explains what your neighborhood means to you, you would essentially be presenting a personal definition of it. The same would be true if you were to write about any favorite spot, whether it be a tree house from your childhood or a park bench. To some, a park bench may be an eyesore or a necessity or a plain park bench, whereas to you it may hold particular meaning as the place where you find peace and quiet.

Perhaps you merely want your readers to reexamine a term and consider its importance. *Education* is a word familiar to all, and you and your classmates have had years of experience with it, but it may well mean different things to different people. Were you to write about the word within the context of your college education, you might begin by chasing down its etymology, which would bring you to the Latin *educatus*, meaning brought up, taught. From there you might speculate on how the meaning of education has shifted, slipping from the general—conveying general knowledge and developing reason and judgment—to the particular—emphasizing skills and preparation for a profession. At that point, you would have the makings of a good argument against or in favor of the change.

EXAMPLE   To flesh out the definition of a term, you can draw on a number of sources. You might make a quick connection with your reader's experience, for instance, by drawing examples from the world of athletics. An essay defining *grace* can cite Michael Jordan's drive to a basket, just as one on *bizarre* might well put Dennis Rodman at the head of the list for his habit of dyeing his hair different colors and cross-dressing. Citing examples of well-known figures from film, television, the arts, and politics is also a quick way to remind your readers of what they know and to make use of that to explain the unfamiliar. While contemporary figures probably come to mind first, historical ones will serve just as well, with the additional advantage of broadening the base of your information and adding to your credibility, your **persona**, the self you present behind the prose in the essay. A brief mention of the grace of a Donatello bronze or the bizarre world of Hieronymus Bosch extends the range of your definition while also revealing the depth of your knowledge. The point is not to drop names but to use what you know to make your point.

OTHER MODES   Definition, perhaps more than any other rhetorical pattern, depends on other modes to serve its purpose. While example is the most obvious, all the others may also come into play. Were you to write an essay on *honesty*, for example, you might begin your discussion with a narrative, a brief story about a friend who bought a magazine at a newsstand and received too much change for a twenty-dollar bill. The narrative can then lead to comparison and contrast, making a distinction between honest and dishonest. And if the friend kept the money but feels guilty about it, then you would be dealing with cause and effect.

While an essay that depends primarily on definition can be developed as a personal narrative, one that is organized as straightforward exposition will also involve other patterns of organization. If you were writing a short research paper on the common cold, comparison would help you distinguish it from the flu and process would enable you to trace its progress from the first sore throat to the last sniffle. In between, you might discuss possible ways to relieve symptoms, which would bring in classification. Although you may use many different modes, your primary one would still be definition.

THESIS AND ORGANIZATION   Although a definition can play a key role in an essay, it is not the essay's thesis. The thesis rises from the author's assertion about the definition. Sometimes your title can serve as your thesis or at least hint at it, as in "Honesty Isn't Easy" or "No Cure for the Common Cold." The explicit thesis is also obvious, usually found in one sentence in the introduction. Sometimes, however, you want the reader to infer the thesis by combining the ideas in two or more sentences. Far more subtle is the implied thesis, which is what you have here:

> Pile on onions, lettuce, tomato, cheese, even mushrooms and jalapeño peppers, douse it with ketchup, mustard, mayonnaise, and still you can't hide the classic American hamburger—a quarter pound or so of relatively lean grilled beef snuggled into a soft but not spongy round roll. If the meat's too lean, the hamburger is too dry, but if it's not lean enough, the juice soaks the roll and the whole creation falls apart.

The thesis? Several are possible but two come quickly to mind, variations on "You can't spoil the classic American hamburger" and "The classic American hamburger is a splendid creation." Either way, what you have is a definition and an assertion about it.

Like the thesis, an essay's organization can be straightforward or somewhat complex. At times, you may want to use a roughly chronological pattern of organization, starting at one point in time and moving forward to another. Structuring an essay so that it moves from the least to the most important point is another obvious pattern, one used by several of the writers in this chapter. You might also consider organizing your paper by question/answer, the introduction posing a question and the body of the essay answering it. A variation on that pattern is one in which one part of the essay poses a problem that is then discussed and analyzed in terms of possible solutions. Both those ways of organizing an essay are relatively uncomplicated. Perhaps the hardest to handle successfully is the organization that goes from the particular to the general. Were you to write a paper on the American flag, for example, you might start with the particular—a description of the modern flag—and then discuss the general—what it means as a symbol.

USEFUL TERMS

Connotation   The associations suggested by a word that add to its literal meaning. *Home* and *domicile* have similar dictionary meanings, but they differ radically in their connotation.

Denotation   The literal meaning of a word, its dictionary definition.

Persona   The character of the writer that comes through from the prose.

■ POINTERS FOR USING DEFINITION

Exploring the Topic

1. **What are the denotations of your term?** You should consult an unabridged dictionary and perhaps a more complete or specialized one, such as the *Oxford English Dictionary* or a dictionary of slang.
2. **What are the connotations of your term?** What emotional reactions or associations does it elicit from people? What situations evoke what responses and why?
3. **What other words can be used for your term?** Which are similar?
4. **What are the characteristics, qualities, or components of your term?** Which are most important? Are some not worth mentioning?
5. **What other modes are appropriate?** What modes can you draw on to help support your definition and the organization of the essay? Where can you use description? Narration? What examples can you use to illustrate your term?
6. **Has your word been used or misused in the past?** If so, might that misuse be turned into an introductory narrative? A closing one?

Drafting the Paper

1. **Know your reader.** Review your lists of denotations and connotations together with the characteristics related to your term to see how familiar they are to your reader. Check to see if your reader may have particular associations that you need to redirect or change. Or if your reader is directly affected by your topic, make sure your definition does not offend.
2. **Know your purpose.** Unless your term is unusual, one of your biggest problems is to tell the reader something new about it. Work on your first paragraph so that it will engage the reader from the start. From that point

on, keep your primary purpose in mind. If you are writing a paper that is basically self-expressive or persuasive, make sure you have an audience other than yourself. If your aim is informative, consider narration, example, cause and effect, and analogy as possible ways of presenting familiar material in a fresh light.

3. **Use examples.** Provide examples to illustrate what your key term means. Also consider using negative examples and setting out distinctions between the meaning of your word and other, similar words.

4. **Draw on a variety of sources.** Define your term from several perspectives. Perhaps a brief history of the word would be helpful, or maybe some statistical information is in order. See if a brief narrative might provide additional meaning for the term.

5. **Make a point.** Don't mistake your definition for your thesis. The two are certainly related, but one is an assertion; the other is not. Perhaps your definition is a jumping-off place for a larger point you wish to make or a key part of that point. Or perhaps your term evokes a single dominant impression you want to convey. Whatever purpose your definition serves, it supports your thesis.

I n All Ways a Woman

Maya Angelou

Known to all who watched the inauguration of President William Jefferson Clinton on January 20, 1993, for her reading of her poem "On the Pulse of Morning," Maya Angelou has long been a celebrated writer and speaker. She is as apt to begin a speaking engagement with an acappela blues song as with a narrative from her childhood, a childhood many readers are familiar with through her book I Know Why the Caged Bird Sings. *Author of a large body of poetry, essays, children's books, and memoirs, Angelou is currently Reynolds Professor in the English Department at Wake Forest University. Her published poetry has been collected in* The Complete Collected Poems of Maya Angelou *(1994), and the essay that follows comes from* Wouldn't Take Nothing for My Journey Now *(1993), a collection dedicated to her good friend Oprah Winfrey.*

WHAT TO LOOK FOR   *Changing from the particular to the general or from the personal to the impersonal is often difficult. One choice many writers make involves writing a draft in first person and then shifting out of first person in the next version. Maya Angelou takes a different approach, starting with first person and her own experience, then generalizing about that experience by using one of the categories she belongs to, that of woman. All of us belong to any number of larger groups. Like Angelou, you can generalize based on gender, or you can use any other category that fits—age, occupation, family relationship (father or mother or child), voter, citizen. The list is almost endless.*

1   In my young years I took pride in the fact that luck was called a lady. In fact, there were so few public acknowledgments of the female presence that I felt personally honored whenever nature and large ships were referred to as feminine. But as I matured, I began to resent being considered a sister to a changeling as fickle as luck, as aloof as an ocean, and as frivolous as nature.

2   The phrase "A woman always has the right to change her mind" played so aptly into the negative image of the female that I made myself a victim to an unwavering decision. Even if I made an inane and stupid choice, I stuck by it rather than "be like a woman and change my mind."

3   Being a woman is hard work. Not without joy and even ecstasy, but still relentless, unending work. Becoming an old female may require only being born with certain genitalia, inheriting long-living genes and the fortune not to be run over by an out-of-control truck, but to become and remain a woman command the existence and employment of genius.

4   The woman who survives intact and happy must be at once tender and tough. She must have convinced herself, or be in the unending process of convincing herself, that she, her values, and her choices are important. In a time and world where males hold sway and control, the pressure upon women to yield their rights-of-way is tremendous. And it is under those very circumstances that the woman's toughness must be in evidence.

5   She must resist considering herself a lesser version of her male counterpart. She is not a sculptress, poetess, authoress, Jewess, Negress, or even (now rare) in university parlance a rectoress. If she is the thing, then for her own sense of self and for the education of the ill-informed she must insist with rectitude in being the thing and in being called the thing.

6   A rose by any other name may smell as sweet, but a woman called by a devaluing name will only be weakened by the misnomer.

7   She will need to prize her tenderness and be able to display it at appropriate times in order to prevent toughness from gaining total authority and to avoid becoming a mirror image of those men who value power above life, and control over love.

8   It is imperative that a woman keep her sense of humor intact and at the ready. She must see, even if only in secret, that she is the funniest, looniest woman in her world, which she should also see as being the most absurd world of all times.

9   It has been said that laughter is therapeutic and amiability lengthens the life span.

10   Women should be tough, tender, laugh as much as possible, and live long lives. The struggle for equality continues unabated, and the woman warrior who is armed with wit and courage will be among the first to celebrate victory.

Thesis and Organization

1. What paragraph or paragraphs introduce the essay? What reasons do you have for your choice?

2. Where and what is the essay's thesis? What reasons can you find for its placement? Explain whether you find that placement effective.
3. Where in the essay does Angelou use comparisons? What do they contribute to the thesis?
4. What do paragraphs 2 and 9 have in common? How do they relate to the thesis?
5. Given that essays can be organized in a number of ways—such as chronological, particular/general (or vice versa), dramatic, problem/solution—how would you characterize Angelou's sequencing of paragraphs?

Technique and Style

1. Explain the ways in which the title fits the essay's thesis and content.
2. What reasons can you find for Angelou's use of sayings and associations in paragraphs 1 and 2?
3. To what extent, if any, does Angelou make use of race in the essay? What purpose does it or the lack of it serve?
4. Angelou alludes to Shakespeare's *Romeo and Juliet* in paragraph 6 and to Maxine Hong Kingston, author of *Woman Warrior*, in paragraph 10. What do these allusions contribute to the essay?
5. Although the audience for the essay is a general one, the piece focuses almost exclusively on women. Discuss the degree to which that focus limits the essay. What is in it for men?

Suggestions for Writing

Journal

1. Use your journal to explore what Angelou means by *tender*. What examples can you find in your own experience that fit the definition?
2. If you prefer, explore what Angelou means by *tough*. Again, flesh out her definition with examples from your own experience.

Essay

Write your own "in all ways" essay, drawing on a category or group to which you belong. The tone of your essay may be serious, like Angelou's, or humorous. Either tone would work, for instance, if you were to write "In All Ways a Student" or "In All Ways Underpaid." Other suggestions:

a parent (or child or sibling)
a winner (or loser)
a reader (or writer)
a fan

 **the Porch**

Garrison Keillor

Anyone who has heard "Prairie Home Companion" is familiar with Garrison Keillor, whose radio show makes rural living downright attractive, so much so that the shows have been made into tapes, videocassettes, and compact discs. More recently, Keillor has turned his talents to children's stories such as Cat, You Better Come Home *(1995) and* The Sandy Bottom Orchestra *(1996). Whether he's relating the story of a cowboy named Lonesome Shorty or speculating on the midlife crisis of the Greek god Dionysus in his collection* The Book of Guys *(1994), Keillor is always entertaining. In the essay below, you'll recognize the same tone that's in "Prairie Home Companion," a gentle and good-humored nostalgia for all things rural. It's no wonder we should pity the poor city dweller with no porch and therefore no company, no friends, no comfort, no grace. The essay appeared in Keillor's 1989 collection* We Are Still Married.

WHAT TO LOOK FOR *Metaphor and simile come into play in definition because they help clarify the term under discussion and make it valid. Keillor uses a simile in paragraph 8 to make the reader feel what a home without a porch is like. As you write your own definition paper, think of what metaphor and simile can add.*

1   Of porches there are two sorts: the decorative and the useful, the porch that is only a platform and the porch you can lie around on in your pajamas and read the Sunday paper.

2   The decorative porch has a slight function, similar to that of the White House portico: it's where you greet prime ministers, premiers, and foreign potentates. The cannons boom, the band plays, the press writes it all down, and they go indoors.

3   The true porch, or useful porch, incorporates some of that grandeur, but it is screened and protects you from prying eyes. It strikes a perfect balance between indoor and outdoor life.

4   Indoors is comfortable but decorous, as Huck Finn found out at the Widow's. It is even stifling if the company isn't right. A good porch gets you out of the parlor, lets you smoke, talk loud, eat with your fingers—without apology and without having to run

away from home. No wonder that people with porches have hundreds of friends.

5   Of useful porches there are many sorts, including the veranda, the breezeway, the back porch, front porch, stoop, and now the sun deck, though the veranda is grander than a porch need be and the sun deck is useful only if you happen to like sun. A useful porch may be large or not, but ordinarily it is defended by screens or large shrubbery. You should be able to walk naked onto a porch and feel only a slight thrill of adventure. It is comfortable, furnished with old stuff. You should be able to spill your coffee anywhere without a trace of remorse.

6   Our family owned a porch like that once, attached to a house overlooking the St. Croix River east of St. Paul, Minnesota, that we rented from the Wilcoxes from May to September. When company came, they didn't stop in the living room but went straight through to the porch.

7   You could sit on the old porch swing that hung from the ceiling or in one of the big wicker chairs or the chaise lounge, or find a spot on the couch, which could seat four or accommodate a tall man taking a nap. There was a table for four, two kerosene lanterns, and some plants in pots. The porch faced east, was cool and shady from midday on, and got a nice breeze off the river. A lush forest of tall ferns surrounded this porch so the occupants didn't have to look at unmowed lawn or a weedy garden and feel too guilty to sit. A brook ran close by.

8   In the home-building industry today, a porch such as that one is considered an expensive frill, which is too bad for the home buyer. To sign up for a lifetime of debt at a vicious rate of interest and wind up with a porchless home, a home minus the homiest room—it's like visiting Minnesota and not seeing the prairie. You cheat yourself. Home, after all, doesn't belong to the bank, it's yours. You're supposed to have fun there, be graceful and comfortable and enjoy music and good conversation and the company of pals, otherwise home is only a furniture showroom and you may as well bunk at the YMCA and get in on their recreation programs.

9   The porch promotes grace and comfort. It promotes good conversation simply by virtue of the fact that on a porch there is no need for it. Look at the sorry bunch in the living room standing in little clumps and holding drinks, and see how hard they work to keep up a steady dribble of talk. There, silence indicates boredom and unhappiness, and hosts are quick to detect silence and rush

over to subdue it into speech. Now look at our little bunch on this porch. Me and the missus float back and forth on the swing, Mark and Rhonda are collapsed at opposite ends of the couch, Malene peruses her paperback novel in which an astounding event is about to occur, young Jeb sits at the table gluing the struts on his Curtiss biplane. The cats lie on the floor listening to birdies, and I say, "It's a heck of a deal, ain't it, a *heck* of a deal." A golden creamy silence suffuses this happy scene, and only on a porch is it possible.

10   When passersby come into view, we say hello to them, but they don't take this as an invitation to barge in. There is something slightly *forbidding* about the sight of people on a porch, its grace is almost royal. You don't rush right up to the Queen and start telling her the story of your life, and you don't do that to porch sitters either. We are Somebody up here even if our screens are torn and the sofa is busted and we're drinking orange pop from cans. You down there are passersby in a parade we've seen come and go for years. We have a porch.

11   It is our reviewing platform and observation deck, our rostrum and dais, the parapet of our stockade, the bridge of our ship. We can sit on it in silence or walk out naked spilling coffee. Whatever we do, we feel richer than Rockefeller and luckier than the President.

12   Years ago, my family moved from that luxurious porch to a porchless apartment in the city. Our friends quit visiting us. We felt as if we had moved to Denver. Then we moved to a big old house with two porches, then to another with a long veranda in front and a small sleeping porch in back. Now we have arrived in Manhattan, at an apartment with a terrace. A porch on the twelfth floor with a view of rooftops, chimney pots, treetops, and the street below. A canvas canopy, a potted hydrangea, and two deck chairs. Once again, we're ready for company.

Thesis and Organization

1. Keillor introduces his essay in paragraphs 1–3. How does he use comparison and contrast? Cause and effect? What working thesis does the introduction establish?

2. In the body of the essay (paragraphs 4–11), how does Keillor use cause and effect? Comparison and contrast? Description? Example? Classification? What does each pattern of organization contribute to his definition?

3. In paragraphs 6 and 7, Keillor refers to where he has lived, a subject that comes up again in his conclusion (paragraph 12). What do those references add to his definition?

4. Add up all the positive qualities Keillor attributes to the "true porch." What is his definition? Think about the cause-and-effect relationships in the essay and that definition. What is Keillor's thesis?

Technique and Style

1. Garrison Keillor is probably best known for his radio show "The Prairie Home Companion." If you are familiar with that show, describe the personality Keillor reveals there and compare it to the one in this essay. If you don't know that program, examine Keillor's use of diction, point of view, simile, and sentence structure and describe the personality he creates for himself.

2. In general, writers choose one point of view and stick with it, but here, Keillor keeps shifting his point of view from *you* to *we*. Analyze his point of view by figuring out exactly to whom the pronouns refer. For example, does the second person in paragraph 1 refer to the same person as the second person in paragraph 10? What justification can you find for the switching of point of view?

3. Examine the allusions Keillor makes: Huck Finn and the Widow Douglas (paragraph 4), the Minnesota prairie (paragraph 8), the Curtiss biplane (paragraph 9), and Rockefeller and the president (paragraph 11). What generalizations can you make about these allusions? What do they add to Keillor's tone?

4. In an earlier version of this essay, Keillor used three similes in paragraph 8: " . . . it's like ordering Eggs Benedict and saying 'Hold the hollandaise'; it's like buying a Porsche with a Maytag motor; it's like flying first-class and being seated next to a man who bores the eyeballs right out of you." He replaced those three with " . . . it's like visiting Minnesota and not seeing the prairie." What might account for Keillor's decision to rewrite this passage using just one simile? What function does the simile serve? Create one of your own that would fit with or substitute for the one Keillor uses.

5. Keillor relies heavily on description to make his point in paragraph 9. What do the descriptive details add to his tone? How are they framed?

Suggestions for Writing

Journal

1. Explain whether or not you would like to meet Garrison Keillor.

2. Keillor says that porches "promote grace and comfort." What objects in your life do the same? Pick one and describe it.

Essay

Write your own "O the _____" essay, finding a topic among the everyday objects around you. Suggestions:
   easy chair, sofa, television set
   hamburger, ice cream cone, pizza
   jeans, backpack, cap, jogging shoes
   backyard, barbecue grill, garage

*P*icket Fences

J. Decker

Since this essay was first published, J. Decker has graduated with honors from the University of New Orleans. While she was enrolled, she spent much of her free time donning a bite suit to prepare police dogs for duty as well as training dogs and helping friends cope with the peculiarities of their computers. Since that time, she has been working professionally with police dogs in a county near New Orleans, far, far from her native Wisconsin. The essay that follows was written in the spring of 1993 in response to an open-ended assignment—an essay about a person or place.

WHAT TO LOOK FOR *While Decker does indeed define her central term—Wisconsin—she does it by using a variety of organizational strategies. As you read the essay, notice how she uses description, narration, example, comparison, and causal analysis to achieve her definition.*

1   When people ask me where I am from, I often hesitate. Should I admit, to a stranger, that I come from a state that named its professional baseball team after the beer-making industry? Should I admit to sharing a heritage with people who don foam cheese wedge hats and dance in the streets in October? It can be a difficult decision.

2   The first response to my admission that I come from Wisconsin is a tilt of the head. "Oh," they say, scanning their memory banks for a location, "isn't that in Canada?" I am constantly amazed that people who live at the southern end of the Mississippi River don't know the general location of where that same river starts. Even the learned are not immune. In my first semester at U.N.O., my geology professor talked about the "mountainous headwaters of the Mississippi River." There aren't any mountains in Wisconsin or Minnesota that I know of—just a few big hills left over from the last ice age. Granted, Wisconsin is substantially above sea level. Maybe that confuses Louisianians.

3   If the public cannot correctly identify the country Wisconsin belongs to, it's a fairly safe bet that it isn't a holiday hot spot. Wisconsin is one of those places people don't purposely visit. You'll

never hear a family coming back from vacation, "Ah, yes, we vacationed in Wisconsin this summer." Maybe they've switched planes at the (only) airport, but it wasn't an intentional visit. Travelers do sometimes drive through Wisconsin—to get somewhere else—but those who do cut through Wisconsin generally don't even know they've been there. In their minds, they've detoured straight from Illinois into Minnesota.

4   There may be some basis for this evasion. Wisconsin is the land of the Green Bay Packers, most of the serial killers you've seen on television, three cows for every person, and the Cheddar Heads. This alone is enough to scare many longtime residents away, let alone a visitor. Several years ago the state tourism department started a promotion campaign with the slogan "Escape to Wisconsin!" Not only was this slogan hard to fit on a bumper sticker, it was usually marked out to read "Escape Wisconsin!"

5   Perhaps one of the reasons travelers avoid Wisconsin is the way we name our towns. Sure, everyone has heard of Milwaukee, largely due to *Wayne's World* and Jeffrey Dahmer (definitely one of "Milwaukee's Best"). Now try to say Wonewoc, Oconomowoc, Sinsinawa, Memomonee, Chequamegon, or Kewaskum. Hooked on Phonics isn't going to help you here. Add to that the preponderance of people who don't live in any town at all, and you've got a direction-taker's nightmare. I've fielded those desperate calls many times. The conversation goes something like this:

CALLER: Hi, this is Dave. We're lost.
ME: Well, Dave, do you know where you are?
CALLER: The guy at the bar says I'm in Manitowoc.
ME: Are you sure that's not Manitowish, Dave?
CALLER: Oh, yeah, you're right. We're in Magnet Wish.
ME: Now Dave, think very hard. The sign above the bar—
             did it say Sal's, Hal's, or Big Al's?
CALLER (excitedly): It said Hal's! You mean you know where I
             am?
ME: Well, Dave, I know where you are, but I don't know
             who you are.
CALLER (silent for a moment): Is this 2148?
ME: No, it's 2184, but I live just down the road from Bart's.
CALLER: Oh, well maybe you can give me better directions
             than he did. . . .

Even if the names aren't all that hard to say, they can still be confusing. It's usually hard for non-natives to keep track of small towns that all sound like cheeses: Edam, Colby, Monterey, Edelweiss.

6   While it's not all rural, the entire state of Wisconsin has a reputation for being somewhat "hokey." By that, I mean that outsiders picture us milking cows named Betsy or Lola by hand while singing "What do the simple folk do?" But the state of Wisconsin is not entirely backwards, it just appears that way. After all, what is it that folks see on the news about our state? You see thousands of intoxicated people wearing orange cheese hats and holding steins as they run through the streets of Milwaukee during Oktoberfest. Or you might have had the good fortune to see a clip from the most recent cow chip-flinging contest. Yes, it really does go on, and no, gloves are not allowed. The secret is in selecting a well-shaped, thoroughly dried specimen. (Or so I've been told.)

7   Winter is another joy that keeps many people away. It is only a slight exaggeration to say that winter lasts three-quarters of the year. It begins in late September with vigor and ferocity, as if to chase those football fanatics inside, and ends, reluctantly, in mid-May when the tulips start bouncing their heads off the ice sheet that has covered our state.

8   This roughly corresponds to the school year, and for good reason. There's not much hope of skipping school when your bus driver has shovelled his way up your driveway, and besides, there's just no "cool" way to hang around town in snowshoes. The characteristic saunter of truants loses its effect when three feet of rawhide webbing is strapped to each foot.

9   Another tourist-banishing idea is Wisconsin's reputation for producing every serial killer and wacko that has graced the six o'clock news. That is absolutely not true. Just because our two most famous residents liked to upholster furniture with human skin and drill holes into skulls, respectively, there is no reason to classify ours as an overly deviant population. Though some researchers *have* speculated that the abundance of Holstein cows and their resemblance to Rorschach's ink blots has something to do with this "serial" trend. You might go crazy too if all you saw were grazing cattle and cornfields.

10   In spite of the criticisms, people do leave the hustle and hassle of big city life to "escape to Wisconsin." For every news clip show-

casing our problems or idiosyncrasies, there's a TV show reveling in the normalcy ("Happy Days," "Flying High," "Step by Step"), a good-hearted alien landing in our state forest (Star Man), or a supercomputer guru setting up shop (Cray). Wisconsin *is* a nice place to live, but I wouldn't want to visit.

Thesis and Organization

1. Paragraphs 1 and 2 set out what some people do and do not know about Wisconsin. How do those ideas prepare the reader for the rest of the essay?
2. List all the negative features set out in paragraphs 3–9.
3. What positive qualities can you extract from the negative ones?
4. What does the last paragraph bring out? What would the effect of the essay be without it?
5. Given the positives, negatives, and the very last sentence, how does the author define Wisconsin?

Technique and Style

1. What does the dialogue in paragraph 5 add to the reader's impression of Wisconsin?
2. Reread the essay, looking for Decker's use of the second-person pronoun *you*. To whom does it refer? What does this choice of pronoun add to the essay?
3. Look up the use of parentheses in a handbook of grammar and usage. Does Decker's use of them in paragraphs 3, 5, 6, and 10 follow the explanation you find?
4. Given Decker's examples and her thesis, how would you describe the tone of the essay?
5. Throughout the essay, Decker uses details to make her points vivid. Which did you find particularly effective and why?

Suggestions for Writing

Journal

1. What cities have you visited? Make a list, then choose one and jot down your impressions of it.
2. What do people associate with the place—state, city, town, neighborhood, or area—where you live? What examples can you think of to illustrate those associations? You can use this list and your examples to draft an essay.

Essay

Chances are that people have some mistaken ideas about where you live—the town, county, or state. Or perhaps you live in a large city or in a rural area, both places that many people have false ideas about. Cities such as New York and Los Angeles are often thought of as having a mugger on every corner, and small towns and rural areas are considered so dull that watching a traffic light change is an event. Think of your reader as someone who has preconceived ideas about a place you know well and has never been there, and write an essay defining that place in such a way that you either reinforce or refute those ideas. Other suggestions:

the state, city, town, neighborhood, area, or region where you live
the kind of car you drive
the clothes you wear
the way you style your hair

*T*he Myth of the Matriarch

Gloria Naylor

Best known for her novels, Gloria Naylor was born in Queens, a borough of New York City, and received her first library card at the age of four. After graduating from Brooklyn College and earning a master's degree at Yale, she began her career as a writer. Her first novel, The Women of Brewster Place, *was published in 1982 and received the American Book Award for best first novel. Her most recent,* Bailey's Café, *rounds off what Naylor calls her "novel quartet." A winner of the National Book Award for her fiction, Naylor is also noted for editing* Children of the Night: The Best Short Stories by Black Writers, 1967 to the Present *(1996). The essay that follows was published in* Life *in the spring of 1988. The neighborhood she grew up in and her travels have given Naylor lots of opportunity to observe both the myth and the reality of the matriarch.*

WHAT TO LOOK FOR   *When you think of the term* paragraph, *you probably imagine a fairly large chunk of prose that illustrates and develops a particular point that's stated or implied as a topic sentence. But paragraphs serve other functions as well, as Naylor's essay shows. Her essay is complex, which makes the need for clear transitions between paragraphs important, but providing a transition from one major part of the essay to another is more difficult. Naylor does it by using a short paragraph in which she poses a question that she then answers in the paragraphs that follow.*

1   The strong black woman. All my life I've seen her. In books she is Faulkner's impervious Dilsey, using her huge dark arms to hold together the crumbling spirits and household of the Compsons. In the movies she is the quintessential Mammy, chasing after Scarlett O'Hara with forgotten sunbonnets and shrill tongue-lashings about etiquette. On television she is Sapphire of *Amos 'n Andy* or a dozen variations of her—henpecking black men, herding white children, protecting her brood from the onslaughts of the world. She is the supreme matriarch—alone, self-sufficient and liking it that way. I've seen how this female image has permeated the American consciousness to the point of influencing everything from the selling of pancakes to the structuring of welfare benefits.

But the strangest thing is that when I walked around my neighborhood or went into the homes of family and friends, this matriarch was nowhere to be found.

2   I know the statistics: They say that when my grandmother was born at the turn of the century as few as 10 percent of black households were headed by females; when I was born at mid-century it had crept to 17 percent; and now it is almost 60 percent. No longer a widow or a divorcée as in times past, the single woman with children today probably has never married—and increasingly she is getting younger. By the time she is 18, one out of every four black unmarried women has become a mother.

3   But it is a long leap from a matrifocal home, where the father is absent, to a matriarchal one, in which the females take total charge from the males. Though I have known black women heading households in different parts of the country and in different social circumstances—poor, working class or professional—none of them has gloried in the conditions that left them with the emotional and financial responsibility for their families. Often they had to take domestic work because of the flexible hours or stay in menial factory or office jobs because of the steady pay. And leaving the job was only to go home to the other job of raising children alone. These women understood the importance of input from black men in sustaining their families. Their advice and, sometimes, financial assistance were sought and accepted. But if such were not forthcoming, she would continue to deal with her situation alone.

4   This is a far cry from the heartwarming image of the two-fisted black woman I watched striding across the public imagination. A myth always arises to serve a need. And so it must be asked, what is it in the relationship of black women to American society that has called for them to be seen as independent Amazons?

5   The black woman was brought to America for the same reason as the black man—to provide slave labor. But she had what seemed to be contradictory roles: She did the woman's work of bearing children and keeping house while doing a man's work at the side of the black male in the fields. She worked regardless of the advanced stages of pregnancy. In the 19th century the ideal of the true woman was one of piety, purity, domesticity and submissiveness; the female lived as a wife sheltered at home or went abroad as a virgin doing good works. But if the prevailing belief was that the natural state of women was one of frailty, how could the black female be explained? Out in the fields laboring with their

muscled bodies and during rest periods suckling infants at their breasts, the slave women had to be seen as different from white women. They were stronger creatures: they didn't feel pain in childbirth; they didn't have tear ducts. Ironically, one of the arguments for enslaving blacks in the first place was that as a race they were inferior to whites—but black women, well, they were a little *more* than women.

6   The need to view slavery as benign accounted for the larger-than-life mammy of the plantation legends. As a house servant, she was always pictured in close proximity to her white masters because there was nothing about her that was threatening to white ideas about black women. Her unstinting devotion assuaged any worries that slaves were discontented or harbored any potential for revolt. Her very dark skin belied any suspicions of past interracial liaisons, while her obesity and advanced age removed any sexual threat. Earth mother, nursemaid and cook, the mammy existed without a history or a future.

7   In reality, slave women in the house or the field were part of a kinship network and with their men tried to hold together their own precarious families. Marriages between slaves were not legally recognized, but this did not stop them from entering into living arrangements and acting as husbands and wives. After emancipation a deluge of black couples registered their unions under the law, and ex-slaves were known to travel hundreds of miles in search of lost partners and children.

8   No longer bound, but hardly equal citizens, black men and women had access to only the most menial jobs in society, the largest number being reserved solely for female domestics. Richard Wright wrote a terribly funny and satirical short story about the situation, "Man of All Work." His protagonist is unable to find a job to support his family and save his house from foreclosure, so he puts on his wife's clothes and secures a position as a housekeeper. "Don't stop me. I've found a solution to our problem. I'm an army-trained cook. I can clean a house as good as anybody. Get my point? I put on your dress. I looked in the mirror. I can pass. I want that job."

9   Pushed to the economic forefront of her home, the 19th century mammy became 20th century Sapphire. Fiery, younger, more aggressive, she just couldn't wait to take the lead away from the man of the house. Whatever he did was never enough. Not that he wanted to do anything, of course, except hang out on street corners, gamble and run around with women. From vaudeville of the

1880s to the advent of *Amos 'n Andy*, it was easier to make black men the brunt of jokes than to address the inequities that kept decent employment from those who wanted to work. Society had not failed black women—their men had.

10   The truth is that throughout our history black women could depend upon their men even when they were unemployed or underemployed. But in the impoverished inner cities today we are seeing the rise of the *unemployable*. These young men are not equipped to take responsibility for themselves, much less the children they are creating. And with the increasing youth of unwed mothers, we have grandmothers and grandfathers in their early thirties. How can a grandmother give her daughter's family the traditional wisdom and support when she herself has barely lived? And on the other side of town, where the professional black woman is heading a household, usually because she is divorced, the lack of a traditional kinship network—the core community of parents, uncles, aunts—makes her especially alone.

11   What is surprising to me is that the myth of the matriarch lives on—even among black women. I've talked to so many who believe that they are supposed to be superhuman and bear up under all things. When they don't, they all too readily look for the fault within themselves. Somehow they failed their history. But it is a grave mistake for black women to believe that they have a natural ability to be stronger than other women. Fifty-seven percent of black homes being headed by females is not natural. A 40 percent pregnancy rate among our young girls is not natural. It is heartbreaking. The myth of the matriarch robs a woman caught in such circumstances of her individuality and her humanity. She should feel that she has the *right* at least to break down—once the kids are put to bed—and do something so simple as cry.

Thesis and Organization

1. Paragraphs 1–3 introduce the essay. In what ways do they set the stage for what follows?
2. Paragraph 3 introduces the concepts of matrifocal and kinship relationships, and Naylor refers to these concepts again in paragraphs 7 and 10. What is her point?
3. Naylor states that "A myth always arises to serve a need" (paragraph 4). Reread paragraphs 5–9 and explain the needs served by the myth of the matriarch.

4. How does Naylor's description of the present situation relate to the idea of the myth of the matriarch?

5. The essay concludes with the negative effects of the myth. What are they? Given those negative effects and the history of the myth explained in paragraphs 4–9, what is Naylor's thesis?

Technique and Style

1. The essay opens with allusions to fiction and television shows. How would you update them?

2. Paragraphs 2 and 11 introduce statistics into the essay. What do they contribute?

3. Naylor describes the role of black women in the days of slavery and the attitudes of whites toward them. Explain whether you find her tone more objective than subjective or the opposite.

4. What does the irony in paragraph 5 add to the idea of myth?

5. How would you describe Naylor's audience?

Suggestions for Writing

Journal

1. Test your own experience against Naylor's myth of the strong black woman. Does the myth exist or not? Write a journal entry in which you describe what you discovered.

2. In what ways have you been affected by a myth? List those that may apply to you, choose one, and write down your response to it.

Essay

The myth of the matriarch is just one of the many myths in our culture that have given rise to stereotypes similar to the mammies and Sapphires that Naylor points out. These stereotypes show up frequently in popular culture—in films, books, television shows—thus furthering the myth. Mull over recent movies or television shows you've seen or popular fiction you've read. Once you've focused on a myth, search your memory for other examples of it and for how it may show up in real life. Your paper may turn out like Naylor's, defining the myth and showing its harmful and false side, or you may prefer a simpler route, exploring only the myth. Suggested myths:

>   the hero
>   the "Wild West"
>   the supermom
>   the adorable child
>   the nightmare slasher
>   the happy homemaker

*D*iscrimination Is a Virtue

Robert Keith Miller

Robert Keith Miller teaches English at the University of St. Thomas, and his scholarly publications include work on authors as diverse as Willa Cather, Oscar Wilde, and Samuel Clemens (Mark Twain). Given his interest in the written word, it's natural that sloppy language would bother him, but most of us would not think that dis-crimination is often misused. Miller, in his essay, proves us wrong. By examining the connotations and denotations of the word, Miller shows us not only that we misuse it, but that its misuse points to a flaw in our "public policies." As you read his essay, note how he uses example and narration, as well as two other modes—process and causal analysis—to make his case. For the latter, look for places where Miller examines how the meaning of the word has changed and the effect that change has had. Miller's essay appeared in the "My Turn" column in Newsweek *in 1980. His argument stills holds.*

WHAT TO LOOK FOR *Look up rhetorical questions in a handbook of grammar and usage and then be on the lookout for how Miller uses them. When you write your next paper, see if a rhetorical question or two can function as a transition or can be used for emphasis.*

1   When I was a child, my grandmother used to tell me a story about a king who had three daughters and decided to test their love. He asked each of them "How much do you love me?" The first replied that she loved him as much as all the diamonds and pearls in the world. The second said that she loved him more than life itself. The third replied "I love you as fresh meat loves salt."

2   This answer enraged the king; he was convinced that his youngest daughter was making fun of him. So he banished her from his realm and left all of his property to her elder sisters.

3   As the story unfolded it became clear, even to a 6-year-old, that the king had made a terrible mistake. The two older girls were hypocrites, and as soon as they had profited from their father's generosity, they began to treat him very badly. A wiser man would have realized that the youngest daughter was the truest. Without

attempting to flatter, she said, in effect, "We go together naturally; we are a perfect team.*"*

4   Years later, when I came to read Shakespeare, I realized that my grandmother's story was loosely based upon the story of King Lear, who put his daughters to a similar test and did not know how to judge the results. Attempting to save the king from the consequences of his foolishness, a loyal friend pleads, "Come sir, arise, away! I'll teach you differences." Unfortunately, the lesson comes too late. Because Lear could not tell the difference between true love and false, he loses his kingdom and eventually his life.

5   We have a word in English which means "the ability to tell differences." That word is *discrimination.* But within the last 30 years, this word has been so frequently misused that an entire generation has grown up believing that "discrimination" means "racism." People are always proclaiming that "discrimination" is something that should be done away with. Should that ever happen, it would prove to be our undoing.

6   Discrimination means discernment; it means the ability to perceive the truth, to use good judgment and to profit accordingly. The *Oxford English Dictionary* traces this understanding of the word back to 1648 and demonstrates that for the next 300 years, "discrimination" was a virtue, not a vice. Thus, when a character in a nineteenth-century novel makes a happy marriage, Dickens has another character remark, "It does credit to your discrimination that you should have found such a very excellent young woman."

7   Of course, "the ability to tell differences" assumes that differences exist, and this is unsettling for a culture obsessed with the notion of equality. The contemporary belief that discrimination is a vice stems from the compound *discriminate against.* What we need to remember, however, is that some things deserve to be judged harshly: we should not leave our kingdoms to the selfish and the wicked.

8   Discrimination is wrong only when someone or something is discriminated against because of prejudice. But to use the word in this sense, as so many people do, is to destroy its true meaning. If you discriminate against something because of general preconceptions rather than particular insights, then you are not discriminating—bias has clouded the clarity of vision which discrimination demands.

9   One of the great ironies of American life is that we manage to discriminate in the practical decisions of daily life, but usually fail to discriminate when we make public policies. Most people are

very discriminating when it comes to buying a car, for example, because they realize that cars have differences. Similarly, an increasing number of people have learned to discriminate in what they eat. Some foods are better than others—and indiscriminate eating can undermine one's health.

10   Yet in public affairs, good judgment is depressingly rare. In many areas which involve the common good, we see a failure to tell differences.

11   Consider, for example, some of the thinking behind modern education. On the one hand, there is a refreshing realization that there are differences among children, and some children—be they gifted or handicapped—require special education. On the other hand, we are politically unable to accept the consequences of this perception. The trend in recent years has been to group together students of radically different ability. We call this process "mainstreaming," and it strikes me as a characteristically American response to the discovery of differences: we try to pretend that differences do not matter.

12   Similarly, we try to pretend that there is little difference between the sane and the insane. A fashionable line of argument has it that "everybody is a little mad" and that few mental patients deserve long-term hospitalization. As a consequence of such reasoning, thousands of seriously ill men and women have been evicted from their hospital beds and returned to what is euphemistically called "the community"—which often means being left to sleep on city streets, where confused and helpless people now live out of paper bags as the direct result of our refusal to discriminate.

13   Or to choose a final example from a different area: how many recent elections reflect thoughtful consideration of the genuine differences among candidates? Benumbed by television commercials that market aspiring officeholders as if they were a new brand of toothpaste or hair spray, too many Americans vote with only a fuzzy understanding of the issues in question. Like Lear, we seem too eager to leave the responsibility of government to others and too ready to trust those who tell us whatever we want to hear.

14   So as we look around us, we should recognize that "discrimination" is a virtue which we desperately need. We must try to avoid making unfair and arbitrary distinctions, but we must not go to the other extreme and pretend that there are no distinctions to be made. The ability to make intelligent judgments is essential both

for the success of one's personal life and for the functioning of society as a whole. Let us be open-minded by all means, but not so open-minded that our brains fall out.

Thesis and Organization

1. Paragraphs 1–4 use narration. What is the "lesson" of the narrative? Why might Miller have chosen a narrative to introduce the essay?
2. Paragraph 5 deals with the popular connotations of *discrimination*. What are they? What other paragraph or paragraphs bring out the misuse of the word?
3. Paragraph 6 presents the denotative meaning of the word. What other paragraph or paragraphs emphasize that meaning?
4. Where does Miller maintain that the idea of differences runs counter to our notion of equality? How is that idea related to paragraphs 9–13?
5. Paragraph 14 concludes the essay. Consider the essay's title and the last paragraph. What is a full statement of Miller's thesis? Is the essay primarily expressive, informative, or persuasive?

Technique and Style

1. Consult a handbook of grammar and usage for discussion of the rhetorical question. Where in the essay do you find examples of this device? To what extent do the examples fit the handbook's definition?
2. What modes does Miller use to define his central terms? Which does he use most frequently?
3. Note all the times Miller uses quotation marks. What different functions do the quotation marks serve?
4. What sort of a person does Miller seem to be? In what ways does his persona fit his tone? How would you characterize his tone?
5. What sources does Miller draw his examples from? Group them according to the generalizations they support. In what ways are they appropriate or inappropriate to the generalizations? What do the examples add to Miller's persona?

Suggestions for Writing

Journal

1. Test Miller's point by writing an entry that explains what you mean by the word *discrimination*.
2. British author Rudyard Kipling (1865–1936), said that "Words are, of course, the most powerful drug used by mankind." What words hold power for you? Choose one and explain why.

Essay

Think of a word that is commonly misused or has outworn its meaning and make a case for its linguistic correction or restoration. Commonly misused words can be found in a handbook of grammar and usage, usually in its glossary. Suggestions:

virtually

disinterested

flaunt

irritate

As for worn-out words, they are all around us particularly in advertisements:

fabulous

lovely

elegant

Or if you like, think of a situation or example for which there is no adequate word and make one up.

T he Handicap of Definition

William Raspberry

Although William Raspberry is the urban affairs columnist for the Washington Post, *he is better known as the author of a syndicated column that runs in more than 200 newspapers. His commentary on issues such as rap music, crime, and AIDS earned him a Pulitzer Prize in 1994. In the essay that follows, he writes about the terms* black *and* white, *words that have connotations we don't often think about. Raspberry shows us that if we stop to think about* black, *we'll see that it has so narrow a definition that it is "one of the heaviest burdens black Americans—and black children in particular—have to bear." Not much has changed since 1982, when this essay first appeared in Raspberry's syndicated column.*

WHAT TO LOOK FOR   *Somewhere along the line, we've all been warned never to begin a sentence with a conjunction such as* and, but, *and the like. But as long as you know how to avoid the trap of a sentence fragment, beginning a sentence with a conjunction can lend a conversational tone to your essay. As you read Raspberry's essay, notice how often he uses this technique.*

1   I know all about bad schools, mean politicians, economic deprivation and racism. Still, it occurs to me that one of the heaviest burdens black Americans—and black children in particular—have to bear is the handicap of definition: the question of what it means to be black.

2   Let me explain quickly what I mean. If a basketball fan says that the Boston Celtics' Larry Bird plays "black," the fan intends it—and Bird probably accepts it—as a compliment. Tell pop singer Tom Jones he moves "black" and he might grin in appreciation. Say to Teena Marie or The Average White Band that they sound "black" and they'll thank you.

3   But name one pursuit, aside from athletics, entertainment or sexual performance in which a white practitioner will feel complimented to be told he does it "black." Tell a white broadcaster he talks "black," and he'll sign up for diction lessons. Tell a white reporter he writes "black" and he'll take a writing course. Tell a white lawyer he reasons "black" and he might sue you for slander.

4   What we have here is a tragically limited definition of blackness, and it isn't only white people who buy it.

5   Think of all the ways black children can put one another down with charges of "whiteness." For many of these children, hard study and hard work are "white." Trying to please a teacher might be criticized as acting "white." Speaking correct English is "white." Scrimping today in the interest of tomorrow's goals is "white." Educational toys and games are "white."

6   An incredible array of habits and attitudes that are conducive to success in business, in academia, in the nonentertainment professions are likely to be thought of as somehow "white." Even economic success, unless it involves such "black" undertakings as numbers banking, is defined as "white."

7   And the results are devastating. I wouldn't deny that blacks often are better entertainers and athletes. My point is the harm that comes from too narrow a definition of what is black.

8   One reason black youngsters tend to do better at basketball, for instance, is that they assume they can learn to do it well, and so they practice constantly to prove themselves right.

9   Wouldn't it be wonderful if we could infect black children with the notion that excellence in math is "black" rather than white, or possibly Chinese? Wouldn't it be of enormous value if we could create the myth that morality, strong families, determination, courage and love of learning are traits brought by slaves from Mother Africa and therefore quintessentially black?

10   There is no doubt in my mind that most black youngsters could develop their mathematical reasoning, their elocution and their attitudes the way they develop their jump shots and their dance steps: by the combination of sustained, enthusiastic practice and the unquestioned belief that they can do it.

11   In one sense, what I am talking about is the importance of developing positive ethnic traditions. Maybe Jews have an innate talent for communication; maybe the Chinese are born with a gift for mathematical reasoning; maybe blacks are naturally blessed with athletic grace. I doubt it. What is at work, I suspect, is assumption, inculcated early in their lives, that this is a thing our people do well.

12   Unfortunately, many of the things about which blacks make this assumption are things that do not contribute to their career success—except for that handful of the truly gifted who can make it as entertainers and athletes. And many of the things we concede to whites are the things that are essential to economic security.

13   So it is with a number of assumptions black youngsters make about what it is to be a "man": physical aggressiveness, sexual prowess, the refusal to submit to authority. The prisons are full of people who, by this perverted definition, are unmistakably men.

14   But the real problem is not so much that the things defined as "black" are negative. The problem is that the definition is much too narrow.

15   Somehow, we have to make our children understand that they are intelligent, competent people, capable of doing whatever they put their minds to and making it in the American mainstream, not just in a black subculture.

16   What we seem to be doing, instead, is raising up yet another generation of young blacks who will be failures—by definition.

Thesis and Organization

1. Examine paragraphs 1–4 as a unit. What sentence functions as the major assertion for this group of paragraphs? What examples support that assertion? What conclusion does Raspberry draw from the examples? How is that conclusion related to the paragraphs that follow?

2. Take paragraphs 5–7 as a unit and analyze it also, looking for the controlling assertion, the examples, and the conclusion.

3. Paragraphs 8–11 also form a paragraph block. What is its controlling assertion? What examples support it? What conclusion does Raspberry draw?

4. Examine paragraphs 12–16 as a concluding paragraph block. What is the relationship between paragraph 12 and the preceding paragraphs? In what way is the point raised in paragraph 13 an analogy? Is the analogy apt or false? What is the function of paragraph 14? Paragraphs 15 and 16 look to the future and assess the present. What cause-and-effect relationship do they point out?

5. Consider the controlling ideas that guide the paragraph blocks and the conclusions Raspberry draws from the examples that support those assertions. Stated fully, what is Raspberry's thesis? Do you agree or disagree with this thesis? Why or why not?

Technique and Style

1. This essay was one of Raspberry's syndicated columns; as a result, it appeared in a large number of newspapers with equally large readerships, mostly white. What evidence can you find that Raspberry is trying to inform his white audience and persuade his black readers?

2. How and where does Raspberry establish his credibility as a writer on this subject? What grammatical point of view does he use? What is the effect of that point of view?
3. Where in the essay does he qualify or modulate his statements? What is the effect of that technique?
4. Many techniques can be used to give a paragraph coherence, but an often neglected one is syntax. Examine paragraphs 2, 3, 5, and 9 to discover the similar sentence structure at work. What do you find?
5. Paragraphs 3, 7, 13, and 14 all begin with a conjunction. What effect does this technique achieve? Consult a handbook of grammar and usage for a discussion of this device. To what extent does Raspberry's usage conform to the handbook's advice?
6. Paragraph 16 is an example of a rhetorical paragraph, a one-sentence paragraph that gives dramatic emphasis to a point. If you eliminate the dash or substitute a comma for it, what happens to the dramatic effect? What does the pun add?
7. A militant who read this essay would argue that Raspberry is trying to make blacks "better" by making them white. Is there any evidence to support this view? Explain.
8. A feminist who read the essay would argue that it is sexist. Is there any evidence to support this view? Explain.

Suggestions for Writing

Journal

1. Raspberry's essay was published in 1982. Write a journal entry explaining whether his point holds true today.
2. Write down any examples you can think of that can substitute for those Raspberry uses, but focus on women. In a paragraph or two, explain how the substitutions would add to or detract from his point.

Essay

Find a word that has accumulated broad connotations and then see what definitions have evolved and their effect. Like Raspberry, you may want to consider two terms but emphasize only one. Possibilities:

man
hero
student
woman
worker
lover
politician

Division and Classification

*T*he next time you shop in a supermarket or clean out a closet, think about how you are doing it and you will understand the workings of **division and classification**. "How often do I wear those shoes?" and "I never did like that sweater" imply that dividing items according to how frequently you wear them would be a good principle for sorting out your closet. Supermarkets, however, do the sorting for you. Goods are divided according to shared characteristics—all dairy products in one section, meat in another, and so on—and then items are placed in those categories. The process looks easy, but if you have ever tried to find soy sauce, you know the pitfalls: Is it with the spices? Sauces? Gourmet foods? Health foods? Ethnic products?

To divide a subject and then classify examples into the categories or classes that resulted from division you must be able to examine a subject from several angles, work out the ways in which it can be divided, and then discern similarities and differences among the examples you want to classify. A huge topic such as animals invites a long list of ways they can be divided: wild animals, work animals, pets; ones that swim, run, crawl; ones you have owned, seen, or read about. These groups imply principles for division—by degree of domesticity, by manner of locomotion, by degree of familiarity. Division and classification often help define each other in that having divided your subjects, you may find that once you start classifying, you have to stop and redefine your principle of division. If your division of animals is based on locomotion, for instance, where do you put the flying squirrel?

Division and classification is often used at the paragraph level. If your essay argues that a particular television commercial for a toilet

cleaner insults women, you might want to introduce the essay by enu-
merating other advertisements in that general category—household
products—that you also find insulting to women. From Julius Caesar's "Gaul is divided into three parts" to a ten-year-
old's "animal, vegetable, or mineral," classification and division has had
a long and useful history. And, of course, it has a useful present as
well. In each of the essays in this chapter, you will see that the system
of division and classification supports a thesis, though the essays use
their theses for different purposes: to entertain, to explain, to argue.

AUDIENCE AND PURPOSE   Knowing who your readers are and
what effect you want to have on them will help you devise your system
of classification and sharpen your thesis. Imagine that you are writing
an essay for a newsletter put out by a health club or by students in a
physical education program and that your subject is the benefits of garlic. You would know that your readers are interested in the positive effects of herbs, but you would also know that their noses may well
wrinkle at the mere mention of garlic. Given the negative associations
your audience may have, you would do well to begin with the unpleasant connotation, thus starting with what your readers already
know, connecting your subject with their experience, and immediately
addressing their first and probably negative ideas about garlic. After
that, you might move quickly to the many good uses to which garlic
can be put, categorizing them according to the herb's different effects.
Thus you would inform your readers and at the same time argue for its
positive qualities and the idea that garlic should be more than a pizza
topping.

To explain, however, is the more obvious use of division and classification. You may well find that when you start off on a topic that lends
itself to this pattern of organization, you need to define some of your
terms. Writing about the ways in which a one-year-old can both annoy
and delight you, for instance, you may want to define what you mean
by your central terms. In so doing, you have a chance to link the **definitions** to your audience's experiences, so that even if some of your
readers have never spent much time around a baby, they can still appreciate your points. For *annoy*, you might define your reaction as similar to hearing a car alarm going off in the middle of the night, and for
delight, you might remind your readers of how they felt when opening

an unexpected but well-chosen present. Both definitions help explain while at the same time drawing on common experiences. Should you tackle that same topic with a humorous tone, you will not only be informing your audience but entertaining them as well. But humor comes in many forms, evoking everything from belly laughs to giggles to knowing smiles. To produce those responses, you may find yourself using exaggeration, also known as **hyperbole**, or **irony**, or **sarcasm** or a combination of all three, and more. Your title can tip off your readers to your tone: "Baby Destructo" (exaggeration); "Little Baby, Big Problem" (irony); "The Joys of Parenthood" (sarcasm).

SYSTEM OF CLASSIFICATION   To work effectively, a system of classification must be complete and logical. The system that governs how goods are arranged in a supermarket needs to be broad enough to cover everything a supermarket might sell, and it needs to make sense. Can openers should be with kitchen implements, not with vegetables; cans of peas should be with other canned goods, not with milk.

So, too, when you are writing an essay all your examples should be in the correct category. If you were thinking of the subject of campaign spending in the 1996 presidential election and, in particular, who contributed what to which political party, you would first concentrate on the Republicans and the Democrats, ignoring the campaigns of the minor political groups (the money they raised being minor in comparison). Then you would sort out the kinds of contributions—small donations from private citizens, large ones from individuals, money from PACs, from corporations, and the like—made to each of those two political parties. At that point, you would find you had so much material that you would be better off narrowing your subject, but no matter what you did, you wouldn't mix in intangible gifts such as a volunteer's time or tangible ones such as the "free" donuts handed out to the campaign workers.

More likely, however, as you think about your topic and work on your draft, you will find your classifications are not watertight. Yet you can account for the occasional leak by explaining it or by adjusting your system of division. In the example of campaign contributions, for instance, it would be impossible to put an accurate price tag on the time spent by volunteers or on the goods and services donated to the two political parties, though it's reasonable to assume that the dollar figure would be high. And that's all you need to say. You've explained why you have omitted those kinds of contributions. Adjusting the system of division, the other alternative, so that it included every conceivable kind of donation isn't a reasonable solution as it would make an already large topic even larger, impossibly so.

OTHER PATTERNS OF ORGANIZATION   Earlier in this chapter, you read about what definition can add to classification and division, but description, narration, and example are useful as well. The essay on political contributions, for instance, might open with a brief narrative recounting your having been besieged by a telephone caller who was trying to raise money for a particular candidate. And if that narrative described your having discovered the plea by listening to the caller's recorded message talking to your answering machine, then you could also underscore your point that raising money for campaigns has reached absurd heights (or depths).

Examples are also essential to classification, usually in the form of multiple illustrations. Your practice in using examples in other papers will help you here, for as you know, you can select examples from your own experience or that of others or both. Outside sources such as evidence drawn from books and magazines are also helpful, showing your reader that you have looked beyond your personal experience. When using examples, however, you need think through the most effective way to sequence them, which will often be according to dramatic effect—moving from least to most dramatic—or in chronological order.

THESIS AND ORGANIZATION   Some writers begin their essays by first dividing the subject into their system of classification, then moving on to focus on one of the classes. Say you chose as a topic the electronic gizmos we often take for granted. You might have found yourself making notes that include a huge list. Thinking through that list you might have noticed that you can divide it into machines that can be controlled with a remote device and those that cannot. In one category are items such as microwaves, answering machines, and computers, and in the other you've lumped together CD players, television sets, VCRs. Your lists grow longer, and you begin to wonder what the life of the American consumer will be like in a remote-controlled world. The question interests you and you want it to interest your audience. If you want the reader to think along with you, you might begin your essay by recreating the process of division that you thought through before focusing on life in the remote lane.

On the other hand, you may find your central question so intriguing that you want to get right to it, in which case you wouldn't need to discuss the division at all; instead, you can leap straight into presenting the category of remote-controlled objects, illustrating it with multiple examples. But before you make up your mind to jump into the subject, consider a third alternative: discussing both remote and nonremote classes, piling examples into each class without telling your reader how you arrived at them.

Perhaps the greatest trap in writing an essay that uses division and classification is that your means don't add up to an end, that what you have is a string of examples that don't lead anywhere. All your examples are well developed, yes, but they don't support an assertion. It's the cardinal sin—an essay without a thesis.

If you find yourself headed in that direction, one solution is to answer your own questions. In the course of thinking about your subject, you may well have come up with a solid, focused, central question, such as "What kind of life will the American consumer have in a remote-controlled world?" Your one-sentence answer to that question can be your thesis.

Often it helps to think of writing as a sort of silent dialogue with yourself. Reading a sentence in your draft and thinking about it, you find that thought leads to another sentence, and so on till you've filled up a number of pages. By the time you have stopped, you may realize that your first draft could more accurately be called a discovery draft, for in the course of writing it, you have found out what you want to say. Sum it up in one sentence that has a debatable point and you have your thesis.

If you are using division and classification to develop only one part of your paper, then where you place it depends on where you think it would be most effective. But if your essay, like most of those in this chapter, is structured primarily by division and classification, then you would do best to use a straightforward pattern of organization, devoting the body of the paper to developing the category or categories involved. Your reader can then follow your reasoning and understand how it supports your thesis. For the sake of clarity—readers can sometimes get lost in a tangle of examples—you may opt for an explicit thesis in an obvious place, such as at the end of your introduction.

USEFUL TERMS
Definition   The dictionary definition of a word, with all its denotative and connotative meanings.

Division and classification   Methods of examining a subject. Division involves the process of separating, first dividing the subject into groups so that they can be sorted out—classified—into categories; classification focuses on shared characteristics, sorting items into categories that share a similar feature.

Hyperbole   Obvious overstatement, exaggeration.

Irony   A statement or action in which the intended meaning or occurrence is the opposite of the surface one.

Sarcasm   A caustic or sneering remark or tone that is usually ironic as well.

▓ POINTERS FOR USING DIVISION AND CLASSIFICATION

Exploring the Topic

1. **How can your topic be divided?** What divisions apply? Of those you list, which one is the best suited?
2. **What examples can you think of?** What characteristics do your examples have in common? Which do you have the most to say about?
3. **Are your categories for classification appropriate?** Are the categories parallel? Do they overlap? Do you need to make any adjustments?
4. **Do your examples fit your categories?** Are you sure the examples have enough in common? Are they obvious? Which are not?
5. **What is your principle for classification?** Have you applied it consistently to each category?
6. **Are your categories complete?** Do they cover the topic? Do they contain enough examples?
7. **How can your categories be sequenced?** From simple to complex? Least to most important? Least to most effective?

8. **What is your point?** What assertion are you making? Does your system of classification support it? Are your examples appropriate?
9. **What is your purpose?** Are you primarily making your point to express your feelings, to inform, to persuade, or to entertain?

Drafting the Paper

1. **Know your reader.** Where does your reader stand in relation to your system of classification? Is the reader part of it? If so, how? If the reader is not part of your system, is he or she on your side, say a fellow student looking at teachers? What does your audience know about your topic? about your system of classification? What does the reader not know? Your audience might be biased toward or against your subject and classification system. How can you best foster or combat the bias?
2. **Know your purpose.** If your primary purpose is to express your feelings, make sure that you are not just writing to yourself and that you are not treading on the toes of your audience. Similarly, if you are writing to persuade, make sure you are not convincing only yourself. Check to see that you are using material that may convince someone who disagrees with you or who, at the least, is either sitting on the fence or hasn't given the matter much thought. Writing to inform is probably the easiest here, for though your subject may be familiar, your system of classification is probably new. On the other hand, writing to entertain is difficult and requires a deft use of persona.
3. **Set up your system of classification early in the paper.** You may find that a definition is in order or that some background information is necessary, but make your system clear and bring it out early.
4. **Explain the principle behind the system.** To give your system credibility, you need to provide an explanation for your means of selection. The explanation can be brief—a phrase or two—but it should be there.
5. **Select appropriate examples.** Perhaps you can best illustrate a class by one extended example, or maybe it would be better to pile on examples. If your examples are apt to be unfamiliar to your audience, make sure you give enough detail so that they are explained by their contexts.
6. **Make a point.** Remember that what you have to say about your subject is infinitely more interesting than the subject itself. So, too, your major assertion is more important than your system of classification: it is what your system of classification adds up to. It's easy, in writing this kind of paper, to mistake the means for the end, so make sure that you use classification to support an overall assertion.

N̲ot Sold by Intellectual Weight

Tom Kuntz

The Money & Business section of the Sunday New York Times *is a place where you would expect to see all kinds of tables reporting stock prices and mutual funds, information on investing and business trends, as well as news stories related to the subjects its title proclaims, but it also has a lighter side and human voices. Tom Kuntz's essay is one example. When it appeared in the newspaper in 1995 it was headlined "Sold Not by Intellectual Weight But Lots of Volume."*

WHAT TO LOOK FOR *Kuntz's essay intersperses his comments with direct quotations from cereal boxes. To guide the reader through this technique, the essay is formatted so that Kuntz's comments are in italics and the quotations are in roman type, a printing choice that makes it possible to eliminate quotation marks that would clutter up the essay. As you read, try to listen for the two distinct voices behind the different printing fonts.*

1   Ah, those dewy, yawn-filled childhood morns at the breakfast table, when a glazed perusal of the cereal box during milky-sweet crunches of flakes was just the ritual to clear the brain's cobwebs for a new day of rascality. Such nostalgia powerfully stokes today's $8 billion market for breakfast cereal, which is eaten by an estimated 80 million adults, adolescents and children daily. It's not surprising, given such numbers, that the cereal box has become practically a metaphor for artifice and packaging in modern American life. Yet it's the stuff inside that usually gets all the publicity, especially from nutritional critics who say a lot of it is just vile, sweet, overpriced junk. They overlook cereal boxes' cultural value.

2   Which you may not think much of either. Still, boxes can command hundreds of dollars on the nostalgia market. More important: "Walk into any grocery store, stroll down the cereal aisle, and you'll realize that cereal is more than a food—it's an all-American form of entertainment," writes Chuck McCann, the original voice of Sonny, the Cocoa Puffs cuckoo bird ("Wuuwk . . . I'M CUCKOO FOR COCOA PUFFS!"). He wrote this in the foreword to "Cerealizing America: the Unsweetened Story of American Break-

fast Cereal," by Scott Bruce and Bill Crawford, a new book that tracks cereal's Elvis-like trajectory from turn-of-the-century wholesomeness to the corny excesses of modern times.

3   If Mr. McCann is right, what's been playing in the cereal aisle lately? From the scores of varieties on the shelves, it's possible to discern several distinct types of boxes.

4   *First up: kiddie cereals. Gone for the most part are the once-common trade-in boxtops and prizes inside (thanks to new marketing methods and greater product liability). Today's boxes are typically cartoonish and character-driven (Tony the Tiger, Cap'n Crunch), offering a crass mix of forced excitement and promotional tie-ins to perhaps the world's most credulous consumers. On the back of Kellogg's Cocoa Krispies is "Coco the Monkey's Marshmallow Adventure," an unchallenging maze through jungle terrain marked by mini-marshmallows (a "free bonus" pack is included inside):*

5   Hey kids! Follow Coco on his adventure through the jungle to discover how Coco uses his mini-marshmallows.

6   "Which weighs more: a pound of marshmallows or a pound of mud?" asks a spotted feline creature leaning on a mug of cocoa.

7   "They both weigh the same, but marshmallows sure taste better," says Coco.

8   "How many S'mores can an elephant eat?" asks an elephant.

9   "As many as he wants," says Coco.

10   (See S'mores Treats recipe on side panel.)

11   *The trail leads to a giant bowl of Cocoa Krispies, watched over, inexplicably, by two thug-like hippopotamuses in dark shades and business suits:*

12   Thanks for joining Coco on his jungle adventure. Have fun trying out all the new ways you can use your mini-marshmallows. How many jungle animals did you see along the way?

13   *Curiously, Rice Krispies, the less-sweet cousin of Cocoa Krispies, pushes dental hygiene on its box, after a fashion, by offering Timmy the Tooth Character Cards. These include the Cavity Goon—a guy with choppers so bad he looks like he OD'd on Cocoa Krispies. Kiddie boxes also resort to self-promotional fun facts:*

14   Get to the center of great taste with [General Mills'] Hidden Treasures. There's a discovery in every bite. That's because inside *some* crunchy sweet squares is a delicious, fruit-flavored center. . . .

Here are a few more cool things with surprise centers to grab your attention!

15   • Geode rocks appear common on the outside, but when you break into one, you'll find a crystal treasure center. The treasure you'll find inside Hidden Treasures is a tasty center of fruit-flavored filling inside special pieces.

16   • What's inside of a neon light is actually a colorless gas. The only way to shed some light on neon is to pass electricity through it. Give your mouth a charge when you bite into Hidden Treasures.

For Kids of All Ages

17   *Then there are cereals like Wheaties and Corn Flakes aimed at both kids and adults—in particular adults who still like the cereal they ate as whelps. By including sports starts on the boxes, the cereals achieve cross-generational appeal, and attract both sports and non-sports collectors. And hey kids! Hey anti-smoking lobby! Check out the subtle way the brand name Winston repeatedly appears on the recent Kellogg's Raisin Bran box featuring the father–son stock car racers Darrell and Michael Waltrip. No, the cigarettes and the cereal don't have the same corporate owners. Still, because the racers' tunics are plastered with corporate plugs, the box has four displays of the logo for the Winston Cup, sponsored by that famous maker of tobacco products hazardous to young lungs! Plus five other mentions of the Winston Cup!*

18   Darrall Waltrip has "finished 9th in Winston Cup series points . . . Has won 3 Nascar Winston Cup championships ('81, '82, '85) . . . trails only Dale Earnhardt and Bill Elliott in career Winston Cup earnings. . . ."

19   *Some boxes continue the tradition of insisting that cereal is not simply cereal. For example, America's Choice Corn Flakes:*

20   That crispy corn taste is just right in the morning with milk and your favorite fruit.

But Don't Stop There!

21   • Top off your casseroles with the crunchy goodness of Corn Flakes.

22   • Use crushed Corn Flakes as a coating for oven-fried chicken or fish.

23   • Mix with any yogurt to add delicious flavor and texture.

24 • Great taste and wholesome goodness make Corn Flakes much more than a breakfast cereal!

25 *You want wholesome? How about Rice Krispies Treats? "Easy to make and low fat!" though the recipe cautions, "Do not use diet or low-fat margarine."*

For Health

26 *It's enough to make you take up health food. But while the smaller "organic" cereal brands eschew additives, you're not likely to find the phrase "piety- and self-congratulation free!" on any of the boxes:*

27 Health Valley's "Save the Earth" Policy: the grains and fruit in these flakes were *grown without chemical fertilizers, herbicides or pesticides* by farmers using organic methods. Health Valley uses more *certified organic* ingredients than any other food company in the world because George Mateljan, the founder of Health Valley, wants to provide you with nutritious, good tasting foods without polluting our precious water supplies or diminishing our topsoil. . . .

28 *Some organic cereals can be downright depressing:*

29 Remember the Irish potato famine? Billions of rows of genetically identical cereal grains are now planted each year, making entire crops vulnerable to a single rapidly evolving pest or disease. This sameness of fields sown horizon to horizon without interruption demands costly and often dangerous reliance on chemicals to protect crops. And every year what we find in our stores tastes less and less like real food.

30 *Your salvation supposedly can begin with the cereal inside the box, Nature's Path Heritage O's. Also sounding the alarums are Rainforest cereals, launched in 1991 by members of the Grateful Dead:*

31 **Action Alert:** The rubber tappers of the Xapuri Co-op (birthplace of the movement once headed by Chico Mendes, assassinated in 1988, and home of the first Brazil nut-collecting and processing co-op) are under increasing attacks by ranchers & some local government officials. . . .

32 **What You Can Do:** Send a letter to Dra. Maria Tapajos Santana Areal & Dr. Erick Cavalcante Linhares, (address) Rua Floriano Peixoto S/N, 69.930-000 Xapuri-Acre, Brasil. . . . Let them know the world is watching. . . .

33 *Who are these people? The box doesn't say.*

For Grown-Ups

34   *Much gauzier, Madison Avenue–style verbiage can be found on the boxes of adult-oriented cereals developed by the big cereal manufacturers in response to the health-food upstarts:*

35   Imagine sitting in the kitchen, enjoying a delicious slice of home-baked banana nut bread. Now imagine that wonderful taste—in a cereal. . . . Real banana oven-baked into crunchy oat clusters, mixed with crispy whole wheat flakes and chopped walnuts . . . [Post] Banana Nut Crunch cereal. The delicious taste of home-baked banana nut bread—in a cereal.

36   *But for those who don't need their breakfast prose dripping with syrup, you can't get much blunter than the discrete warning on Kellog's All-Bran:*

37   Increase your fiber intake gradually. Intestinal gas may occur until your body adjusts. If digestive pain occurs consult your doctor and avoid laxatives.

Thesis and Organization

1. Paragraphs 1 and 2 set out two different functions for the prose on cereal boxes. What are they?
2. Identify the four classifications for the different cereals. What reasons can you find for presenting them in the order Kuntz uses?
3. Which category contains the most examples? Choose one example and evaluate its effectiveness.
4. Paragraphs 36 and 37 end the essay. How effectively do they serve as its conclusion?
5. Kuntz poses a question in paragraph 3. What is his answer? How does it relate to the two functions you identified in question 1?

Technique and Style

1. Choose one of the categories Kuntz uses. How would you characterize Kuntz's voice and tone? That of the example he presents?
2. How would you describe Kuntz's humor?
3. The diction level in the essay varies from slang to archaic, as paragraph 17 exemplifies. What reasons can you discern for such a wide range?
4. Look up *irony* in an unabridged dictionary. What example can you find in the essay that fits the definition?
5. Throughout the body of the essay, Kuntz uses his paragraphs as transitions. Select one and explain any other functions the paragraph has.

Suggestions for Writing

Journal

1. If you eat a particular brand of cereal, take a look at the box it comes in and write a paragraph or two analyzing the box's entertainment value.
2. Kuntz has divided cereal into those ready to eat and the kind that has to be cooked, then classifying the former into various categories. Write a journal entry on what the ready-to-eat variety might imply about our culture.

Essay

We live in a consumer culture, so it follows that every day we are bombarded with advertisements for one product or another. Take a popular magazine and look through the ads, isolating one category of products and then collecting all of the ads that fall within that category. Sort the advertisements into categories that make sense to you. Draw up a statement for each of the categories you have identified. What overall conclusions can you deduce? Choose one of them as a working thesis, and then draft your paper, using the statements as topic sentences and the ads as examples. Products that may lend themselves to such an essay:

cars
lingerie
men's underwear
liquor
beer
perfume
men's cologne
jeans

A lways, Always, Always

Bill Rohde

The essay that follows was written for a class required for students who intended to teach English. Focusing on both writing and the teaching of writing, the course asked students to analyze their own writing habits, including elements in the writing process that gave them problems. No matter what their stage of experience, most writers hit at least one question that sends them to the nearest handbook. The assignment here asked the class to choose one matter of grammar or usage that sent them in search of answers, then to research what the handbooks had to say, and to write an essay explaining both the question and the answers. Since the students were prospective English teachers, they were to use the Modern Language Association's (more familiarly known as the MLA) system of documentation and their audience was the class itself. Bill Rohde questioned the necessity of using a comma before the last item in a series.

WHAT TO LOOK FOR   *It's difficult to write a paper about a dry, well-researched subject in such a way that it has a light tone and an identifiable voice, but that's what Bill Rohde does. As you read the essay, try to imagine the person behind the prose. Also keep in mind that Rohde creates a distinct personality for the narrator of the essay without ever using the first-person I.*

1   A student inquiring about the "correctness" of the serial comma finds conflicting advice in her *Harbrace,* her teacher's *MLA Style Manual,* and the library's *Washington Post Deskbook on Style. Harbrace* tells her she may write either

The air was raw, dank, and gray.

or

The air was raw, dank and gray.

Ever accommodating, the tiny, red handbook considers the comma before the conjunction "optional" unless there is "danger of misreading" (132). *The MLA Style Manual,* with its Bible-black cover, neither acknowledges ambivalence nor allows for options. "Commas are required between items in a series," it clearly states in Section 2.2.4., after which it provides a typically lighthearted sample sentence:

The experience demanded blood, sweat, and tears. (46)

The paperback *Post Deskbook,* so user-friendly it suggests right in the title the handiest place to keep it, advises the student to "omit commas where possible," as before the conjunction in a series (126–27). Apparently written on deadline, the book offers sample sentence fragments:

red, white, green and blue; 1, 2 or 3 (127)

2   What should you, the composition teacher, tell this puzzled student when she approaches with her problem? Tell her she must always use the serial comma—no ifs, ands, or buts about it. Regardless of whether you believe this to be true, you must sound convincing. If the student appears satisfied with your response and thanks you, you may go back to grading papers. If, however, she wrinkles her nose or bites her lip in a display of doubt, then you may safely label her a problem student and select one of the following tailor-made responses.

3   *The struggling student* appreciates any burden a teacher can remove. You should explain to her that out of sympathy for her plight—so much to keep track of when writing—you have just given her one of the few hard-and-fast rules in existence. Tell her to concern herself with apostrophes or sentence fragments, and not with whether the absence of a serial comma might lead to a misreading.

4   *The easily intimidated student* (often ESL) should have accepted your unequivocal answer, but perhaps you do not (yet) strike her as an authority figure. Go for the throat. Say, "Obey the MLA. It is the Bible (or Koran or Bhagavad-Gita) of the discourse community to which you seek entry. Expect blood, sweat, and tears if you do not use the serial comma."

5   *The skeptic* needs an overpowering, multifarious theory to be convinced, so pull out Jane Walpole's *A Writer's Guide* and read the following:

[A]ll commas indicate an up-pause in the voice contour, and this up-pause occurs after *each* series item up to the final one. Listen to your voice as you read this sentence:

Medical science has overcome tuberculosis, typhoid, small pox, and polio in the last hundred years.

Only *polio,* the final series item, lacks an up-pause; and where there is an up-pause, there should be a comma. The "comma and" combination before the final item also tells your readers that the series is about to close, thus reducing any chance of their misreading your sentence. (95)

While that's still soaking in, drop the names of linguists who have stated that writing is silent speech and reading is listening. Then tell her that omitting the serial comma represents an arrogant, foolish, and futile attempt to sever the natural link between speech and text.

6   Show *the visually oriented student,* possibly an artist, how

Chagall, Picasso, and Dali

are nicely balanced, but

Chagall, Picasso and Dali

are not.

7   Tell *the metaphor-happy student* that commas are like dividers between ketchup, mustard, and mayonnaise; fences between dogs, cats, and chickens; or borders between Israel, Syria, and Lebanon. Without them, messes result. (Dodge the fact that messes may result even if they are present.)

8   If the student is *a journalism major* who cites the *Deskbook* as proof of the serial comma's obsolescence, point out that her entire profession is rapidly approaching obsolescence. Add that editors who attempt to speed up reading by eliminating commas in fact slow down comprehension by removing helpful visual cues.

9   One hopes that reading, seeing, and hearing so many strong arguments in favor of the serial comma has so utterly convinced you

of its usefulness that every student from here on in will accept your rock-solid, airtight edict without question.

WORKS CITED

Achtert, Walter S., and Joseph Gibaldi. *The MLA Style Manual.* New York: MLA, 1985.

Hodges, John C., et al. *Harbrace College Handbook.* New York: Harcourt, 1990.

Walpole, Jane. *A Writer's Guide.* Englewood Cliffs: Prentice, 1980.

Webb, Robert A. *The Washington Post Deskbook on Style.* New York: McGraw, 1978.

Thesis and Organization

1. Paragraphs 1 and 2 introduce the essay. What points do they convey to the reader?
2. At what point in the essay does Rohde use division? What does he divide and into what groups?
3. Rohde begins his classification in paragraph 3 and ends it with paragraph 8. What reasons can you infer for the order in which he presents his categories?
4. Where in the essay do you find Rohde's thesis? How effective is that placement?
5. Rohde's thesis is explicit, but what does the essay imply about English teachers? About students? About punctuation and usage?

Technique and Style

1. How would you describe Rohde's tone? his persona? What does his research on the topic contribute to his persona?
2. Who is the *you* in the essay? How effective do you find the direct address?
3. Note the use of parentheses in paragraph 4. Check out what your handbook says about parentheses. To what extent does Rohde's use fit the handbook's explanation?
4. A writer's choice of pronoun has become an issue ever since the once generic *he* lost its general nature and gained a specific gender connotation. What is Rohde's solution? Explain why you do or do not find his choice of pronoun effective.
5. The point of documentation is to provide specific and relevant references in an unobtrusive manner. Evaluate how well Rohde uses his research and how well he documents it.

Suggestions for Writing

Journal Entry

1. Write out your response to Rohde's persona. Would you like to have him as your teacher? Would you like to have him in your class?

2. Commas give many writers fits. Thinking about your own writing, jot down the kinds of problems you have with commas. When you've finished, reread what you have written. Do you find a pattern?

Essay

Given that people's personalities range over a continuum with extremes at either end, the extremes can be good subjects for an essay that uses division and classification. Think about virtually any activity people are involved in and identify the behavior that represents the two extremes, thus dividing the subject. Then choose one of those groups and consider the categories your choice can be classified into. Suggestions:

    drivers
    readers
    writers
    teachers
    professional athletes

*T*he New York Walk: Survival of the Fiercest

Caryn James

Division and classification may seem to play a small part in Caryn James's essay, but it's a crucial one, for misreading the kind of man who hassles women on a city street can have serious consequences. Central to James's essay is the initial division between "a harmless gesture and a threat" (paragraph 13). Faced with either, most women adopt the " 'don't mess with me' glare" that James finds natural. But most also wonder about the long-term effects of that glare on the glarer. As the essay explains, James lives in New York City. Her essay was, appropriately, published in the New York Times, *October 17, 1993.*

WHAT TO LOOK FOR   *As you write, you'll probably discover that you use a number of patterns of organization. James, for example, begins and ends with narration and description, and the body of her essay incorporates division and classification, example, process, cause and effect, and comparison and contrast. The mixture of modes may make the essay hard to classify, but it also gives it variety.*

1   I know better than to talk back to guys who hassle women on the street. But on one weird August afternoon, I was caught in pedestrian gridlock in Times Square and the humidity turned my common sense to mush. A young man so average-looking he belonged in a Nike commercial planted himself on the sidewalk in front of me, purposely blocking my path, and offered some not-poetic variation on "Hey, baby."

2   What I did next was something no short, slight, sane person should ever do: I stamped my little foot and snapped at him in unprintable terms to get out of my way, right now! And while I was wondering why I had chosen a response that was both ineffectual *and* ridiculous, the street hassler smiled, stepped aside and said in a good-natured, singsong voice, "You're gonna learn to love me."

3   Humor is a desirable quality in a man, but this remark did not make him a person to take home. He was visibly affected by some

161

chemical or other, so I made sure to stay behind him as he woozed his way toward traffic. A basic rule of navigating the New York sidewalks, like driving anyplace, is that it's safer to be behind the drunk driver or drug-addled walker than in front of him.

4   And I didn't want him to see that my deliberately off-putting scowl was turning into a laugh.

5   For an instant I had almost lost the protective covering, the "don't mess with me" glare, that so many of us wear on crowded urban streets. Then I remembered that danger is real—the humor made him seem harmless, but his swaying toward an intersection suggested someone seriously out of control—and that walking in the city is a precise defensive maneuver.

6   This is especially, though not exclusively, true for women. Men are hassled, too, but physical size and social conditioning have made women more likely to be picked on. Walking can become an exhausting series of paralyzing questions. Should you slow down for the guy who seems, quite obviously, about to ask for directions? (I tried it once and was asked to join a theater group.) When is someone being innocently friendly, and when is he sidling up to get a better grip on your wallet or purse? When is a comment an invisible weapon, and when is it just a remark?

7   What's more, 30 years of raised feminist consciousness has taught us all that when men yell out to women on the street, whether to comment on a smile or issue a crude invitation, no compliment is involved. The average street hassler is not a fussy type, and while he may keep an eye out for a 17-year-old with no thighs, he will happily go after whoever crosses his line of vision: your mother, your granny, your self.

8   So most women have mastered the New York Walk for avoiding unpleasant encounters: eyes ahead but with good peripheral vision, bag clutched to your side, a purposeful stride and an unfriendly look. If someone talks to you, think of him as an obscene phone caller. Hang up. Do not acknowledge that he exists. In a big city, this is as necessary as locking your doors, and only a naïf would think otherwise.

9   Most of the time, this survival strategy doesn't bother me. I've always thought that my chilly, don't-talk-to-strangers New England upbringing has given me a Darwinian advantage; I've been naturally selected for this urban life. Ignoring strangers who talk to me

in Times Square—people to whom I have not, after all, been properly introduced—makes me feel right at home.

10   I could have evolved differently. My sister transplanted herself to Virginia, and while walking with her there on a civilized cobblestoned street once, I was shocked to hear her say: "You know, you don't have to grab your bag like that. You're not in New York anymore."

11   At moments like that, it's easy to wonder about the psychic cost of living in a city where such guardedness becomes second nature. Is it even possible, when you step into your house or office, to drop the hostile mask quite so easily or thoroughly as you imagine you can?

12   What residue of snarling distrust must build up over the years, so slowly you'd never notice it accumulating? Those are finally moot questions for someone like me, for whom New York will always be tinged with Holly Golightly glamour. Assuming a defensive posture while walking down the street seems a reasonable trade-off for the advantages of living here. Just as a matter of personal preference. I'd rather be hassled outside the Metropolitan Museum or Tiffany's than on a farm or in the 'burbs. (Don't say it doesn't happen.)

13   Maybe the best one can do is to savor those rare episodes during which it is easy to tell the difference between a harmless gesture and a threat. On another summer day, by a fluke in the law of averages, I happened to be the only person walking by a real-life cliché: a scaffold full of construction workers having lunch at a site on Broadway. As I passed, glare in place and prepared for anything, they started to sing a cheerful version of an oldies song: "There she goes, a-walkin' down the street/Singin' doo-wah-diddy-diddy-dum-diddy-do."

14   Hours later as I left my office, several blocks away, I passed a man who gave a big surprised wave. "Hey, I know you!" he said with a friendly smile of recognition as he passed by. "We sang to you!" I almost said hello.

Thesis and Organization

1. What is the point of James's opening narrative?
2. Paragraph 6 briefly describes various categories of men who approach women on the street. What are they?

3. Paragraph 7 tells the reader that "no compliment is involved." What is?
4. The essay ends with an example of "a harmless gesture" (paragraph 13). What is James's reaction?
5. Think about the division that James makes, her glare and its "psychic cost" (paragraph 11), and in your own words, state the thesis.

Technique and Style

1. Though the essay is certainly a literate one, James includes a number of words that best fit the category of slang. What, if anything, do they add to the essay?
2. What evidence can you find to disprove the idea that the essay deals only with the hassling of women?
3. How would you describe James's tone?
4. Where in the essay does James use process? Cause and effect?
5. Explain whether you find James's mixing of modes adds or detracts from the essay.

Suggestions for Writing

Journal

1. Have you ever been followed, or whistled or yelled at, on the street? Write a paragraph or two about how it made you feel.
2. Describe your behavior when you walk along a crowded street. What do you do or not do? Why?

Essay

We interact with strangers in many different ways according to many different circumstances. The next time you find yourself in one of those situations, note how people act. Think about how various people behave and what categories they can be placed into. Then, when you draft your paper, make your categories come alive through description, narration, and example. Likely spots to observe behavior:

    traffic jams
    elevators
    lines (at a bank, supermarket, movie, cafeteria)
    train stations or airports

I ntense!

Richard Brookhiser

An editor for the National Review, *Brookhiser is also the author of numerous articles and books, most recently a biography of George Washington,* Founding Father *(1996), and* Rules for Civility *(1997). The latter book is an update of 110 principles based on earlier ones formed by French Jesuits in the fifteenth century that Washington had copied out in the 1740s and used to guide how he lived his life. As you may infer, Richard Brookhiser is an astute observer of people and society and their quirks. The subtitle of Brookhiser's essay— "Reflections on a Paradoxical Personality Type"—points out a particular quirk, so be on the lookout for what's paradoxical about the truly intense. You'll also find that the essay weaves definition into its division. The essay was first published in the* Atlantic *in May, 1993, then reprinted in the* Utne Reader *in the November/December issue of that same year.*

WHAT TO LOOK FOR   *If you are writing a reflective essay, a collection of thoughts on a particular subject, you may find it difficult to find a way to bring those thoughts together. Brookhiser does it by weaving his ideas around a conversation with his wife, who provides a kind of audience for his thoughts. You can use a similar device if you set up an opening dialogue.*

1   My wife and I were having lunch. She was talking. "What do my friends mean," she asked, "when they call me intense?"

2   I didn't know what to answer at first, not because I didn't know what she was talking about but because I knew so perfectly that it was hard to put into words.

3   My wife is five feet tall. Of the pocket dictionary of pet names I have bestowed on her over the years, most of which have had a half-life of about a month, one was "bundle," short for "bundle of energy." When I think of her as a car, I think of a sports car, usually a Miata, red—or the cars in the cartoons I watched on TV as a kid, which walked down highways on tire feet and had eyelashes over their headlights and grins for grillwork. If a pet squirrel accomplished anything by running around in a wheel—if the shaft of the wheel turned on a gas jet, which heated a tea kettle, whose

steam floated a small parachute that brushed a light switch as it rose—and if the squirrel understood the process and desired the result, then my wife could be that squirrel.

4   *Intense,* I told my wife, was the word my pothead friends used in college, in the '70s, when they were at that stage of being stoned in which they were fully conscious of the activities of the unstoned but lacked the desire or the capacity to participate in any way. What normal activity is to the stoned, the activity of those who are intense is to those who are normal.

5   I was not making any headway, so I decided to list intense people. "Hillary is intense," I said. "Bill is not." Our forty-second president: hand pumper, hugger, hugger of the tree hugger, smiler, glows with the flow, interested in a hundred policies, committed to about three. Resilient, intelligent, eager to please and be pleased—he is all these things. But he is not intense. The first lady: author of articles in law journals, this year earning less money than her husband probably for the first time in her life, lived in Arkansas not because she was born there but because she chose to. She is intense. My wife began to see.

6   I went through other presidents. Bush: not intense. Reagan: not intense. Carter: intense. Ford: come on. Nixon: so intense that he will probably live, on pure intensity, to give a sound bite at Clinton's funeral. Johnson: not intense (paradoxical—I'll get back to it). Kennedy: not intense. Eisenhower: very intense, though he pretended not to be. George Washington: the most intense president we have ever had. Goebbels, I added, was also intense, though Hitler was not. Lenin was intense. Trotsky was not. Madonna is intense; Marilyn was not.

7   "Give me explanations!" my wife howled. How intense of her, I thought. Here goes.

8   The defining quality of intense is that the motor never stops. The engine always runs, the battery always hums. Within the psychic boiler room of the intense person there is always at least a skeleton crew, and that crew never takes a break.

9   Intense cuts across such categories as good and evil, great and mediocre, success and failure, happiness and the lack of it. Jimmy Carter in office was decent, piddling, unsuccessful, and troubled, whereas Lenin was wicked, grand, triumphant, and possibly happy (he was known to laugh at the murder of his enemies). But from each man came the whir of wheels endlessly turning.

10   Activity, to be intense, must also be deliberate, directed, self-propelled. Intense requires an exercise of will. This is what distinguishes the achievements of the intense from those of the non-intense.

11   You can be busy without being intense. This thoughtless quality characterizes busy but not intense types—Lyndon Johnson, William F. Buckley Jr., and Francis of Assisi. Even when they seem to be consciously choosing, their choices are driven by uncontrollable personal forces (in Johnson's case, ambition and grievance). Their activity is an exfoliation of their natures. They do not do, they are.

12   Are the intense ever happy? As often as anyone else in this world. The intense are happy when they're coming down the home stretch. Do the intense ever rest? Never.

13   Are you intense? This is the sort of question no one can ever answer for himself. Each of us thinks he is more complicated than anyone else does, possibly more complicated than anyone actually is. If you want to know which you are, ask a friend. If you do, you are probably intense.

Thesis and Organization

1. Paragraphs 1–3 serve as an introduction. What do they lead you to expect about the author's tone?
2. Brookhiser sets out one definition in paragraph 4. What other paragraphs help define the central term?
3. Division enters paragraphs 5 and 6, then is followed by definition. Where does Brookhiser return to his division?
4. Multiple examples make up paragraphs 5, 6, 9, and 11. What are the advantages of using so many examples?
5. Like many reflective essays, this one contains no one sentence that can work as the thesis. Instead, the reader must deduce the thesis from bits and pieces of Brookhiser's ideas about intense people. What is the thesis?

Technique and Style

1. Brookhiser uses analogy in paragraph 3. How effective do you find his comparisons?
2. What does Brookhiser achieve by the comparison in paragraph 11?
3. What does the dialogue add to the essay?

4. Brookhiser brings in the topic of happiness in paragraph 12. What reasons can you think of for introducing that idea?
5. Who is the "you" in paragraphs 11 and 13?

Suggestions for Writing

Journal

1. Use your journal to describe someone you know who, by Brookhiser's definition, is intense.
2. Analyze the degree to which you would call yourself intense or not intense. What examples support your opinion?

Essay

You can write your own "Intense!" essay by drawing up your own list of friends or public figures, using Brookhiser's definitions or your own. Or if you prefer, pick a different category and figure out who belongs where. For examples, you can draw on your own experience and the world of public figures or well-known characters from mythology, books, television, or film. If your examples are not that well known, make sure you provide enough information about them so that your reader can see how they fit your categories. You may want to have a working thesis to keep you on track, and then in your final draft, switch from an explicit to an implied thesis. For possible categories, you can think of who or what is or is not:

"with it"
"in"
overpaid
underrated
bizarre

*T*he Plot Against People

Russell Baker

Russell Baker is best known for his light tone, one that many readers enjoyed during the time he was a regular columnist for the New York Times. *Baker is the author of several collections of essays and autobiographical books—*Growing Up *(1982),* The Good Times *(1989),* There's a Country in My Cellar *(1991)—and the editor of* The Norton Book of Light Verse *(1986) and* Russell Baker's Book of American Humor *(1993). The essay that follows typifies the humorous side of Baker's style, for he has discovered the principles behind the continuing battle between humans and inanimate objects. He discusses these principles as he neatly divides things into three categories and then places objects into his classifications.*

WHAT TO LOOK FOR *Transitions between paragraphs can be wooden, so obvious that they leap off the page to say "Look at me! I'm a transition." The more effective variety is subtle, and one way to bring that about is to pick up a key word from the previous sentence and repeat it in the first sentence of the paragraph that follows. After you've read Baker's essay, go back over it searching for his transitions between paragraphs.*

1   Inanimate objects are classified into three major categories—those that don't work, those that break down and those that get lost.

2   The goal of all inanimate objects is to resist man and ultimately to defeat him, and the three major classifications are based on the method each object uses to achieve its purpose. As a general rule, any object capable of breaking down at the moment when it is most needed will do so. The automobile is typical of the category.

3   With the cunning typical of its breed, the automobile never breaks down while entering a filling station with a large staff of idle mechanics. It waits until it reaches a downtown intersection in the middle of the rush hour, or until it is fully loaded with family and luggage on the Ohio Turnpike.

4   Thus it creates maximum misery, inconvenience, frustration and irritability among its human cargo, thereby reducing its owner's life span.

5   Washing machines, garbage disposals, lawn mowers, light bulbs, automatic laundry dryers, water pipes, furnaces, electrical fuses, television tubes, hose nozzles, tape recorders, slide projectors—all are in league with the automobile to take their turn at breaking down whenever life threatens to flow smoothly for their human enemies.

6   Many inanimate objects, of course, find it extremely difficult to break down. Pliers, for example, and gloves and keys are almost totally incapable of breaking down. Therefore, they have had to evolve a different technique for resisting man.

7   They get lost. Science has still not solved the mystery of how they do it, and no man has ever caught one of them in the act of getting lost. The most plausible theory is that they have developed a secret method of locomotion which they are able to conceal the instant a human eye falls upon them.

8   It is not uncommon for a pair of pliers to climb all the way from the cellar to the attic in its single-minded determination to raise its owner's blood pressure. Keys have been known to burrow three feet under mattresses. Women's purses, despite their great weight, frequently travel through six or seven rooms to find a hiding space under a couch.

9   Scientists have been struck by the fact that things that break down virtually never get lost, while things that get lost hardly ever break down.

10   A furnace, for example, will invariably break down at the depth of the first winter cold wave, but it will never get lost. A woman's purse, which after all does have some inherent capacity for breaking down, hardly ever does; it almost invariably chooses to get lost.

11   Some persons believe this constitutes evidence that inanimate objects are not entirely hostile to man, and that a negotiated peace is possible. After all, they point out, a furnace could infuriate a man even more thoroughly by getting lost than by breaking down, just as a glove could upset him far more by breaking down than by getting lost.

12   Not everyone agrees, however, that this indicates a conciliatory attitude among inanimate objects. Many say it merely proves that furnaces, gloves and pliers are incredibly stupid.

13   The third class of objects—those that don't work—is the most curious of all. These include such objects as barometers, car

clocks, cigarette lighters, flashlights, and toy train locomotives. It is inaccurate, of course, to say that they never work. They work once, usually for the first few hours after being brought home, and then quit. Thereafter, they never work again.

14　　In fact, it is widely assumed that they are built for the purpose of not working. Some people have reached advanced ages without ever seeing some of these objects—barometers, for example—in working order.

15　　Science is utterly baffled by the entire category. There are many theories about it. The most interesting holds that the things that don't work have attained the highest state possible for an inanimate object, the state to which things that break down and things that get lost can still only aspire.

16　　They have truly defeated man by conditioning him never to expect anything of them, and in return they have given man the only peace he receives from inanimate society. He does not expect his barometer to work, his electric locomotive to run, his cigarette lighter to light or his flashlight to illuminate, and when they don't, it does not raise his blood pressure.

17　　He cannot attain that peace with furnaces and keys and cars and women's purses as long as he demands that they work for their keep.

Thesis and Organization

1. In what ways does the introduction, paragraphs 1–2, set up both the system of classification and the major principle at work among inanimate objects?

2. Paragraphs 3–6 explain the first category. What effects does the automobile achieve by breaking down? How do those effects support Baker's contention about "the goal of all inanimate objects"? What other examples does Baker put into his first category? What example does not fit?

3. Paragraphs 7–12 present the second classification. What causes, reasons, or motives are attributed to the examples in this group?

4. Paragraphs 13–16 describe the third group. What are its qualities? Why might Baker have chosen to list it last? What principle of organization can you discern beneath Baker's ordering of the three groups?

5. Consider how each group frustrates and defeats people together with the first sentence of paragraph 2. Combine this information into a sentence that states the author's thesis.

Technique and Style

1. In part, the essay's humor arises from Baker's use of anthropomorphism, attributing human qualities to inanimate objects. How effectively does he use the technique?
2. Baker has a keen eye for the absurd, as illustrated by paragraph 10. What other examples can you find? What does this technique contribute to the essay?
3. Baker's stance, tone, and line of reasoning, while patently tongue-in-cheek, are also mock-scientific. Where can you find examples of Baker's explicit or implied "scientific" trappings?
4. The essay's transitions are carefully wrought. What links paragraph 3 to paragraph 2? Paragraph 7 to paragraph 6? Paragraph 10 to paragraph 9? Paragraph 12 to paragraph 11?
5. How an essay achieves unity is a more subtle thing. What links paragraph 8 to paragraph 6? Paragraph 9 to paragraphs 3–6? Paragraph 16 to paragraph 2? Paragraph 17 to paragraphs 10–12 and paragraphs 3–5?

Suggestions for Writing

Journal

1. Describe a fight you have had with an inanimate object.
2. Of all the inanimate objects that can frustrate you, which one tops the list and why?

Essay

Write your own "plot" essay, imagining something else plotting against people. Like Baker, you can take a "scientific" stance or you may prefer your own humorous tone. Suggestions:

> clothes
> food
> pets
> the weather
> plants
> traffic

Comparison and Contrast

"**W**hat's the difference?" gets at the heart of **comparison and contrast**, and it is a question that can fit into any context. In college, it often turns up in the form of essay questions; in day-to-day life, it implies the process behind most decisions: "What shall I wear?" "Which movie will I see?" "Should I change jobs?" All these questions involve choices that draw on comparison and contrast. Like description, narration, example, and classification, comparison and contrast forces you to observe, but here you are looking for similarities and differences. In a way, comparison and contrast is the simplest and most analytical form of division and classification in that you are examining only two categories, or perhaps only one example from each of the two categories. "Which sounds better, tapes or records?" compares two categories; "Which sounds better, compact discs or records?" compares two items in the same category.

No matter what you select, however, you need to be sure that the comparison is fair. Deciding where to go out to dinner often depends on how much you are willing to spend, so comparing a fast-food place to an elegant French restaurant doesn't have much of a point unless you want to treat the comparison humorously. If neither is worth the money, however, you have a serious assertion to work from, but you have to work carefully.

Sometimes the similarities will not be readily apparent. If you were writing a paper on Senator Jack Kemp and his 1996 campaign as the Republican's nominee for Vice-President, you might well wonder how he connected his football days with serving in public office. But as you think about what being a quarterback for a professional football team has in common with his experience serving in the United States Senate, similarities begin to emerge: both positions require teamwork and leadership; both depend on the ability to make quick decisions based on complex situations; both call for stamina and training, including what could be called homework. A cynic might add that both involve fancy footwork and the ability to dodge the opposition, but if you want to keep to a serious tone and carry the comparison further, you'd also realize that both jobs call for many public appearances and the ability to be at ease in front of cameras, to be a public figure, if not a celebrity.

There the similarity ends. One position is relatively short-lived and may pay millions. The other is at least a six-year term and not nearly so well remunerated. And no matter how seriously you take football, it is essentially a game, a sport, whereas the other may well affect every citizen in the United States and potentially—as foreign policy is involved—citizens elsewhere as well.

Essays that depend primarily on other modes, such as description, narration, and definition, often use comparison and contrast to heighten a difference or clarify a point, but the pieces in this section rely on comparison and contrast as their main principle of organization, even though their purposes differ.

AUDIENCE AND PURPOSE   Often you may want only to inform your reader: x is better or worse than y; x has a lot in common with y, though not obviously so; x is quite different from y, though superficially similar. If, for instance, your college is primarily residential, you might be interested in how it differs from a nonresidential institution. Assuming that your classmates are your audience, they might be surprised to find that on the average, students at nonresidential campuses are quite different. Compared to those at residential institutions, they are older, work more hours at jobs, miss more classes, carry fewer hours, attend fewer sports events, participate in fewer on-campus activities, and take longer to earn a degree.

You could easily turn what started out as an informative essay into an argumentative one if in the course of writing, you decide that living on a campus that is primarily residential has some drawbacks that may not be apparent at first. A dorm room may not be half as pleasant as an apartment off campus, and eating in the cafeteria can be monotonous. On the other hand, living on campus makes it easier to form solid friendships, and classes don't have to be over at the bell—the discussion can continue without the pressure of having to race off for a job downtown. As you come up with more and more information, you are able to assess the pros and cons and, therefore, to construct a strong argument in favor of the side you believe is best.

Comparison can also be used to entertain your readers. A seemingly simple job such as washing the dog can be as much of a challenge as performing major surgery. At least at hospitals, you don't have to catch the patient first.

ANALOGY   One useful form of comparison is **analogy**, for it can emphasize a point or illuminate an idea. If you are writing about an abstraction, for example, you can make it more familiar by using an analogy to make it concrete and therefore more understandable. An intangible word such as *rumor* becomes more distinct, more memorable, if you write of it as cancer. Or, if you are explaining a process, analogy can often make the unfamiliar familiar; many a tennis instructor has said, "Hold your racquet as though you are shaking hands with a person."

An analogy is an extended **metaphor**, in which a primary term is equated with another quite dissimilar term. The process of writing, for example, is a far cry from making music, but if you think of all the elements of the writing process—coming up with a topic and ideas about it, planning how to organize what you want to say, working on drafts, editing as you go along—then you can see how you can extend the description into a metaphor. You, the writer, are the leader of the orchestra. Organizing your ideas for an essay is rather like getting all the members of the orchestra to play the same tune. Can't find quite the right word? That's similar to having a musician missing from the string section. Wonder if that comma is in the right place? One of the horns skipped a note. Tone not quite what you want it to be? Some of the musicians are flat. Once you have a solid draft, however, it's as though rehearsal is over and the piece is ready for an audience.

So in exposition, analogy clarifies—because by making x analogous to y, you bring all the associations of y to bear on x. If you were to compare the differences in the style of two television newscasters, you might find that one delivers the news in a rush, like a machine gun firing, while the other is more like a single-shot target rifle. The machine gun person fires rapid lines and barely pauses for breath, a sharp contrast to the target rifle person, who hesitates between sentences as though to reload an idea before aiming it at the viewers.

But to use analogy well, you have to use it cautiously. Often writers use it sparingly, working one into a sentence or paragraph instead of using it as the basic structure for an entire essay. Five pages of the ship of state can make you and your readers seasick.

METHOD OF COMPARISON   Comparison-and-contrast essays group information so that the comparison is made by **blocks** or **point by point** or by a combination of the two. If you were to write an essay explaining the differences between an American feast, such as Thanksgiving, and a Chinese one, here is what the two major types of organization would look like in outline form:

Type	**Structure**	**Content**
Block	Paragraph 1	Introduction
	Block A, paragraphs 2–4	American culture
	Point 1	Preparation
	Point 2	Courses & types of food
	Point 3	Manners
	Block B, paragraphs 5–7	Chinese culture
	Point 1	Preparation
	Point 2	Courses & types of food
	Point 3	Manners
	Paragraph 8	Conclusion
Point by Point	Paragraph 1	Introduction
	Point 1, paragraph 2	Preparation
		Chinese
		American
	Point 2, paragraph 3	Courses & types of food
		Chinese
		American

And so on. As you can see, sticking rigorously to one type of organization can become boring or predictable, so writers often mix the two.

In this chapter you'll find essays organized by block, point by point, and by a combination of the two. Outlining an essay readily reveals which type of organization the writer depends on. In your own writing, you might first try what comes easiest; then, in a later draft, you might mix the organization a bit and see what you find most effective. Fortunately word processing makes such changes easy, but if you don't have a word processor, try writing each paragraph on a separate piece of paper. Shuffling them around is then a simple task, though you'll have to supply some transitions after you decide on the best sequence for your paragraphs.

OTHER MODES   A close look at any of the essays that follow will show how you can use other modes, such as description, narration, and cause and effect, to help flesh out the comparison and contrast. A brief narrative or anecdote is often a good way to begin an essay as it usually sets a conversational tone and establishes a link between writer and reader. Examples can clarify your points and description can make them memorable, while exploring why the differences or similarities exist or what effect they may have will lead you into pondering cause-and-effect relationships.

THESIS AND ORGANIZATION   The one-sentence thesis placed at the end of an introductory paragraph certainly informs your readers of your subject and stance, but you might find your paper more effective if you treat your thesis more subtly, trying it out in different forms and positions. While some of the essays in this chapter save their major assertion until last, others combine ideas from various points in the essay to form a thesis. And, of course, not all theses are explicit, but if you want to imply it, you have to be sure your implication is clear or the reader may miss the point.

Although some writers begin the writing process with a thesis clearly set out, many find that it is easier to write their way into one. As a result, you may find that the last paragraph in your draft will make a very good introductory one, for by the time you write it, you have refined your thesis. At that point, you'll find writing a new introduction isn't the task it was to begin with; you already know where you ended up and how you got there.

USEFUL TERMS

Analogy   An analogy examines a subject by comparing it point by point to something seemingly unlike but more commonplace and less complex. An analogy is also an extended metaphor.

Block comparison   A comparison of x to y by grouping all that is to be compared under x and then following with the same information under y.

Comparison and contrast   An examination of two or more subjects by exploring their similarities and differences. Similarities and differences are usually developed through literal and logical comparisons within like categories.

Metaphor   An implied but direct comparison in which the primary term is made more vivid by associating it with a quite dissimilar term. "Life is a bed of roses" is a familiar metaphor.

Point by point   A comparison that examines one or more points by stating the point, then comparing subject *x* to subject *y,* and then continuing to the next point.

▪ POINTERS FOR COMPARISON AND CONTRAST

Exploring the Topic

1. **What are the similarities?** What characteristics do your two subjects share? Are the two so similar that you have little to distinguish them? If so, try another subject; if not, pare down your list of similarities to the most important ones.
2. **What are the differences?** In what ways are your two subjects different? Are they so different that they have little in common? If so, make sure you can handle a humorous tone or try another subject; if not, pare down your list of differences to the most important ones.
3. **Should you emphasize similarities or differences?** Which pattern of organization best fits your material? Block? Point by point? A combination of the two?
4. **What examples will work best?** If your reader isn't familiar with your topic, what examples might be familiar? What examples will make clear what may be unfamiliar?
5. **What metaphor does your subject suggest?** Given the metaphor and your subject, what characteristics match? How can the metaphor be extended into an analogy? How can you outline the analogy as an equation? What equals what?
6. **What other modes are appropriate?** What modes can you draw on to help support your comparison and the organization of the essay? Do you need to define? Where can you use description? narration? example? Do any of your comparisons involve cause and effect?
7. **What is your point? your purpose?** Do you want to entertain, inform, persuade? Given your point as a tentative thesis, should you spell it out in the essay or imply it? If you are writing to inform, what information do you want to present? If you are writing to persuade, what do you want your reader to believe or do?
8. **What persona do you want to create?** Is it best for you to be a part of the comparison and contrast or to be an observer? Do you have a strongly held conviction about your subject? Do you want it to show? Does your persona fit your audience, purpose, and material?

Drafting the Paper

1. **Know your reader.** Use your first paragraph to set out your major terms and your general focus, and to prepare the reader for the pattern of organization and tone that will follow. Reexamine your list of similarities and differences to see which ones may be unfamiliar to your reader. Jot down an illustration or brief description by each characteristic that the reader may not be familiar with. If your reader is part of the group you are examining, tread carefully, and if your teacher may have a bias about your topic, try to figure out what the bias is so you can counter it. Reread your paper from the perspective of the reader who is biased so that you can check your diction as well as your choice of examples and assertions.

2. **Know your purpose.** If you are writing to persuade, keep in mind the reader's possible bias or neutral view and see how you can use your persona as well as logical and emotional appeals to get the reader on your side. Informative papers run the risk of telling readers something they already know, so use description, detail, example, and diction to present your information in a new light. If your paper's main purpose is to entertain, these techniques become even more crucial. Try adding alliteration, allusions, paradox, and puns to the other techniques you draw on.

3. **If you use an analogy, double-check it.** Make sure your analogy is an extended metaphor, not a statement of fact. See what you want to emphasize. Also make sure the placement is effective by trying out the analogy in different positions. Perhaps it works best as a framing device or standing alone in a sentence or paragraph.

4. **Use other modes to support your comparison.** Description and example are probably the most obvious modes to use, but consider narration, cause and effect, definition, and analogy as well. Perhaps a short narrative would add interest to your paper, or perhaps cause and effect enters into your comparisons. Definition may be vital to your thesis, and analogy may help clarify or expand a point.

5. **Check your pattern of organization.** If you are using block comparison, make sure you have introduced your two subjects and that your conclusion brings them back together. In the body of the paper, make sure that what you cover for one, you also cover for the other. In point-by-point comparison, check to see that your points are clearly set out. You may want to use both types of organization, though one will probably predominate.

6. **Make a point.** Perhaps you want to use your comparison to make a comment on the way we live, perhaps to clarify two items that people easily confuse, perhaps to argue that one thing is better than the other. Whatever your point, check it to make sure it is an assertion, not a mere fact. Whether your purpose is to inform or to persuade, take a stand and make sure that your thesis clearly implies or states it.

# The Writer

Perry James Pitre

For some people, the process of writing is similar to cooking or exercising or designing and building furniture, but for Perry James Pitre it's a roller-coaster ride. Pitre ought to know. At the time he wrote the piece that follows, he was writing against deadlines for his column in the student newspaper, the Driftwood. *The essay that follows was written for an English class at the University of New Orleans in 1990.*

WHAT TO LOOK FOR *More often than not, when you start drafting an essay, you almost automatically find yourself using past tense. And when the action described took place in the past, past tense seems the only alternative. Sometimes, though, present tense can be much more effective because it gives the impression of immediacy, which is why Pitre chooses it. As you read the essay, ask yourself what difference using the past tense would have made.*

1   "Ticket please!"

2   The Writer steps into the roller-coaster car and straps himself in as he anticipates the ride to come. Slowly, agonizingly slowly, the car pulls out onto the track, with the huge first hill before it, seemingly an unconquerable mountain. It climbs the hill slowly, almost glacierlike, as The Writer ponders his ideas. Thoughts are discarded, sifted, rearranged, born, die, mutate; but to the observer, all that is apparent is a creeping climb toward the edge of the precipice.

3   As the car nears the pinnacle, The Writer grows excited, scared, triumphant. He clicks on his word processor (which is a real bitch in a roller coaster, but hey, this is a metaphor), and as the car reaches the crest (the program loads) The Writer peers down the incline as the words begin to . . .

4   COME! . . . as the car shrieks down the incline as the words pour out in a torrential flood. Hugging the curves, straining the rails, the car careens down the track, up the next hill, through the 180 degree curve, as the words flow, seemingly directly from his

brain onto the screen, in an almost sexual release of stored, tensed thought.

5   Then, it's over. The car slows, as The Writer loads Spell-Check, observes his handiwork, takes a deep breath, savors a cup of hot chocolate, and lights a cigarette. The car stops, abruptly, as The Writer looks up. . . .

6   "Ticket please!"

Thesis and Organization

1. State the analogy in your own words.
2. What principle lies behind the sequencing of paragraphs 2–5?
3. Spell out the various stages of the analogy and what stands for what.
4. What emotions are associated with those stages?
5. What is the essay's thesis?

Technique and Style

1. In paragraph 3, Pitre destroys the credibility of the roller-coaster ride by including a word processor. How does he account for it? How effective is the device he uses?
2. How would you characterize Pitre's diction? As formal? Informal? What? What effect does he achieve with his choice of diction level?
3. Look up the use of ellipses in your handbook. Does Pitre's use conform to what you found? In what ways does it or does it not?
4. What words, structure, or devices does Pitre use to create a sense of motion?
5. How effective do you find the essay's framework? What meaning do you infer from the final " 'Ticket please' "?

Suggestions for Writing

Journal

1. To what extent does Pitre's description of how he writes coincide with your own experience? Write a brief entry in your journal that explains your answer.
2. Some writers would say that Pitre's analogy gets across the exhilaration of writing, while others would say it communicates the terror involved. Analyze the role fear plays in your own writing process.

Essay

Often a metaphor or analogy can help you discover something new about a familiar subject, or at least force you to think about it from a different perspective. Choose a subject that holds some interest for you and think about an analogy that you can use to explore it. Suggestions:

    friendship
    work
    politics
    football
    boredom

F ashions in Funerals

Shana Alexander

A career journalist, Shana Alexander has published essays in Life *and* Newsweek, *and has been a commentator on* 60 Minutes. *She has also written a number of nonfiction books ranging from* Shana Alexander's State-by-State Guide to Women's Legal Rights *(1977) to her most recent, an autobiography,* Happy Days: My Mother, My Father, My Sister & Me *(1995). She has always been drawn to the unusual: Patty Hearst and her kidnapping; Jean Harris, best known as the boarding-school head who shot and killed Herman Tarnower, the diet doctor; and, indeed, her own family. Her taste for the bizarre may be what drew her to the subject of the essay that follows. While the jungles of New Guinea are a long way from Nashville, Tennessee, she finds that when it comes to funeral customs, the two cultures are perhaps not so far apart after all. The piece was included in Alexander's* Talking Woman *(1976).*

WHAT TO LOOK FOR *Getting started, writing that opening paragraph, can often be difficult. One way to search for ideas is to keep an eye out for the unusual when flipping through your local newspaper or a magazine. That may be just what got Shana Alexander thinking. Whatever brought the story of the New Guinea "funeral" to mind, she uses a narrative to begin her essay, a technique you can adopt for your own writing.*

1   A man in the remote jungles of New Guinea not long ago murdered another man with an ax. Tribal justice ensued. First the murderer was shot and killed with an arrow, and then seven other members of the tribe cut him up and ate him.

2   When word of the feast reached civilization, the authorities concluded that on this occasion justice had literally been served, and perhaps a bit too swiftly, so they hauled the seven cannibals into court, where a wise Australian judge dismissed all the charges, and acquitted the seven men. "The funerary customs of the people of Papua and New Guinea," he explained, "have been, and in many cases remain, bizarre in the extreme."

3   What, I wonder, would the judge have to say about the new, high-rise mausoleum now under construction in Nashville, Ten-

nessee? When completed, this model of modern funerary design will be twenty stories high, fully air-conditioned, and capable of holding 65,000 bodies. A second slightly less deluxe tower on an adjoining site will have facilities to entomb 63,500 more. Nashville's enterprising mortician entrepreneur points out that his high-rise mortuary will be self-contained on only 14 acres, whereas it would require 129 acres to contain all these caskets in the, uh, conventional manner.

4   Well, not exactly caskets. In the new-style funeral, you will be laid out—after embalming, of course—on something called a "repose," described as a "bedlike structure," complete with white sheets, pillow, and blanket. When the ceremonies are ended, bed, pillow, sheet, and blanket are all whisked away; a fiberglass lid snaps down over what remains; and—zap—it's into the wall, stacked seven-high, with a neat bronze marker attached to the face of the crypt.

5   The forward-looking undertaker who thought all this up is already respected, in the trade, for bringing to Nashville the one-stop funeral.

6   But the most important advantage of the high-rise mausoleum is that by putting everything-but-everything under one roof you cut down on the high cost of dying. Maybe so, maybe so. But I can't help thinking it would be even cheaper to die in New Guinea, where the funerary customs are certainly no less bizarre, and a lot more practical.

Thesis and Organization

1. Which paragraphs emphasize New Guinea? Which emphasize Nashville? What sentence summarizes the point the author wishes to make about New Guinea?
2. What sentence serves as a transition between New Guinea and Nashville? What sentence summarizes the point the author wishes to make about Nashville?
3. What paragraph covers both New Guinea and Nashville? What sentence presents that paragraph's major assertion? Explain how that sentence is or is not the thesis of the essay.
4. What is Alexander's attitude toward "the new-style funeral"? Is she attempting to persuade the reader to adopt that attitude or is she simply informing the reader about the latest fashion in funerals and making a

comment about it? What evidence can you find in the essay to support your view? Has she convinced you of anything? Why or why not?

Technique and Style

1. How would you characterize the author's tone? Is it earnest, lighthearted, sarcastic, ironic, tongue-in-cheek, what? What examples can you find to support your answer? Is the tone effective? Why or why not?
2. Where in the essay does the author use narration? Description? How do those modes support the author's use of comparison and contrast?
3. Why might Alexander have chosen to begin the essay in the third person with an objective point of view? Where and why does she introduce first person? Second person? How does her choice of point of view relate to her thesis?
4. How would you characterize the author's level of diction? Is it colloquial? Conversational? Formal? Fancy? What examples support your view? What relationship do you find between Alexander's tone and her level of diction?
5. Where in the essay does Alexander use fragments? What important parts of speech do those sentences lack? Rewrite the sentences as complete sentences. What is lost? gained?

Suggestions for Writing

Journal

1. Look up the word *bizarre* in the dictionary. Consider what has happened to you recently or the news stories you have read or listened to. What strikes you as *bizarre?* Explain how the word fits your experience.
2. Think about the rituals you have developed for studying or writing. Perhaps you need the radio on or have to sit in a certain chair or have a particular kind of pen. Describe your ritual, which may or may not be bizarre.

Essay

Write an essay in which you compare and contrast two fads or fancies from different times or cultures. Suggestions:
 gold-fish swallowing or flagpole sitting of the 1920s versus one of the
  odder pursuits of today
 the Icarus myth versus hang gliding
 tattooing in primitive cultures versus tattooing today in America
 killing enemies with primitive weapons versus killing people you
  don't even know with cars
 polygamous marriage versus serial marriage

*T*hat Lean and Hungry Look

Suzanne Britt

A professor of English and a freelance writer, Suzanne Britt uses example and description to reinforce the humor in her essay, which was published in Newsweek's *"My Turn" column in 1976. The essay is also a good example of the implied thesis, for underneath the obvious assertion she makes in her essay is a critique of our culture. We may worship the "lean and hungry look," but the more fools are we, she implies in her point-by-point comparison of thin people and fat ones.*

WHAT TO LOOK FOR   *Allusions are a form of comparison that make a connection between what the writer is focusing on and the reader's knowledge of cultural or historical events or quotations. Britt uses allusions ironically, but they can take on any spin the writer gives them. Allusions can also help you come up with ideas for what you are writing about. If, for example, you had to write a paper on trees, you could get some help from a dictionary of quotations. You'll find an index in the back of such a dictionary that will list all the quotations that mention trees.*

1   Caesar was right. Thin people need watching. I've been watching them for most of my adult life, and I don't like what I see. When these narrow fellows spring at me, I quiver to my toes. Thin people come in all personalities, most of them menacing. You've got your "together" thin person, your mechanical thin person, your condescending thin person, your tsk-tsk thin person, your efficiency-expert thin person. All of them are dangerous.

2   In the first place, thin people aren't fun. They don't know how to goof off, at least in the best, fat sense of the word. They've always got to be a-doing. Give them a coffee break, and they'll jog around the block. Supply them with a quiet evening at home, and they'll fix the screen door and lick S&H green stamps. They say things like "There aren't enough hours in the day." Fat people never say that. Fat people think the day is too damn long already.

3   Thin people make me tired. They've got speedy little metabolisms that cause them to bustle briskly. They're forever rubbing

their bony hands together and eyeing new problems to "tackle." I like to surround myself with sluggish, inert, easygoing fat people, the kind who believe that if you clean it up today, it'll just get dirty again tomorrow.

4   Some people say the business about the jolly fat person is a myth, that all of us chubbies are neurotic, sick, sad people. I disagree. Fat people may not be chortling all day long, but they're a hell of a lot *nicer* than the wizened and shriveled. Thin people turn surly, mean and hard at a young age because they never learn the value of a hot-fudge sundae for easing tension. Thin people don't like gooey soft things because they themselves are neither gooey nor soft. They are crunchy and dull, like carrots. They go straight to the heart of the matter while fat people let things stay all blurry and hazy and vague, the way things actually are. Thin people want to face the truth. Fat people know there is no truth. One of my thin friends is always staring at complex, unsolvable problems and saying, "The key thing is. . . ." Fat people never say that. They know there isn't any such thing as the key thing about anything.

5   Thin people believe in logic. Fat people see all sides. The sides fat people see are rounded blobs, usually gray, always nebulous and truly not worth worrying about. But the thin person persists. "If you consume more calories than you burn," says one of my thin friends, "you will gain weight. It's that simple." Fat people always grin when they hear statements like that. They know better.

6   Fat people realize that life is illogical and unfair. They know very well that God is not in his heaven and all is not right with the world. If God was up there, fat people could have two doughnuts and a big orange drink anytime they wanted it.

7   Thin people have a long list of logical things they are always spouting off to me. They hold up one finger at a time as they reel off these things, so I won't lose track. They speak slowly as if to a young child. The list is long and full of holes. It contains tidbits like "get a grip on yourself," "cigarettes kill," "cholesterol clogs," "fit as a fiddle," "ducks in a row," "organize," and "sound fiscal management." Phrases like that.

8   They think these 2000-point plans lead to happiness. Fat people know happiness is elusive at best and even if they could get the

kind thin people talk about, they wouldn't want it. Wisely, fat people see that such programs are too dull, too hard, too off the mark. They are never better than a whole cheesecake.

9   Fat people know all about the mystery of life. They are the ones acquainted with the night, with luck, with fate, with playing it by ear. One thin person I know once suggested that we arrange all the parts of a jigsaw puzzle into groups according to the size, shape and color. He figured this would cut the time needed to complete the puzzle by at least 50 percent. I said I wouldn't do it. One, I like to muddle through. Two, what good would it do to finish early? Three, the jigsaw puzzle isn't the important thing. The important thing is the fun of four people (one thin person included) sitting around a card table, working a jigsaw puzzle. My thin friend had no use for my list. Instead of joining us, he went outside and mulched the boxwoods. The three remaining fat people finished the puzzle and made chocolate, double-fudged brownies to celebrate.

10   The main problem with thin people is they oppress. Their good intentions, bony torsos, tight ships, neat corners, cerebral machinations and pat solutions loom like dark clouds over the loose, comfortable, spread-out, soft world of the fat. Long after fat people have removed their coats and shoes and put their feet up on the coffee table, thin people are still sitting on the edge of the sofa, looking neat as a pin, discussing rutabagas. Fat people are heavily into fits of laughter, slapping their thighs and whooping it up, while thin people are still politely waiting for the punch line.

11   Thin people are downers. They like math and morality and reasoned evaluation of the limitations of human beings. They have their skinny little acts together. They expound, prognose, probe and prick.

12   Fat people are convivial. They will like you even if you're irregular and have acne. They will come up with a good reason why you never wrote the great American novel. They will cry in your beer with you. They will put your name in the pot. They will let you off the hook. Fat people will grab, giggle, guffaw, gallumph, gyrate and gossip. They are generous, giving and gallant. They are gluttonous and goodly and great. What you want when you're down is soft and jiggly, not muscled and stable. Fat people know this. Fat people have plenty of room. Fat people will take you in.

Thesis and Organization

1. How does the introduction prepare the reader for the essay's pattern of organization? Its tone? Its thesis?
2. Paragraphs 2–5 and 8–10 use point-by-point comparison to support the essay's thesis. What point or points are raised in each of those paragraphs?
3. Why might the author change her paragraph structure in paragraphs 6 and 7 and paragraphs 11 and 12? In each pair of paragraphs, which paragraph deals with what type of person? Why might the author have chosen to present them in that order? How does the order of paragraphs 11 and 12 affect Britt's thesis?
4. The thesis of the essay is obvious, but its purpose is somewhat complex. The humorous tone of the essay and the author's wordplay suggest that the essay's purpose is to entertain, but the author's unusual perspective provides the reader with a fresh way of looking at a familiar topic; at the same time, the reader suspects that underneath the humor there may lurk a serious point and a persuasive one. Citing evidence from the essay, make a case for what you think is the author's main purpose.

Technique and Style

1. The title of the essay is an allusion that is picked up in the first sentence. What is being alluded to? What other allusion can you spot in paragraph 1? in paragraph 9? What do the allusions add to the writer's persona?
2. Britt relies heavily on details to make her points vivid. How many specific details can you find in paragraph 10? What assertion about thin people is supported by details? What assertion about fat people is implied by details?
3. Frequently, the author relies on a short declarative sentence to open a paragraph. What effect does this technique have on the paragraph? On the essay as a whole?
4. Britt achieves her comic effect by taking words at their face value, by putting clichés to use as clichés, and by employing alliteration. Where in the essay do you find examples of these techniques? Choose a sentence that uses one of the techniques and analyze its specific effect. What does it contribute to the thesis and purpose of the essay and to its tone?

Suggestions for Writing

Journal

1. Analyze how you feel about the thin and the fat, comparing your reactions.
2. If you had to be thin or fat, which would you choose and why? This journal entry may become the draft of an essay that uses comparison and contrast.

Essay

Like Britt, your essay can have a humorous (even satiric) tone but a serious point underneath it. Using her essay as a model, you can make a case for

the villain instead of the hero

the ordinary instead of the beautiful

the poor instead of the rich

the hungry instead of the fed

the loser instead of the winner

If you prefer a straightforward essay, think of making a case for something few people might value, such as a worn-out pair of blue jeans, a long-forgotten toy, a vegetable such as parsnips. Along the way, you will be using comparisons.

*T*wo Ways to Belong in America

Bharati Mukherjee

You will find out much about Bharati Mukherjee as you read the essay that follows. What she does not say, however, is that she is the author of five novels, two short story collections, and two nonfiction books. Her sixth novel, Leave It to Me, *was published in 1997. Her essay also does not mention the numerous awards she has received, among them the 1988 National Book Critics' Circle Award (for her collection* The Middleman and Other Stories*) as well as Guggenheim and Canada Council grants and fellowships. Much of Mukherjee's writing focuses on the experiences of immigrants. That is also the focus of the essay that follows, one that appeared in the Op-Ed section of the* New York Times *on September 22, 1996, a time when the U.S. Congress, along with many states, was considering bills that would severely curtail the benefits of legal immigrants.*

WHAT TO LOOK FOR   *Like Mukherjee, you may at times find yourself directly affected by a proposed law or political debate and you may want to make yourself heard about it. When that happens, you will probably want to begin by explaining how the proposal affects you personally. Yet to make your point to a wider audience, you will need to broaden it so that you speak not just for yourself, but for a larger group. As you read Mukherjee's essay, look for the ways in which she does just that, moving from the particular to the general, from personal narrative to a more universal stance.*

1 This is a tale of two sisters from Calcutta, Mira and Bharati, who have lived in the United States for some 35 years, but who find themselves on different sides in the current debate over the status of immigrants. I am an American citizen and she is not. I am moved that thousands of long-term residents are finally taking the oath of citizenship. She is not.

2 Mira arrived in Detroit in 1960 to study child psychology and pre-school education. I followed her a year later to study creative writing at the University of Iowa. When we left India, we were almost identical in appearance and attitude. We dressed alike, in saris; we expressed identical views on politics, social issues, love

and marriage in the same Calcutta convent-school accent. We would endure our two years in America, secure our degrees, then return to India to marry the grooms of our father's choosing.

3   Instead, Mira married an Indian student in 1962 who was getting his business administration degree at Wayne State University. They soon acquired the labor certifications necessary for the green card of hassle-free residence and employment.

4   Mira still lives in Detroit, works in the Southfield, Mich., school system, and has become nationally recognized for her contributions in the fields of pre-school education and parent-teacher relationships. After 36 years as a legal immigrant in this country, she clings passionately to her Indian citizenship and hopes to go home to India when she retires.

5   In Iowa City in 1963, I married a fellow student, an American of Canadian parentage. Because of the accident of his North Dakota birth, I bypassed labor-certification requirements and the race-related "quota" system that favored the applicant's country of origin over his or her merit. I was prepared for (and even welcomed) the emotional strain that came with marrying outside my ethnic community. In 33 years of marriage, we have lived in every part of North America. By choosing a husband who was not my father's selection, I was opting for fluidity, self-invention, blue jeans and T-shirts, and renouncing 3,000 years (at least) of caste-observant, "pure culture" marriage in the Mukherjee family. My books have often been read as unapologetic (and in some quarters overenthusiastic) texts for cultural and psychological "mongrelization." It's a word I celebrate.

6   Mira and I have stayed sisterly close by phone. In our regular Sunday morning conversations, we are unguardedly affectionate. I am her only blood relative on this continent. We expect to see each other through the looming crises of aging and ill health without being asked. Long before Vice President Gore's "Citizenship U.S.A." drive, we'd had our polite arguments over the ethics of retaining an overseas citizenship while expecting the permanent protection and economic benefits that come with living and working in America.

7   Like well-raised sisters, we never said what was really on our minds, but we probably pitied one another. She, for the lack of structure in my life, the erasure of Indianness, the absence of an unvarying daily core. I, for the narrowness of her perspective, her uninvolvement with the mythic depths or the superficial pop culture of this society. But, now, with the scapegoating of "aliens"

(documented or illegal) on the increase, and the targeting of long-term legal immigrants like Mira for new scrutiny and new self-consciousness, she and I find ourselves unable to maintain the same polite discretion. We were always unacknowledged adversaries, and we are now, more than ever, sisters.

8   "I feel used," Mira raged on the phone the other night. "I feel manipulated and discarded. This is such an unfair way to treat a person who was invited to stay and work here because of her talent. My employer went to the I.N.S. and petitioned for the labor certification. For over 30 years, I've invested my creativity and professional skills into the improvement of *this* country's pre-school system. I've obeyed all the rules, I've paid my taxes, I love my work, I love my students, I love the friends I've made. How dare America now change its rules in midstream? If America wants to make new rules curtailing benefits of legal immigrants, they should apply only to immigrants who arrive after those rules are already in place."

9   To my ears, it sounded like the description of a long-enduring, comfortable yet loveless marriage, without risk or recklessness. Have we the right to demand, and to expect, that we be loved? (That, to me, is the subtext of the arguments by immigration advocates.) My sister is an expatriate, professionally generous and creative, socially courteous and gracious, and that's as far as her Americanization can go. She is here to maintain an identity, not to transform it.

10   I asked her if she would follow the example of others who have decided to become citizens because of the anti-immigration bills in Congress. And here, she surprised me. "If America wants to play the manipulative game, I'll play it too," she snapped. "I'll become a U.S. citizen for now, then change back to Indian when I'm ready to go home. I feel some kind of irrational attachment to India that I don't to America. Until all this hysteria against legal immigrants, I was totally happy. Having my green card meant I could visit any place in the world I wanted to and then come back to a job that's satisfying and that I do very well."

11   In one family, from two sisters alike as peas in a pod, there could not be a wider divergence of immigrant experience. America spoke to me—I embraced the demotion from expatriate aristocrat to immigrant nobody, surrendering those thousands of years of "pure culture," the saris, the delightfully accented English. She retained them all. Which of us is the freak?

12   Mira's voice, I realize, is the voice not just of the immigrant South Asian community but of an immigrant community of the millions who have stayed rooted in one job, one city, one house, one ancestral culture, one cuisine, for the entirety of their productive years. She speaks for greater numbers than I possibly can. Only the fluency of her English and the anger, rather than fear, born of confidence from her education, differentiate her from the seamstresses, the domestics, the technicians, the shop owners, the millions of hard-working but effectively silenced documented immigrants as well as their less fortunate "illegal" brothers and sisters.

13   Nearly 20 years ago, when I was living in my husband's ancestral homeland of Canada, I was always well-employed but never allowed to feel part of the local Quebec or larger Canadian society. Then, through a Green Paper that invited a national referendum on the unwanted side effects of "nontraditional" immigration, the Government officially turned against its immigrant communities, particularly those from South Asia.

14   I felt then the same sense of betrayal that Mira feels now. I will never forget the pain of that sudden turning, and the casual racist outbursts the Green Paper elicited. That sense of betrayal had its desired effect and drove me, and thousands like me, from the country.

15   Mira and I differ, however, in the ways in which we hope to interact with the country that we have chosen to live in. She is happier to live in America as expatriate Indian than as an immigrant American. I need to feel like a part of the community I have adopted (as I tried to feel in Canada as well). I need to put roots down, to vote and make the difference that I can. The price that the immigrant willingly pays, and that the exile avoids, is the trauma of self-transformation.

Thesis and Organization

1. It's possible to identify Mukherjee's introduction as her first paragraph or as paragraphs 1–5. Make a case for what you find best serves to introduce the essay.
2. Trace the essay's pattern of organization. Is it block, point by point, or a mixture of the two? If the latter, which paragraphs conform to which pattern?
3. Paragraphs 13 and 14 provide a brief narrative of Mukherjee's experience in Canada. What happened and how did it affect her?
4. Where in the essay does Mukherjee broaden the base of her narrative? Why might she have chosen the examples she uses?

5. The essay deals with a number of topics—the "trauma of self-transformation" (paragraph 15), the injustice of the proposed laws, the concept of citizenship, the plight of the immigrant, the question of what it means to hold a green card. What do you find to be the essay's major focus and what is Mukherjee saying about that subject?

Technique and Style

1. How would you describe Mukherjee's tone? Does it change in the course of the essay and if so, where and how?
2. Mukherjee makes extensive use of quotation marks (paragraphs 5–8 and 10–13). To what different uses does she put them? What do they add to the essay?
3. What facts do you come to know about Mukherjee's family? What do they add to the essay's point? To Mukherjee's persona?
4. *Immigrant* has many connotations. What are some of them? Where in the essay does Mukherjee allude to the word's connotations? Why does she do so?
5. Mukherjee poses a question at the end of paragraph 11. What is her implied answer? How does her answer relate to the essay's thesis?

Suggestions for Writing

Journal

1. Write a page or two that records your associations with the word *immigrant.*
2. If you were to move to another country and work there, would you be more likely to become like Mukherjee or her sister?

Essay

Mukherjee describes two ways of looking at a culture, from the outside looking in and from the inside looking out—perspectives all of us are used to. Write your own essay comparing the two views, drawing on your own experiences and that of others to make your point. For suggestions, think of two ways of examining a topic:

what you thought college was going to be like and what you actually found it to be like

what you expected from a job and what you learned

If you prefer, write an essay in which you analyze what it means to have a certain privilege compared to not having it. Suggestions:

a driver's license

a voter's card

membership in a certain group

a green card

an, Bytes, Dog

James Gorman

Few people would think of evaluating a dog in terms of the characteristics of a computer, but that's what James Gorman does to discover which is man's best friend. This unlikely comparison appeared in the New Yorker *in 1984. Gorman is now a contributing editor for the* New York Times Magazine.

WHAT TO LOOK FOR *Comparing two very dissimilar things can often get a writer into trouble if the major point is a serious one. Gorman, however, uses the dissimilarity to construct a satire that makes an underlying serious statement about dogs and computers.*

1   Many people have asked me about the Cairn Terrier. How about memory, they want to know. Is it IBM compatible? Why didn't I get the IBM itself, or a Kaypro, Compaq, or Macintosh? I think the best way to answer these questions is to look at the Macintosh and the Cairn head on. I almost did buy the Macintosh. It has terrific graphics, good word-processing capabilities, and the mouse. But in the end I decided on the Cairn, and I think I made the right decision.

2   Let's start out with the basics:
Macintosh
Weight (without printer): 20 lbs.
Memory (RAM): 128 K
Price (with printer) $3,090
Cairn Terrier
Weight (without printer): 14 lbs.
Memory (RAM): Some
Price (with printer) $250

3   Just on the basis of price and weight, the choice is obvious. Another plus is that the Cairn Terrier comes in one unit. No printer is necessary, or useful. And—this was a big attraction to me—there is no user's manual.

4   Here are some of the other qualities I found put the Cairn out ahead of the Macintosh.

5   **Portability:** To give you a better idea of size, Toto in *The Wizard of Oz* was a Cairn Terrier. So you can see that if the young Judy Garland was able to carry Toto around in that little picnic basket, you will have no trouble at all moving your Cairn from

place to place. For short trips it will move under its own power. The Macintosh will not.

6   **Reliability:** In five to ten years, I am sure, the Macintosh will be superseded by a new model, like the Delicious or the Granny Smith. The Cairn Terrier on the other hand, has held its share of the market with only minor modifications for hundreds of years. In the short term, Cairns seldom need servicing, apart from shots and the odd worming, and most function without interruption during electrical storms.

7   **Compatibility:** Cairn Terriers get along with everyone. And for communications with any other dog, of any breed, within a radius of three miles, no additional hardware is necessary. All dogs share a common operating system.

8   **Software:** The Cairn will run three standard programs, SIT, COME, and NO, and whatever else you create. It is true that, being microcanine, the Cairn is limited here, but it does load the programs instantaneously. No disk drives. No tapes.

9   Admittedly, these are peripheral advantages. The real comparison has to be on the basis of capabilities. What can the Macintosh and the Cairn do? Let's start on the Macintosh's turf—income-tax preparation, recipe storage, graphics, and astrophysics problems:

	Taxes	**Recipes**	**Graphics**	**Astrophysics**
Macintosh	yes	yes	yes	yes
Cairn	no	no	no	no

10   At first glance it looks bad for the Cairn. But it's important to look beneath the surface with this kind of chart. If you yourself are leaning toward the Macintosh, ask yourself these questions: Do you want to do your own income taxes? Do you want to type all your recipes into a computer? In your graph, what would you put on the x axis? The y axis? Do you have any astrophysics problems you want solved?

11   Then consider the Cairn's specialties: playing fetch and tug-of-war, licking your face, and chasing foxes out of rock cairns (eponymously). Note that no software is necessary. All these functions are part of the operating system:

	Fetch	**Tug-of-war**	**Face**	**Foxes**
Cairn	yes	yes	yes	yes
Macintosh	no	no	no	no

12   Another point to keep in mind is that computers, even the Macintosh, only do what you tell them to do. Cairns perform their functions all on their own. Here are some of the additional capabilities that I discovered once I got the Cairn home and housebroken:

13   **Word Processing:** Remarkably, the Cairn seems to understand every word I say. He has a nice way of pricking up his ears at words like "out" or "ball." He also has highly tuned voice recognition.

14   **Education:** The Cairn provides children with hands-on experience at an early age, contributing to social interaction, crawling ability, and language skills. At age one, my daughter could say "Sit," "Come," and "No."

15   **Cleaning:** This function was a pleasant surprise. But of course cleaning up around the cave is one of the reasons dogs were developed in the first place. Users with young (below age two) children will still find this function useful. The Cairn Terrier cleans the floor, spoons, bib, and baby, and has an unerring ability to distinguish strained peas from ears, nose, and fingers.

16   **Psychotherapy:** Here the Cairn really shines. And remember, therapy is something that computers have tried. There is a program that makes the computer ask you questions when you tell it your problems. You say, "I'm afraid of foxes." The computer says, "You're afraid of foxes?"

17   The Cairn won't give you that kind of echo. Like Freudian analysts, Cairns are mercifully silent; unlike Freudians, they are infinitely sympathetic. I've found that the Cairn will share, in a nonjudgmental fashion, disappointments, joys, and frustrations. And you don't have to know BASIC.

18   The last capability is related to the Cairn's strongest point, which was the final deciding factor in my decision against the Macintosh—user friendliness. On this criterion, there is simply no comparison. The Cairn Terrier is the essence of user friendliness. It has fur, it doesn't flicker when you look at it, and it wags its tail.

Thesis and Organization

1. Paragraph 1 begins by setting out the answers to some of the standard journalistic points: *who, what, where, when, why,* and *how.* What answers does paragraph 1 provide?

2. Paragraph 2 summarizes the "basics," and paragraph 3 draws a conclusion from them. What is the thesis suggested by paragraphs 1–3?

3. Paragraphs 5–12 compare the Cairn to the Macintosh. What is the basis of comparison in each paragraph? Which paragraphs focus on the Cairn, the

Macintosh, both? Which pattern of comparison dominates, the point-by-point or block?

4. What sentence introduces paragraphs 13–18? Which paragraphs focus on the Cairn, the Macintosh, both? Which pattern of comparison dominates, the point-by-point or block?

5. Reconsider the thesis of the essay from a broader perspective by summarizing what the dog can do that the computer cannot. What comment might the author be making about dogs? Pets? Computers? Machines? About their relative worth? Consider the essay as a satire, and state its thesis.

Technique and Style

1. Explain how the author's use of punctuation and spelling in the title establishes the tone of the essay.

2. Humor often stems from improbable juxtapositions. Given that the fundamental comparison fits that idea, what other examples can you find of Gorman's using this technique?

3. What effect does the author achieve by including the two charts? What do the charts contribute to the satire?

4. The tone of the essay is at times informal, almost as though the author were talking to the reader. How is that tone reinforced by point of view? By diction? By the examples Gorman includes? Why did he choose this tone?

5. In paragraphs 5, 8, and 16, Gorman relies on the short sentence. Choose an example from one of those paragraphs and rewrite it, combining the sentence with another. What is gained? Lost?

Suggestions for Writing

Journal

1. Write a paragraph that describes an analogy for your pet, or, if you don't have a pet, for a dog or cat (or other animal) you have known.

2. Assuming that you have used a word processor, compare writing by hand with writing on a word processor.

Essay

Write an essay that compares two quite dissimilar subjects in order to make a satiric point about one of them. Suggestions:

    going to a party versus studying
    raising a garden versus children
    playing poker versus football
    owning a bicycle versus a car
    eating junk food versus cooking

If you prefer, write a serious paper evaluating two products to determine which is better.

Of Prophets and Protesters

Robert C. Maynard

At first thought, the lives of Huey Newton and Martin Luther King, Jr., would seem to have more differences than similarities. After all, Newton epitomized a radical approach to asserting one's civil rights while King espoused nonviolence. Robert Maynard, however, finds some significant commonalities: concern, passion, charisma, and—unhappily—violent death. Maynard's essay was published in 1989, appearing in his syndicated column carried by the Times-Picayune *of New Orleans.*

Until his death in 1993, Maynard, one of the most prominent African Americans in American journalism, was the editor and publisher of the Oakland Tribune *and was well known for his efforts to encourage minority journalists. As for Martin Luther King, Jr., biographies abound, and information on Huey Newton is readily available. The most recent account of Newton's life is Hugh Pearson's* The Shadow of the Panther: Huey Newton and the Price of Black Power in America *(Addison-Wesley, 1994).*

WHAT TO LOOK FOR *When you write about a controversial subject, you have to be careful not to arouse the reader's negative associations. As you read Maynard's essay, notice how he deals with readers who may think of Huey Newton as a racist and radical.*

1   If Huey Newton and Martin Luther King, Jr., ever met, they certainly formed no bond. They are bound nonetheless today by the common threads of how they lived and how each died. In one of history's curious accidents, their deaths help tell the tale of their times.

2   Dr. King and Huey Newton shared a deep concern for their people and for the plight of the poor. They aroused the passions of their generations. They were charismatic figures whose words were remembered and repeated. In different ways, the movements they led helped change America.

3   Dr. King was gunned down in Memphis, probably at the instigation of a hate group. Newton was gunned down in West Oakland, probably the victim of criminal street activity. The full extent of his own criminal involvement is not altogether clear.

4   What is clear in the first half-light of history is how the two men differed. The work of one is revered in much of the nation, yet the activity of the other was reviled.

5   Newton was representative in the sixties and seventies of sharp and chic radical diversion from the mainstream of the civil rights movement. There were others, such as Stokely Carmichael and H. Rap Brown. Their criticism of Dr. King and the nonviolent movement was that it was too passive, even "Uncle Tom."

6   I covered many of those leaders before and after the split in the movement. I found the differences fascinating. So were some of the similarities. All agreed on one basic tenet: Racism was destroying black lives by the millions.

7   Newton, Carmichael, and Brown, though all critics of Dr. King, differed in their styles and approaches. They shared with each other and with Dr. King a great talent at articulating the nature of the inequities in our society.

8   The radicals differed among themselves and with Dr. King in the solutions they advocated. Newton and the Panthers were socialists and allied themselves with other fringe groups in the white community. Carmichael and Brown preached black nationalism and racial separation.

9   Dr. King preached democracy. He resisted those who would change ours to a socialist system. He also had no patience for those who advanced the idea that black people should have a state of their own. Dr. King believed black Americans contributed mightily to the shaping of America and were entitled to their fair share of the American dream.

10   The struggle of differing views did not die with Dr. King in 1968. Some of those arguments went full force into the decade of the seventies. By then, the Voting Rights Act and other reforms of the nonviolent movement began showing tangible results.

11   The fringe movements died. Their leaders had their 15 minutes of fame. H. Rap Brown took a Muslim life-style and name, and leads a very low-profile life. Stokely Carmichael pops up now and again, but he has a small following.

12   Dr. King, even in death, continues to command the conscience of the nation. This is so because his choice of a remedy was to resort to basic American principles of justice, fairness and equality.

13   To see the urban underclass is to recognize how much remains to be done. It is also worth noting that the violent streets that

spawned the radical movements remain violent streets. It was on those streets that Huey Newton's life ended.

14   His death is a reminder that the civil rights movement spawned prophets and protesters. Dr. King pronounced a prophecy that remains a challenge to the conscience of our society. And, although Huey Newton and Dr. King differed on solutions, their deaths are joined as reminders of the nation's unfinished business.

Thesis and Organization

1. What tentative thesis does paragraph 1 suggest?
2. Which paragraphs focus on similarities?
3. Which paragraphs focus on differences? On both similarities and differences?
4. Paragraphs 10–14 deal with the time since Martin Luther King, Jr.'s, death. What has changed? What has not changed?
5. Consider your answer to question 1 and the last sentence in paragraph 14. What is the essay's thesis?

Technique and Style

1. In what ways does the title fit the essay?
2. Huey Newton was a controversial figure who many readers may think of negatively. What is Maynard's view of Newton? How does he take negative opinions of Newton into account?
3. Maynard frequently uses parallelism to emphasize his points. Choose one example and rewrite the sentence so that the parallelism disappears or is strengthened. What is gained? Lost?
4. To what extent does Maynard rely on first person? What reasons can you find for his use of it?
5. Alliteration, the use of similar initial sounds, is a technique usually associated with poetry, not prose. What examples can you find in Maynard's essay? What do they add?

Suggestions for Writing

Journal

1. Compare two people you admire and explain why you prefer one over the other.
2. Make a list of the characteristics Maynard associates with Huey Newton, and then explain why Newton should or should not be admired.

Essay

Think about two people who were different yet had an influence on those around them. Once you have chosen your subjects and jotted down some information about them, you are ready to draft an essay about them. The subjects you choose may be people you know or figures drawn from a more public arena. Suggestions based on your personal experience:

    relatives
    teachers
    religious persons

For suggestions based on general experience, think of figures who influenced their fields:

    sports
    music
    film
    medical research
    history
    politics

Process

*I*f you have ever been frustrated in your attempts to put together a barbecue grill or hook up a stereo system, you know the value of clear and complete directions. And if you have tried to explain how to get to a particular house or store, you also know that being able to give clear directions is not as easy as it seems. We deal with this practical, how-to kind of **process analysis** every day in recipes, user's manuals, and instruction booklets. Basic to this process is dividing the topic into the necessary steps, describing each step in sufficient detail, and then sequencing the steps so they are easy to follow. You can also help by anticipating trouble spots. If you are writing a set of directions for a barbecue grill, for example, you might start by describing the parts that must be put together so that you familiarize the reader with them and force a quick inventory. And if the plans call for 12 screws but the packaging includes 15, telling the reader that there are three extra will stave off the inevitable "I must have done it wrong" that leftover parts usually elicit.

But writing directions is only one kind of process analysis. "How does it work?" and "How did it happen?" are questions that get at other sorts of processes—the scientific and the historical. Lab reports exemplify scientific process analysis, as do the kinds of papers published in *Scientific American* or the *New England Journal of Medicine*. Like the practical, how-to process paper, the report of an experiment or explanation of a physical process clearly marks the steps in a sequence. The same is true of essays that rely on historical process, though sometimes it's harder to discern the steps. A paper that analyzes how the United States became involved in the Vietnam War, for instance, identifies the major stages of involvement and their chronology, the steps that led up to open warfare. Essays that focus on a historical process often condense time in a way that practical or scientific process analysis does not, but the chronology itself is still important.

Although process analysis is usually associated with specialized subjects—how to do *x*, how *y* works, or how *z* came about—it also finds its way into less formal prose. If you were to write about how you got interested in a hobby, for instance, you would be using process analysis, as you would if you were writing an explanatory research paper on the history of Coca-Cola. Process analysis is also useful as a means of discovery. If you were to analyze the process you go through to revise a draft of one of your papers, you might find out that you overemphasize a particular stage or leave out a step. It's easy to underrate process analysis as a way of thinking and expressing ideas, because it is often equated with the simpler forms of how-to writing.

AUDIENCE AND PURPOSE   The concept of audience is crucial to process essays, for you must know just how familiar the reader is with the topic in order to know what you need to explain and how to explain it. Familiar topics present you with a challenge, for how can you interest your readers in a subject they already know something about? The answer lies in what you have to say about that subject and how you say it. A seemingly dull topic such as making bread can be turned into an interesting paper if you start with the negative associations many readers have about the topic—air bread, that tasteless, white compactible substance better suited to bread ball fights than human consumption—and then go on to describe the process that produces the kind of bread that is chewy, substantive, tasty, worth $4.50 a loaf in a specialty food store.

Your purpose in such an essay is informative, but if you want your essay to be read by people who don't have to read it, then you need to make your approach to your subject interesting as well. A straightforward, follow steps 1–10, how-to essay will get the job done, but unless the need for the information is pressing, no one will read it. If you relate the process so that your reader enjoys the essay, even the person who would never willingly enter a kitchen will probably keep reading.

If what you have to say involves a personal subject, you need to present the information in a believable way, and at the same time, adjust it to the level of the audience. The process involved in friends growing apart, for instance, can be explained in terms so personal that only the writer could appreciate it. If that were your topic, you would need to gear your description to the general reader who may have experienced something similar. That way, you would place your personal narrative into a larger, more general context.

On the other hand, if you know not only more, but also more specialized information than the reader, you must be careful to make sure your audience is following every step. Sometimes a writer explores a process to inform the reader and other times to persuade, but always the writer has an assertion in mind and is trying to affect the reader. If, for example, you enjoy scuba diving and you're trying to describe the physiological effects the body is subject to when diving, you might first describe the necessary equipment and then take the reader on a dive, emphasizing the different levels of atmospheric pressure—the instant and constant need to equalize the air pressure in your ears, the initial tightness of your mask as you sink to 10 feet, the gradual "shrinking" of your wet suit as the pressure increases with the depth of the dive. Then after a quick tour of the kinds of fish, sea creatures, and coral formations you see during the dive, you would return your reader to the surface, stopping at 15 feet to release the buildup of nitrogen in the blood. The whole process may strike your reader as not worth the risk, so you would want to make sure not only that your thesis counters that opinion, but also that you describe what you see, so the attractions outweigh the hazards and momentary discomfort.

SEQUENCE   Chronology is as crucial to process as it is to narration. In fact, it is inflexible. A list of the ingredients in the bread has to precede baking instructions; a quick safety check of the necessary equipment has to come before the dive. And then you must account for all the important steps. If time is crucial to the process, then you have to account for it also, although in a historical process essay, time is apt to be compressed or de-emphasized to underscore a turning point. An essay on the Civil Rights movement, for instance, might well begin with a brief account of the slave trade, even though the body of the paper focuses on the 1950s and 1960s, culminating with the assassination of Martin Luther King in 1968. And if you were to identify King's death as the turning point in the movement, you would emphasize the chronology and character of the events leading up to and following his assassination.

Undergirding the concept of sequence, of course, is the pattern of cause and effect—in the example above, you might want to explore the effect of King's death on the Civil Rights movement. What's most important to process analysis, however, is neither cause nor effect, but the stages or steps, the chronology of events. Without a set sequence or chronology, neither cause nor effect would be clear.

DETAIL AND EXAMPLE   In writing a process analysis, you will draw on the same skills you use for description, narration, and example papers, for without supporting details and examples to further and describe the process, a process essay can be tedious indeed. An essay on the Civil Rights movement would probably need to draw on statistics—such as the percentage of the population held in slavery in 1860—as well as examples of protests and boycotts, and quotations from those involved, both for and against equal rights for African Americans. An essay on scuba diving may bring in examples from mathematics and physiology, as well as from scientific articles on the relative health of coral reefs in the Caribbean. Incorporating references to well-known people—a Mohammed Ali or a Jacques Cousteau—or to current events or adding a narrative example or even an amusing aside can make what might otherwise be little more than a list into an interesting paper.

TRANSITIONS   To make the stages of the process clear, you will need to rely on logically placed transitions that lead the reader from one stage to the next. Most writers try to avoid depending only on obvious links, such as *first, next, next,* and instead use chronology, shifts in tense, and other indicators of time to spell out the sequence. The process itself may have clear markers that you can use as transitions. An essay explaining a historical event, for instance, will have pegs such as specific dates or actions that you can use to indicate the next stage in the sequence.

THESIS AND ORGANIZATION   The body of a process essay almost organizes itself because it is made up of the steps you have identified, and they must occur in a given sequence. Introductions and conclusions are trickier, as is the thesis, for you must not only set out a process, but also make an assertion about it. Your thesis should confront the reader with a point, implicit or explicit, about the process involved, and in so doing, head off the lethal response, "So what?"

USEFUL TERMS

Chronology   The time sequence involved in events; what occurred when.

Process analysis   A type of analysis that examines a topic to discover the series of steps or acts that brought or will bring about a particular result. Whereas cause and effect emphasizes *why*, process emphasizes *how*.

▓ POINTERS FOR USING PROCESS

Exploring the Topic

1. **What kind of process are you presenting?** Is it a practical, "how-to" process? A historical one? A scientific one? Some mixture of types?

2. **What steps are involved?** Which are crucial? Can some be grouped together? Under what headings can they be grouped?

3. **What is the sequence of the steps?** Are you sure that each step logically follows the one before it?

4. **How familiar is your reader with your subject?** Within each step (or group of steps), what information does the reader need to know? What details can you use to make that information come alive? What examples? What connections can you make to what the reader already knows?

5. **Is setting or context important?** If so, what details of the setting or context do you want to emphasize?

6. **What is the point you want to make about the process?** Is your point an assertion? Will it interest the reader?

Drafting the Paper

1. **Know your reader.** Using two columns, list what your reader may know about your topic in one and what your reader may not know in the other. If you are writing about a practical process, figure out what

pitfalls your reader may be subject to. If you are writing about a historical or scientific process, make sure your diction suits your audience. Be on the lookout for events or actions that need further explanation to be understood by a general audience. If your reader is apt to have a bias against your topic, know what that bias is. If your topic is familiar, shape your first paragraph to enlist the reader's interest; if the topic is unfamiliar, use familiar images to explain it.

2. **Know your purpose.** If you are writing to inform, make sure you are presenting new information and that you are making an assertion about your topic. Don't dwell on information that the reader already knows if you can possibly avoid it. If you are writing to persuade, remember that you do not know whether your audience agrees with you. Use your persona to lend credibility to what you say, and use detail to arouse your reader's sympathies.

3. **Present the steps in their correct sequence.** Make sure that you have accounted for all the important steps or stages in the process and that they are set out in order. If two or more steps occur at the same time, make sure you have made that clear. If time is crucial to your process, see that you have emphasized that point. If, on the other hand, the exact time at which an event occurred is less important than the event itself, make sure you have stressed the event and have subordinated the idea of time.

4. **Use details and examples.** Whether you are writing an informative or a persuasive essay, use details and examples that support your purpose. If you are explaining how to make your own ice cream, for example, draw on what the reader knows about various commercial brands and flavors to bolster the case for making your own. After all, your reader may not want to take the time and trouble to complete that process and may have to be enticed into trying it. Choose details and examples that combat your reader's negative associations.

5. **Double-check your transitions.** First mark your stages with obvious transitions or with numbers. After you have turned your notes into a working draft, review the transitions you have used, checking to see that they exist, that they are clear, and that they are not overly repetitious or obvious. Make sure each important stage (or group of stages) is set off by a transition. See if you can indicate shifts by using verb tense or words and phrases that don't call attention to themselves as transitions.

6. **Make a point.** What you say about a subject is far more interesting than the subject itself, so even if you are writing a practical process essay, make sure you have a point. A paper on a topic such as "how to change a tire" becomes unbearable without a thesis. Given an assertion about changing a tire—"Changing my first flat was as horrible as I had expected it to be"—the paper at least has a chance.

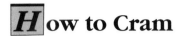ow to Cram

Jill Young Miller

Cramming, deeply embedded as a way of student life, often turns up in nightmares as panic over having to take an exam for a course you never signed up for. Appropriately enough, this essay was published in Campus Voice *(1987), a magazine distributed free on many college campuses.*

WHAT TO LOOK FOR *Often when you write a process analysis, you may find yourself using the imperative form of verbs, as in "Next, take . . . ." But the imperative need not sound rude or bossy. As you read Miller's essay, keep your ear tuned to how her imperatives sound.*

1   Frances Avila learned the hard way not to expect miracles overnight. A chronic crammer, the New York University senior did the usual for her midterm in "Major British Writers" last fall: she pulled an all-nighter. Fighting off fatigue and anxiety, Avila forced herself to concentrate on the novels and her notes through dawn, breaking only to splash cold water on her face. Near noon, she closed her books to head for the test.

2   The first question—"Expand on the gap between her front teeth"—was a lulu. Avila didn't recognize the allusion to Chaucer's Wife of Bath, even though she'd read the section only hours before. "Not only did I blank out, but I was also frightened," she recalls. "I didn't expect the test to be that elaborate." The bad situation only got worse. She fumbled through 14 more stray lines before plunging into part two, which wasn't any easier. Avila had studied innumerable facts for hours, but she knew only one thing for sure: she was in trouble.

3   "I failed the exam," she explains, "because I had to compare and contrast two poets from different time periods. In order to do that, I had to elaborate on all the details within the poetry. But I'd absorbed just enough information the night before to understand what I was reading and not enough to catch all the details."

4   Sound familiar? Almost all of us have stood (and sleepwalked) in Avila's shoes at one time or another. Sometimes push comes to

shove, crunch comes to cram, and before you know it, you have to read 450 pages in six hours. Pour on the caffeine, you mumble.

5   About 90 percent of all students cram, estimates Don Dansereau, a psychology professor at Texas Christian University, who defines cramming as "intense studying the night before or the day of a test." Quips Ric Schank, a University of Florida senior, "Down here, it's the rule rather than the exception."

6   Despite its popularity, cramming gets low marks from educators and memory experts, who claim that the last-minute nature of the act kills your chances for payoff at test time.

7   A quick stroll down memory lane explains why. Most experts identify three types of memory: immediate, short-term, and long-term. You use your immediate memory as you read this, remembering each word just long enough to make the transition to the next.

8   Short-term memory is limited, too. For example, you use it when you look up a phone number, close the book, and dial. Short-term memory can supposedly hold a maximum of seven items for only a few seconds.

9   Long-term memory is the big daddy, the one that holds everything you know about the world. It's the memory that last-minute learners need to respect.

10   How well you organize information on its way into your long-term memory determines how quickly you can retrieve it later, or whether you retrieve it at all. Think of a backpack you'd take on a hike, says Laird Cermak, a research psychologist at the Boston Veterans Administration Hospital and the author of *Improving Your Memory* (McGraw-Hill, 1975). "If your backpack is organized and you get bit by a snake, you can go right for the snakebite kit," he explains.

11   The magic lies in spacing your study over days, weeks, or even months. That gives you time to mull over the new stuff, relate it to what you already know, and organize it for exam-time recall. "The reason you forget the information is not because it was learned the night before," Cermak explains. "It's because when you crammed you didn't give yourself good ways to remember it in the future." In other words, last-minute studying limits the number of mental retrieval routes you can create.

12   But it doesn't take a psychologist to explain why cramming often fails. "You throw things into your mind, knowing that you're going to spit them out in a couple of hours and forget them. It's

not a good way to learn at all," says NYU journalism senior David Reilly.

13   No quick-and-dirty detours to long-term retention and instant recall exist. But if you're forced into a late-night, last-minute study session, the results don't have to be disastrous. Here's some advice to help make the morning after less anxious than the night before:

14   **Find out what kind of test you're in for.** If you cram, you're likely to fare better on multiple-choice and fill-in-the-blank tests because they jog your memory with cues, Cermak says.

15   **Find a quiet place to study.** When Avila crams, she seeks out a small room at the library that's devoid of distractions. "I'm cornered," she says. "I have no choice but to look at the print."

16   If you like to study with music in the background, go for something without lyrics and keep the volume down low. Classical music such as Bach can have a soothing effect if your nerves are impeding your studies, says Danielle Lapp, a memory researcher at Stanford University and the author of *Don't Forget! Easy Exercises for a Better Memory at Any Age* (McGraw-Hill, 1987).

17   **Compose a scene that you can re-create during the exam.** If you can, study at the desk or in the room where you'll take the test, or do something while you study that you can do again when you take the test. For example, Dansereau suggests that you chew grape gum. "The flavor acts a cuing device," he explains.

18   **Build your concentration.** Spend ten minutes warming up with a novel or magazine before you tackle a tough chapter. Says Cermak, "It helps you block out whatever else is going on."

19   **Watch what you eat and drink.** Avoid heavy meals and alcohol. Both could make you drowsy, cautions Lapp. If you need a cup of coffee to perk up, fine. But putting too much caffeine in your system can make you jittery and break your concentration.

20   **Mark your book.** Even if you only have time to read the chapter once, it helps to highlight important terms and sections. Identifying the key words and passages requires you to be mentally alert and forces you to be an active rather than a passive reader.

21   **Spend time repeating or discussing facts out loud.** Recitation promotes faster learning because it's more active than reading or listening. (Try it out when you study for your next foreign language vocabulary quiz.) Discussion groups are helpful for this reason.

22   **Take short breaks at least every few hours.** They'll help you beat fatigue, which takes a heavy toll on learning. Two hour-long

sittings separated by a 15-minute break are more productive than one two-hour session in which your mind wanders throughout the second half. It doesn't matter what you do during those breaks; just take them.

23 **Experiment with memory techniques.** They impose structure on new information, making it easier to remember at test time. The "house" method is one of the oldest. Let's say you want to remember a list of sequential events for a history exam. Try to imagine the events taking place in separate but connected rooms of your house. When the test asks you to recall the events, take a mental amble through the rooms.

24 Another simple technique involves acronyms. You may have learned the names of the Great Lakes (Huron, Ontario, Michigan, Erie, and Superior) with this one: HOMES.

25 **Try some proven learning strategies.** Richard Yates, a counselor and time management expert at Cleveland State University, recommends the SQ3R method: survey, question, read, recite, review. Survey the material to formulate a general impression; rephrase titles and headings into questions; read through the material quickly to find the main points and the answers to your questions; recite those main ideas, taking brief notes; and review. Even when you're pressed for time, the strategy can help. "It may take a little longer," says Yates, "but it's worth the effort."

26 **Get some sleep.** UF's Schank quit all-nighters after his freshman year. "I'd go into a final and be so wired from staying up all night that I'd lose my concentration," he says. "I'd miss questions that I knew I wouldn't miss if I were in a good frame of mind." Now he crams until about 3 A.M., sleeps for about four hours, and hits the books again at 8 A.M.

27 Psychologists and memory researchers can't specify how much sleep you need—everyone has his or her own threshold—but they do stress its importance. Says Lapp, "You're better off getting some sleep so that your mind is rested for the exam than you are cramming the whole night." Just don't forget to set that alarm clock before you go to bed.

28 For an early-morning exam, it's best to do heavy-duty studying right before you go to sleep. In other words, unless you've got back-to-back exams, don't cram and then do something else for a few hours before a test. Freshly learned material is remembered much better after a period of sleep than after an equal period of daytime activity.

29   **Relax.** It may sound simplistic, but it's key to good test performance. "Anxiety is enemy number one of memory," Lapp explains. She compares a student taking a test to a singer performing onstage. "There's no way a completely anxious singer can utter a sound," she says.

30   Cramming is like going to the dentist; if you have to do it, you want it to be as painless and as productive as it can be. After all, no one goes to college to take a semester-long class and promptly forget all the new information that's been taught. At least Frances Avila didn't. After her disastrous midterm, she didn't dare risk cramming for her "Major British Writers" final exam. This time, she spaced her studying over a period of weeks, earned an A, and salvaged her grade for the semester.

31   That doesn't mean she's quit cramming for good—in fact, she hasn't even tried to. Instead she's perfected her technique. Ditto for Reilly, who's tried unsuccessfully to break the habit. "Every semester I kick myself a million times and scream that I'm not going to cram next semester," he laments. "But it never seems to work."

Thesis and Organization

1. The steps to follow are given in paragraphs 14–29, which leaves almost half the essay taken up by introduction and conclusion. Examine paragraphs 1–13 and identify the use of narration, example, and definition.
2. Analyze the role of narrative in the introduction and conclusion. What effect does Miller achieve with the story of Avila?
3. How necessary is Miller's definition of cramming? Of types of memory? Explain the relationship between the two.
4. What principle do you find behind the sequencing of paragraphs 14–29? How does that principle relate to Miller's informative purpose?
5. Consider what Miller tells you about studying, memory, cramming, and Avila. In your own words, state her thesis.

Technique and Style

1. Miller's paragraphs are shorter than you would usually find in an essay of this length. How can you justify the relative shortness of her paragraphs?
2. What point of view does Miller use in the essay? What reasons can you find for that choice?
3. The imperative can be rude and bossy, as in the command "Shut the door." How would you characterize Miller's use of the imperative? How does she avoid using it rudely?

4. What sources does Miller use in her essay? What purpose do they serve in relation to Miller's information? Her credibility? Why provide full citations in paragraphs 10 and 16?

5. What kind of person does Miller seem to be? If you were taking a study skills course, would you want her as a teacher? Why or why not?

Suggestions for Writing

Journal

1. Describe how you study best. Perhaps you need to have the radio or television on and munchies nearby. Try to account for every detail.

2. At some point, you probably crammed for an exam and so can test Miller's advice against your own experience. How helpful do you find the advice?

Essay

Think about the steps in a process you know well and write your own "how-to" essay. Suggestions:

worrying creatively, handling stress, coping with obnoxious people

throwing a curve ball, returning a serve, spiking a volleyball

making the perfect burger, frying the perfect egg, baking the perfect brownie

*L*ove of the Putrid

Laura Van Dyne

Laura Van Dyne is a Professor of Veterinary Technology and has been involved with the Veterinary Technology program at Colorado Mountain College (Glenwood Springs campus) for a number of years. She also has her own business—The Canine Consultant—training dogs (and owners) or, as she puts it "Helping dogs and their people learn together." She writes a regular column for the Valley Journal, *a weekly newspaper that serves the Roaring Fork Valley, from Aspen to Glenwood Springs. Hers is an advice column, one that takes the form of question and answer, and in this case, process analysis as well. This column appeared in the September 5, 1996, issue.*

WHAT TO LOOK FOR   *Anyone who has ever washed a dog knows some of the pitfalls, but Van Dyne is careful to explain some not-so-obvious ones. As you read the essay, look for those subtle directions that help you avoid problems you may not have been aware of.*

"The rankest compound of villainous smell that ever offended nostril."
William Shakespeare

1   **Question:** *My dog Jessica went out today and rolled in the most disgusting pile of dead, rotting stuff! Why do dogs do that?*

2   **Answer:** Because they are dogs . . . it's their job! Well, perhaps a little more information would help to explain.

3   Consider the evolutionary roots of *candis.* A wild dog must hunt to survive. Hunting skills include any behavior which will help to camouflage one's odor from prey.

4   If the predator smells like a pile of rotting flesh, rather than a dog, it is more likely to have a successful hunt. We have been selectively breeding dogs for thousands of years and as a result, we have amazing diversity (compare the Chihuahua to the Irish wolfhound) but we have not "bred out" this innate behavior.

5   You would think that such strong odors would be overwhelming for a dog's sensitive nose, since their sense of smell is thought to be from 100–1,000 times more acute than ours.

6   This is not the case.

7   In fact, they seem to be proud of the magnificent stench.

8   A bath might be in order following a "Pass through the putrid," so I'd like to take this opportunity to cover that topic.

9   A good combing will remove all the dead hair before you get the dog wet. If there are any mats or tangles, be sure to remove them before the bath.

10   Matted hair will dry even tighter than before the bath. I suggest expressing anal glands (if you are up to this task) prior to the bath so that any offensive material can be washed out promptly.

11   Trim the toenails and the dog should be ready for the tub.

12   You might put a cotton ball in each ear (the dog's). Use your fingers and a large wad of cotton so water won't run into the ear canal.

13   I like to wash the face last. This is the area which causes the greatest "shake" reaction. When Jessica does try to shake water all over, remember, the whole movement starts at the head. If you control her head and say "No shake" she will get the idea.

14   Dogs do not appreciate warm water as we like it, so tepid water seems to be most comfortable for them.

15   Use a shampoo made for dogs, not a human shampoo, which won't irritate the eyes. I like to dilute the shampoo before application to avoid getting a heavy lather on the spot of application, which is difficult to spread evenly over the hair coat.

16   The thick lather is also very difficult to rinse out. I usually dilute the shampoo about 1:1 with tap water and apply it through a squeeze bottle.

17   If you leave any residue of the shampoo on the skin or hair coat, you will see a skin reaction in a few days. The skin will become very flaky and itchy.

18   To test for a well-rinsed hair coat, just run your fingers through the hair and it should be "squeaky clean." Typical trouble spots are the chest, elbows and between the rear legs. These areas are a little harder to rinse.

19   A good towel drying, followed by a romp in the sunshine, will usually finish the task, but beware! Jessica will be on the lookout for something ripe and fetid, so she can regain that magnificent odor you just removed.

Thesis and Organization

1. Paragraph 2 supplies the short answer to the question that is posed in paragraph 1, and paragraphs 3 and 4 provide a fuller one. What reason or reasons can you give for needing both types of answers?

2. What is the function of paragraphs 5–7?
3. What steps are outlined in paragraphs 9–19? Is anything omitted? Unnecessary?
4. Paragraph 19 both describes the last step and concludes the essay. Explain whether you find it a satisfactory conclusion.
5. You can deduce the thesis of the essay by putting together the problem (stench) and solution (bath). State the thesis in your own words.

Technique and Style

1. Explain what the quotation from Shakespeare adds or does not add to the essay.
2. Van Dyne uses parenthesis in paragraphs 4, 10, and 12. What functions do they serve?
3. Paragraph 6 consists of one sentence. Discuss whether you find it effective.
4. What information was new to you? What did it contribute to the essay?
5. Describe the writer's persona. Would you want her to train your dog? Why or why not?

Suggestions for Writing

Journal

1. Briefly outline the steps involved in a familiar chore—cleaning out the bathroom cabinet, washing the car, mowing the lawn, painting a room. Your outline plus a thesis can be the basis of a longer essay.
2. In some circles, the word *pet* has become "politically incorrect," and the term "animal companion" is preferred. What associations does the word *pet* hold for you?

Essay

Sometimes essays are organized around a solution. Working on your own or with a member of your class, come up with a practical question or problem to which you can respond. Your response can take the form of a traditional essay, or if your instructor approves, of an advice column. For ideas, you might consider the questions or problems that can arise at:
    school
    work
    home
    a sports event
    a concert
    a movie theater

A Room Without a View

Christina Erwin

The title of the essay plays on A Room with a View, *a novel by E. M. Forster, an English writer of novels and essays (1879–1970). The novel was made into a film in 1986 and therefore the title was generally familiar to many, not just readers. An English major, Christina Erwin graduated from the University of New Orleans in the spring of 1994. Among writers, she particularly admires the late Erma Bombeck, and as you read the essay, you'll find echoes of Bombeck's good-natured but wry humor.*

WHAT TO LOOK FOR   *Many a how-to essay plunges into a predictable string of* first, next, next, next, *followed by* finally. *You can avoid that trap by following Erwin's technique, using spatial relationships to establish sequence.*

1   It's the most often used room in my house, yet no one ever admits to having been in there. It's the place we visit each evening when we retire and every morning when we awaken. It's the bathroom. And the two-foot deep cabinet housed within is a room in itself but without a view. It is a volcano on the verge of eruption.

2   Under the pressure of a six P.M. deadline, I knew I'd have to work quickly for my house to pass my mother-in-law's white-glove inspection. I had completed the major events of my cleaning the day before, bulldozing through the laundry, sandblasting the dirty dishes. All that remained was the detail work.

3   After dusting the tops of the canned peas in my pantry, removing the corn chips from beneath the sofa cushion, and fluffing the pillow in my dog's bed, I knew I had to face it: the dreaded bathroom cabinet. Donning rubber gloves, a gas mask, and hip boots, I prepared for combat.

4   Opening the door to the cabinet, I was buried in a lava flow of once-tried shampoos, half-used deodorants, powders, lotions, and hairsprays that failed to make good on their promises. There is no such thing as "all-day hold."

5   If Freud were alive today, he wouldn't have to psychoanalyze his patients to learn how they tick. He could simply peek in their bathroom cabinets (a skill he could learn from my mother-in-law).

His diagnosis of my cabinet—repulsion with body odor, obsession with body hair—incurable! Simply having hair on our heads (which I am still blessed with, although my husband is not so lucky) is not enough for us; we also insist that it be a certain color, thickness, softness, length, and height.

6   If ever a hair product was advertised, I've probably tried it at least once, be it gel, mousse, spray or color—and it was probably still in that cabinet, waiting to be sprung from hair-care penitentiary. I threw out as many bottles as I could bear to part with, creating a toxic mixture in the bottom of the garbage can that I feared would eat its way through to the floor.

7   Beyond the hair-goo, I found medicines that no one in my family would admit to ever having needed. Hemorrhoid ointments, diarrhea tablets, antacids, even petroleum jelly lay hidden in shame behind the classier drugstore items, the ones over-packaged in plastic, endorsed by fashion models. Has someone like Cindy Crawford ever done an ad for wart remover? Would Paul Newman ever hawk athlete's foot powder? I doubt it.

8   I sorted the pills, balms, and salves into three piles—still usable; past the expiration date; and past recognition, those tubes and plastic bottles with labels resembling hieroglyphics. The last two piles I pitched into the trash can, which was beginning to glow.

9   Buried at the back of the cabinet, I found a twelve-roll bargain pack of toilet paper. My husband hides it there, sure that people will think we're weird if there are more than four rolls visible at one time, a fear that his mother instilled in him. What would Dr. Freud have said about that skeleton in our cabinet?

10   Behind the T.P. I found the plunger (that would have saved me a bill from the plumber last week when the kitchen sink backed up), the bonnet-style hairdryer my mother gave me when I moved out, and the hammer we lost while hanging the new shower curtain rod. I also came across a broken steam iron and an overdue book for which I'd received threats of torture from the librarian.

11   I had worked my way down to the sedimentary bed of solo earrings, razor blades, and toenail clippers. While examining a fossilized aspirin, I heard the doorbell ring. I knew it was her. Quickly, I shoved my latest discoveries back into the cabinet and then covered the whole mess with a large beach towel. The battle was over. I waved a white toilet brush in surrender and answered the door.

Thesis and Organization

1. What paragraph or paragraphs provide the introduction?
2. What are the steps in the process Erwin describes?
3. What does the essay imply (good-naturedly) about our culture?
4. How would you describe the writer's attitude toward cleaning?
5. Given your answer to question 4 and the subject of the essay, what is the thesis?

Technique and Style

1. The essay uses two analogies, one from geology (paragraphs 1, 4, 11) and one from war (paragraphs 3, 11). Choose one and explain what it adds to the essay.
2. Exaggeration or hyperbole is a standard comic technique. Select one example from the essay and explain how it achieves its effect.
3. Erwin places the clean-up within the broader context of her mother-in-law's visit. What does that context add to the essay?
4. What effect is achieved by delaying the subject of the first paragraph until the third sentence?
5. Coherence, literally the quality of sticking together, is a characteristic of good prose, prose in which each paragraph flows naturally into the next so that the essay appears a seamless whole. What techniques can you spot in Erwin's essay that contribute to its coherence?

Suggestions for Writing

Journal

1. Describe something you can't bear to throw away and explain why.
2. Think of a process you are used to (washing the car, cooking, studying, packing, playing a sport or the like) and find an analogy that fits all or part of the process. For instance, packing for a trip may be like preparing to climb Mt. Everest—you never know what you are going to need so you take almost everything.

Essay

Sooner or later, all of us have had to take on an unpleasant job, usually one that we have put off as long as possible. Think of all the unpleasant or difficult things you have had to do. Choose one as the basis for a "how-to" paper. The fact that the job is unpleasant or difficult is apt to make examples and steps come readily to mind. Suggestions:

recycle

weed a garden

learn a computer program

change a diaper

organize and file papers

If that idea doesn't appeal to you, write a paper that takes a positive approach to a usually negative action:

how to procrastinate

how to tell a white lie

how to stay awake in class

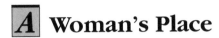 Woman's Place

Naomi Wolf

Naomi Wolf was working on her PhD at Princeton University when she adapted her dissertation into The Beauty Myth: How Images of Beauty Are Used Against Women, *a best-seller published in 1991. As the title of the book implies Wolf is concerned with issues that affect women, an interest that runs through all of her work as she tries to re-define and revive feminism. Her most recent book examines the American version of growing up female,* Promiscuities: An Ordinary American Girlhood *(1997). The essay below, however, is more closely related to an earlier work,* Fire with Fire: The New Female Power and How to Use It *(1993), and is adapted from a commencement address she gave at Scripps College, a women's college in California.*

WHAT TO LOOK FOR *Many writers steer away from beginning a sentence with* and *because they are afraid of creating a sentence fragment. But as long as the sentence has a subject and main verb, it can begin with* and *(or, like this one,* but *or any other conjunction) and still be an independent clause, a complete sentence, with the conjunction serving as an informal transition. To see how effective that kind of sentence can be, notice Wolf's last paragraph.*

1   Even the best of revolutions can go awry when we internalize the attitudes we are fighting. The class of 1992 is graduating into a violent backlash against the advances women have made over the last 20 years. This backlash ranges from a senator using "The Exorcist" against Anita Hill, to beer commercials with the "Swedish bikini team." Today I want to give you a backlash survival kit, a four-step manual to keep the dragons from taking up residence inside your own heads.

2   My own commencement, at Yale eight years ago, was the Graduation from Hell. The speaker was Dick Cavett, rumored to have been our president's "brother" in an all-male secret society.

3   Mr. Cavett took the microphone and paled at the sight of hundreds of female about-to-be Yale graduates. "When I was an undergraduate," I recall he said, "there were no women. The women

went to Vassar. At Vassar, they had nude photographs taken of the women in gym class to check their posture. One year the photos were stolen, and turned up for sale in New Haven's redlight district." His punchline? "The photos found no buyers."

4   I'll never forget that moment. There we were, silent in our black gowns, our tassels, our brand new shoes. We dared not break the silence with hisses or boos, out of respect for our families, who'd come so far; and they kept still out of concern for us. Consciously or not, Mr. Cavett was using the beauty myth aspect of the backlash: when women come too close to masculine power, someone will draw critical attention to their bodies. We might be Elis, but we still wouldn't make pornography worth buying.

5   That afternoon, several hundred men were confirmed in the power of a powerful institution. But many of the women felt the shame of the powerless: the choking on silence, the complicity, the helplessness. We were orphaned from our institution.

6   I want to give you the commencement talk that was denied to me.

7   Message No. 1 in your survival kit: redefine "becoming a woman." Today you have "become women." But that sounds odd in ordinary usage. What is usually meant by "You're a real woman now"? You "become a woman" when you menstruate for the first time, or when you lose your virginity, or when you have a child.

8   These biological definitions are very different from how we say boys become men. One "becomes a man" when he undertakes responsibility, or completes a quest. But you, too, in some ways more than your male friends graduating today, have moved into maturity through a solitary quest for the adult self.

9   We lack archetypes for the questing young woman, her trials by fire; for how one "becomes a woman" through the chrysalis of education, the difficult passage from one book, one idea to the next. Let's refuse to have our scholarship and our gender pitted against each other. In our definition, the scholar learns womanhood and the woman learns scholarship; Plato and Djuna Barnes, mediated to their own enrichment through the eyes of the female body with its wisdoms and its gifts.

10   I say that you have already shown courage: Many of you graduate today in spite of the post-traumatic stress syndrome of acquaintance rape, which one-fourth of female students undergo. Many of you were so weakened by anorexia and bulimia that it took every

ounce of your will to get your work in. You negotiated private lives through a mine field of new strains of VD and the ascending shadow of AIDS. Triumphant survivors, you have already "become women."

11   Message No. 2 breaks the ultimate taboo for women: *Ask for money in your lives.* Expect it. Own it. Learn to use it. Little girls learn a debilitating fear of money—that it's not feminine to insure we are fairly paid for honest work. Meanwhile, women make 68 cents for every male dollar and half of marriages end in divorce, after which women's income drops precipitously.

12   Never choose a profession for material reasons. But whatever field your heart decides on, for god's sake get the most specialized training in it you can and hold out hard for just compensation, parental leave and child care. Resist your assignment to the class of highly competent, grossly underpaid women who run the show while others get the cash—and the credit.

13   Claim money not out of greed, but so you can tithe to women's political organizations, shelters and educational institutions. Sexist institutions won't yield power if we are just patient long enough. The only language the status quo understands is money, votes and public embarrassment.

14   When you have equity, you have influence—as sponsors, shareholders and alumnae. Use it to open opportunities to women who deserve the chances you've had. Your B.A. does not belong to you alone, just as the earth does not belong to its present tenants alone. Your education was lent to you by women of the past, and you will give some back to living women, and to your daughters seven generations from now.

15   Message No. 3: Never cook for or sleep with anyone who routinely puts you down.

16   Message No. 4: Become goddesses of disobedience. Virginia Woolf wrote that we must slay the Angel in the House, the censor within. Young women tell me of injustices, from campus rape coverups to classroom sexism. But at the thought of confrontation, they freeze into niceness. We are told that the worst thing we can do is cause conflict, even in the service of doing right. Antigone is imprisoned. Joan of Arc burns at the stake. And someone might call us unfeminine!

17   When I wrote a book that caused controversy, I saw how big a dragon was this paralysis by niceness. "The Beauty Myth" argues

that newly rigid ideals of beauty are instruments of a backlash against feminism, designed to lower women's self-esteem for a political purpose. Many positive changes followed the debate. But all that would dwindle away when someone yelled at me—as, for instance, cosmetic surgeons did on TV, when I raised questions about silicone implants. Oh, no, I'd quail, people are mad at me!

18   Then I read something by the poet Audre Lorde. She'd been diagnosed with breast cancer. "I was going to die," she wrote, "sooner or later, whether or not I had ever spoken myself. My silences had not protected me. Your silences will not protect you. . . . What are the words you do not yet have? What are the tyrannies you swallow day by day and attempt to make your own, until you will sicken and die of them, still in silence? We have been socialized to respect fear more than our own need for language."

19   I began to ask each time: "What's the worst that could happen to me if I tell this truth?" Unlike women in other countries, our breaking silence is unlikely to have us jailed, "disappeared" or run off the road at night. Our speaking out will irritate some people, get us called bitchy or hypersensitive and disrupt some dinner parties. And then our speaking out will permit other women to speak, until laws are changed and lives are saved and the world is altered forever.

20   Next time, ask: What's the worst that will happen? Then push yourself a little further than you dare. Once you start to speak, people *will* yell at you. They *will* interrupt, put you down and suggest it's personal. And the world won't end.

21   And the speaking will get easier and easier. And you will find you have fallen in love with your own vision, which you may never have realized you had. And you will lose some friends and lovers, and realize you don't miss them. And new ones will find you and cherish you. And you will still flirt and paint your nails, dress up and party, because as I think Emma Goldman said, "If I can't dance, I don't want to be part of your revolution." And at last you'll know with surpassing certainty that only one thing is more frightening than speaking your truth. And that is not speaking.

Thesis and Organization

1. Wolf's essay could easily be retitled "How to Survive the Backlash." What is the backlash?
2. Why does Wolf include the anecdote about Dick Cavett? How is it related to the backlash?

3. What are the four steps for survival?

4. What gender-based stereotypes does Wolf attack?

5. Wolf's essay gives advice and explains how to survive, but it also comments on women's place in society today. Combine those comments with her advice and the result will be the thesis.

Technique and Style

1. What saying does Wolf's title refer to? How does her title set up her essay?

2. Throughout the essay, Wolf uses allusion—Anita Hill (paragraph 1), Plato and Djuna Barnes (paragraph 9), Virginia Woolf (paragraph 16), Audre Lorde (paragraph 19), and Emma Goldman (paragraph 21). Use an encyclopedia to look up one of these allusions so that you can explain to the class how it is (or is not) appropriate.

3. To explore the effect of Wolf's repeated use of *and* in her last paragraph, try rewriting it. What is gained? Lost?

4. The original audience for the essay was women, but it was republished for an audience that also includes men. Explain whether men would find the essay offensive. Is it antimale?

5. Wolf is obviously a feminist, but think of feminism as a continuum ranging from conservative to radical. Based on this essay, what kind of feminist is Wolf? What evidence can you find for your opinion?

Suggestions for Writing

Journal

1. Choose one of Wolf's "messages" and test it out against your own experience. Do you find the advice helpful? Necessary?

2. Relate an experience in which you ran into sexism, either antimale or antifemale. You could use this entry later as the basis for an essay in which you explain how to cope with sexism.

Essay

All of us at one time or another have played a role we didn't believe in or didn't like. Those roles vary greatly. Think about the roles you have had to play and how you broke out of them. Choose one and draft a paper explaining "How to Survive" or "How to Break Out." Some roles to think about:

dutiful daughter
responsible sibling
perfect husband (or wife)
brave man
happy homemaker

ou Sure You Want to Do This?

Maneka Gandhi

Ever wonder what goes into a simple tube of lipstick? Maneka Gandhi tells us, though she also warns us that we may find out more than we wanted to know. Gandhi writes a regular column in the Illustrated Weekly of India, *although this essay was published in the* Baltimore Sun *(1989). A strong voice on the current political scene in India, Maneka Gandhi speaks out in favor of vegetarianism as well as animal rights and protecting the environment. In the essay that follows she uses a technique that you may also find useful—she defines her audience in her first sentence with a very specific* you.

WHAT TO LOOK FOR *Process analysis essays that are built around chronology sometimes fall into predictable transitions such as* first, second, next, then. *Gandhi avoids the obvious, even though chronology is important to her discussion. Be on the lookout for how she gets from one stage to the next.*

1   Are you one of those women who feel that lipstick is one of the essentials of life? That to be seen without it is the equivalent of facial nudity? Then you might like to know what goes into that attractive color tube that you smear on your lips.

2   At the center of the modern lipstick is acid. Nothing else will burn a coloring sufficiently deeply into the lips. The acid starts out orange, then sizzles into the living skin cells and metamorphoses into a deep red. Everything else in the lipstick is there just to get this acid into place.

3   First lipstick has to spread. Softened food shortening, such as hydrogenated vegetable oil, spreads very well, and accordingly is one of the substances found in almost all lipsticks. Soap smears well, too, and so some of that is added as well. Unfortunately, neither soap nor shortening is good at actually taking up the acid that's needed to do the dyeing. Only one smearable substance will do this to any extent: castor oil.

4   Good cheap castor oil, used in varnishes and laxatives, is one of the largest ingredients by bulk in every lipstick. The acid soaks into the castor oil, the castor oil spreads on the lips with the soap and shortening till the acid is carried where it needs to go.

5   If lipstick could be sold in castor oil bottles there would be no need for the next major ingredient. But the mix has to be transformed into a rigid, streamlined stick, and for that nothing is better than heavy petroleum-based wax. It's what provides the "stick" in lipstick.

6   Of course, certain precautions have to be taken in combining all these substances. If the user ever got a sniff of what was in there, there might be problems of consumer acceptance. So a perfume is poured in at the manufacturing stage before all the oils have cooled—when it is still a molten lipstick mass.

7   At the same time, food preservatives are poured into the mass, because apart from smelling rather strongly the oil in there would go rancid without some protection. (Have you smelled an old lipstick? That dreadful smell is castor oil gone bad.)

8   All that's lacking now is shine. When the preservatives and the perfume are being poured in, something shiny, colorful, almost iridescent—and, happily enough, not even too expensive—is added. That something is fish scales. It's easily available from the leftovers of commercial fish-packing stations. The scales are soaked in ammonia, then bunged in with everything else.

9   Fish scales, by the way, mean that lipstick is not a vegetarian product. Every time you paint your lips you eat fish scales. So lipsticks without them actually are marked "vegetarian lipstick."

10   Is that it then? Shortening, soap, castor oil, petroleum wax, perfume, food preservatives and fish scales? Not entirely. There is still one thing missing: color.

11   The orange acid that burns into the lips turns red only on contact. So that what you see in the tube looks like lip color and not congealed orange juice, another dye has to be added to the lipstick. This masterpiece of chemistry and art will be a soothing and suggestive and kissable red.

12   But it has very little to do with what actually goes on your face. That, as we said, is—but by now you already know more than you wanted to.

Thesis and Organization

1. What does paragraph 1 make clear about the essay's audience and subject? What expectations does it set up for the reader?

2. Which paragraphs focus on the ingredients that make lipstick work?

3. Which paragraphs focus on making lipstick attractive?

4. Consider the title of the essay and what Gandhi has to say about what goes into a tube of lipstick. What is her thesis?

5. Given the thesis of the essay, do you find Gandhi's purpose more informative than argumentative or the reverse? Explain.

Technique and Style

1. Considering what you have learned about Gandhi's thesis and purpose, how would you characterize the tone of the essay?

2. What provides the transitions between paragraphs 3 and 4? Between paragraphs 10 and 11? How effective do you find this device?

3. Examine the verbs Gandhi uses in paragraphs 2 and 3. What do they contribute to the essay's tone?

4. Paragraph 9 is more of an aside, a "by the way" comment, than a furthering of the essay's forward motion. What reasons can you think of that make the paragraph appropriate?

5. The last paragraph contains two references that may seem vague at first. What does "it" refer to in paragraph 12's first sentence? What does "That" refer to in the second sentence? Would a summary add to or detract from the conclusion? Explain.

Suggestions for Writing

Journal

1. Did Gandhi's essay change the way you think or feel about lipstick? Write a brief entry explaining how the essay affected you.

2. Get hold of your favorite junk food and jot down what is listed as its ingredients. Write a short entry explaining your response to that list.

Essay

Think about other items we take for granted and then find out if their ingredients contain a few surprises. You might start with a product, first noting the ingredients listed on the package and then consulting an unabridged dictionary. Given that information and your response to it, you are in a position to write an essay similar to Gandhi's. Your thesis would be your response (surprise, disgust, dismay), and the body of the paper would explain the role of the ingredients. Suggestions:

> hot dogs
> marshmallows
> frozen pies or cakes
> shampoo
> perfume or aftershave

D eath by Fasting

Joan Stephenson Graf

"Death by Fasting" sets a scientific process, how the body reacts to prolonged starvation, within a political context, the hunger strike. Here, the hunger strikers are members of the Irish Republican Army held prisoner by the British. Bobby Sands was the first prisoner to die. Graf's essay appeared more than ten years ago in Science 81, a publication of the American Association of the Advancement of Science, but the troubles in Ireland live on.

WHAT TO LOOK FOR *Much of what is published in the social and physical sciences uses process analysis, and now and then that information needs to be written for a nonscientific audience. You may run into the same problem if you are writing a paper on a subject you are very familiar with that is nonetheless aimed at a general audience. When and if that time comes, you'll find Graf's essay a good model. Pay particular attention to how she adjusts technical terms and information.*

1   Bad news travels fast in Northern Ireland. Women and children blow whistles and bang dustbin lids on the pavement to telegraph a grim message: Every 11 days, on the average, a convicted member of the Irish Republican Army dies of starvation in the Maze prison near Belfast.

2   The hunger strike, a strategy IRA inmates are using to pressure their British overlords to reclassify them as political prisoners rather than common criminals, has caught the attention of the entire world. IRA leaders advise prisoners when to begin their fasts so that they will have the most political impact. Last winter, for example, the IRA planned 27-year-old Bobby Sands's fast so that he would die on the anniversary of the bloody Easter Rising of 1916 that led to the original partitioning of Ireland.

3   But Sands did not die on Easter. The human body does not conform precisely to timetables calculated for an "average" person, one who can survive fasting for 50 to 70 days, assuming he has water. Sands lasted 66 days.

4   Early in a fast, the body is comparatively profligate in burning its fuels. A normal, nonfasting person's principal source of energy

is sugar, or glucose. The brain in particular needs glucose to function, but the body's reserve of it, stored in the liver in the form of a starchy carbohydrate glycogen, is exhausted in less than a day. When that supply runs out, the body makes its own glucose from the next most available source, protein in the muscles. If protein were the only energy supply, however, vital muscles in the heart, kidneys, spleen, and intestines would quickly be destroyed, and death would follow soon thereafter.

5   So as early as the first day of the fast, certain tissues begin supplementing their glucose supply with energy derived from fat, which comprises 15 to 20 percent of an average person's body weight. By the third day, when most people lose their hunger pangs, the brain is getting most of its energy from ketone bodies, which are formed in the liver from fatty acids.

6   To protect its vital organs and to conserve energy, the body makes a lot of other adjustments as well. The metabolic rate drops, pulse slows, blood pressure lowers. A starving person feels chilly. The body's thermostat cranks down a notch, an energy-saving strategy akin to maintaining a house at 65 degrees during the winter. According to reports from Belfast, the hunger strikers spend a lot of time in a bed under sheepskin rugs.

7   Fasting produces a lot of side effects: anemia, dry skin, ulcerated mouth, abnormal heart rhythm, erosion of bone mineral, difficulty in walking, blindness, loss of hearing, speech impairment, decrease in sexual drive. Those who visited Bobby Sands in his final days were shocked at his sunken cheeks, emaciated frame, and rapidly thinning brown hair.

8   In the last stages of starvation, when fat is depleted, the body draws exclusively from its protein reserves. At the end of his fast, when his insulating muscle was consumed, Sands was gently laid on a waterbed to cushion his frail skeleton.

9   "The body essentially digests itself," says Arnold E. Andersen, a psychiatrist at Johns Hopkins Medical Institution who treats women suffering from anorexia nervosa, an affliction of young women who exist on a semistarvation diet. "There is a point at which the organs simply stop functioning." Autopsies of the Irish prisoners turn up no single cause of death.

10   As hunters and gatherers, our ancestors adapted to survive when harvests were poor. But the body's heroic efforts to save it-

self while awaiting better nutritional times simply cannot outlast the determined resolve of the Irish hunger strikers.

Thesis and Organization

1. Process essays emphasize *how* something happens, but other concerns such as *who, what, when, where,* and *why* are also apt to be important. Where in this essay does the author first bring out *where? who? what? why?* What device does she use to indicate *when?*
2. At what point does the essay begin to focus on *how?* When does the focus shift again?
3. The mode of cause and effect, like the modes of process and narration, involves sequence. Cause must precede effect. Paragraphs 4, 5, 6, and 7 use cause and effect. Select one of these paragraphs and analyze the cause-and-effect relationship involved.
4. Consider only the scientific process that the author presents. If that alone were the subject of the essay, what would be the author's primary assertion about the subject? Now consider also the political context that the author provides. Given both the process and its context, what is the author's major assertion?
5. What emotions does the author want to elicit from the reader? Is she informing the reader about what some members of the IRA are experiencing or is she persuading the reader to share a particular conviction or take a particular action? What evidence can you cite?

Technique and Style

1. Paragraphs 1–3 set out the overall political context for the essay, but paragraphs 4 and 5 make no mention of it. Where in paragraphs 6–10 is the political context brought back in? How does the author's reintroduction of the context relate to her thesis? purpose? Why might she have chosen to omit it from paragraphs 4 and 5?
2. The essay deals with two levels of conflict: the IRA versus the British and the body versus itself. How does paragraph 10 bring the two conflicts together? What does the paragraph imply about the nature of the Irish hunger striker's "determined resolve"? How does the implication relate to the essay's thesis?
3. The essay first appeared in *Science 81,* a magazine published by the American Association for the Advancement of Science "to bridge the gap between science and citizen." How does the essay serve the magazine's general purpose?

4. Graf chooses her details with care: "sheepskin rugs" (paragraph 6); "sunken cheeks, emaciated frame, and rapidly thinning brown hair" (paragraph 7); "a waterbed to cushion his frail skeleton" (paragraph 8). What purpose do these details reveal? How is their purpose related to that of the essay?

5. Paragraphs 4–9 contain a great deal of technical information. What examples can you cite to show that the author is *not* writing to a technically sophisticated audience?

Suggestions for Writing

Journal

1. When you finished the essay, what did you think about the hunger strikers? Explain your response.

2. The situation in Northern Ireland is obviously very politically charged. For future reference, make a list of the political issues that interest you. Odds are all of them will require some research on your part so that you can write an explanatory or argumentative essay, but at least you'll have a list of topics to work from.

Essay

Make your own "death by" argument, researching the physiological process involved and placing it within a politically sensitive context. Use the *Reader's Guide to Periodical Literature* and the *New York Times Index* to find material to refer to in your argument. Suggestions:

  death by radiation (the danger of nuclear waste disposal)
  death by industrial poisoning (hazardous waste)
  death by diet (anorexia)
  death by digging (black lung disease)
  death by accident (malpractice)

If such topics seem too grim to you, consider writing on a "cure": how you recovered from a broken bone or a major or minor disease.

Cause and Effect

Process analysis focuses on *how;* causal analysis emphasizes *why.* Though writers examine both **cause and effect**, most will stress one or the other. Causal analysis looks below the surface of the steps in a process and examines why they occur; it analyzes their causes and effects, why *X* happens and what results from *X.* All of the examples mentioned in the introduction to process analysis (page 204) can be turned into illustrations of causal analysis.

Let's say you've followed the directions that came with your new stereo system and have finally reached the moment of truth when it's ready. You load your favorite tape, push the switch marked "power," it clicks, nothing happens. The receiver is on, as are the CD player and tape deck, but no sound comes out of the speakers. Probably you first check for the most immediate possible cause of the problem—the hookups. Are all the jacks plugged into the correct sources? Are they secure? Are the speaker wires attached correctly? If everything checks out, you start to search for less immediate causes, only to discover that the wrong switch was depressed on the receiver so that it's tuned to a nonexistent turntable. You push "Tape," and music fills the room. The problem is solved.

Essays that analyze cause and effect usually focus on one or the other. If you are writing about your hobby, which, let's say, happens to be tropical fish, you could emphasize the causes. You might have wanted a pet but were allergic to fur; you might have been fascinated with the aquarium in your doctor's office, and your aunt gave you two goldfish and a bowl. These reasons are causes that you would then have to sort out in terms of their importance. But if you wished to focus on effect, you might be writing on how your interest in tropical fish led to your majoring in marine biology.

You can see how causal analysis can be confusing in that a cause leads to an effect, which can then become another cause. This kind of causal chain undergirds Benjamin Franklin's point that "a little neglect may breed great mischief . . . for want of a nail the shoe was lost; for want of a shoe the horse was lost; and for want of a horse the rider was lost."

You can avoid the traps set by causal analysis if you apply some of the skills you use in division and classification and in process analysis:

1. Divide your subject into two categories—causes and effects.
2. Think about the steps or stages that are involved and identify them as possible causes or effects.
3. List an example or two for each possible cause or effect.
4. Sort out each list by dividing the items into primary or secondary causes and effects, that is, those that are relatively important and those that are relatively unimportant.

When you reach this final point, you may discover that an item you have listed is only related to your subject by time, in which case you should cross it out.

If you were writing a paper on cheating in college, for instance, your notes might resemble these:

	Possibilities	**Examples**	**Importance**
Causes	Academic pressure	Student who needs an A	Primary
	Peer pressure	Everybody does it	Primary
	System	Teachers tolerate it	Secondary
		No real penalty	
	Moral climate	Cheating on income taxes	Secondary
		False insurance claims	
		Infidelity	
		Breakup of family unit	
Effects	Academic	Grades meaningless	Primary
	Peers	Degree meaningless	Primary
	System	Erodes system	Secondary
	Moral climate	Weakens moral climate	Secondary

The train of thought behind these notes chugs along nicely. Looking at them, you can see how thinking about the moral climate might lead to speculation about the cheating that goes undetected on tax and insurance forms, and for that matter, the cheating that occurs in a different context, that of marriage. The idea of infidelity then sets off a causal chain: infidelity causes divorce, which causes the breakup of families. Pause there. If recent statistics show that a majority of students have cheated and if recent statistics also reveal a large number of single-parent households, is it safe to conclude that one caused the other? No. The relationship is one of time, not cause. Mistaking a **temporal relationship** for a causal one is a **logical fallacy** called **post hoc reasoning**.

It is also easy to mistake a **primary cause** or effect for a **secondary** one. If the notes above are for an essay that uses a narrative framework, and if the essay begins by relating an example of a student who was worried about having high enough grades to get into law school, the principle behind how the items are listed according to importance makes sense. To bring up his average, the student cheats on a math exam, justifying the action by thinking, "Everybody does it." The essay might then go on to speculate about the less apparent reasons behind the action—the system and the moral climate. For the student who cheated, the grade and peer pressure are the more immediate or primary causes; the system and climate are the more remote or secondary causes.

AUDIENCE AND PURPOSE   What you know or can fairly safely assume about the intended audience determines both what to say and how to say it. If you went straight from high school into a full-time job, for example, and wanted to write an essay about deciding five years later to enroll in college, you know your reader is familiar with both high school and college but knows nothing about you—your job and what led to your decision. The reality of your work—perhaps you find it isn't sufficiently demanding and that your lack of a higher education stands in the way of promotion—and your expectations of what college will do to enrich your life are the reasons, the causes, behind your change in direction.

Perhaps your subject is less personal but still one that your reader knows something about, say the high school dropout rate. Like your reader, you know that it's high in your city because you remember a story in the local newspaper pointing that out. What you didn't know your reader probably doesn't know either: How high is high? Why do students drop out? What happens to them after that? You'll have to do some research to find out some answers (the news story is a good place to start), but you'll find plenty to say. And as you amass information on your topic, you'll start to sense a purpose. Perhaps you simply want to inform your reader about the magnitude of the problem, or perhaps you will want to argue that more needs to be done about it.

An awareness of the reader and that person's possible preconceptions can also guide your approach to the topic. If, for example, your topic is the single-parent family, and you want to dispel some ideas about it that you think are misconceptions, you might safely assume that your audience regards single-parent families as at best incomplete and at worst irresponsible. It's obvious that you won't win your argument by suggesting that anyone with such ideas is a fool and possibly a bigot, as well; it's also obvious that making your point while not offending some readers requires a subtle approach. One way to avoid offense is to put yourself in the shoes of the reader who has the negative associations. Then just as you learned more about the topic and became enlightened, so, with any luck, may your reader.

VALID CAUSAL RELATIONSHIPS   As noted earlier, it is easy to mistake a temporal relationship for a causal relationship and to assign significance to something relatively unimportant. That's another way of saying that evidence and logical reasoning are essential to cause-and-effect essays. If, for instance, you find yourself drawn to one example, you need to think about how to avoid resting your entire argument on that one example. Writing about collegiate sports, for instance, you might have been struck by the story of a high school basketball star who wanted to play proball but didn't have the educational background necessary to be admitted to an NCAA Division I basketball school. After playing at several junior colleges, he finally transferred to an NCAAI institution, where with tutoring and a lot of individual attention, he was able to keep his grades high enough to maintain his academic eligibility, only to have all the academic support vanish a year short of graduation when he used up his time limit and was no longer eligible to play. The effect—no degree, little education, and few chances for review by pro scouts—was devastating. You want to write about it. You want to argue that college sports take advantage of high school athletes, but you have only one example. What to do?

You can use your one example as a narrative framework, one that is sure to interest your reader. But to make that example more than an attention-getting device that enlists the reader's emotions, you have a number of alternatives. If your research shows that a fair number of athletes have a similar story, then you have multiple examples to support your point. If only a few share the experience, you'll need to modify your thesis to argue that even a few is too many. And if you can't find any other examples, then you have to narrow your argument to fit what you have, arguing that this particular individual was victimized. While you can ask how many more like him there may be, you cannot state that they exist.

THESIS AND ORGANIZATION   Although a cause can lead to an effect that then becomes a cause leading to another effect and so on, most essays are organized around either one or the other: why high school students drop out, why a person returns to college, what happens if a college takes advantage of a basketball player, what a single-parent family really means, what effects being a working mother in a one-parent household can have on the children. That's not to say that if your essay focuses on cause, you have to avoid effect and vice versa. Whichever one you don't emphasize can make a good conclusion. You will probably want to put your thesis in your introduction so that the reader can follow the logical relationships between ideas as you develop your main point.

USEFUL TERMS

Cause and effect   An examination of a topic to discover, explain, or argue why a particular action, event, situation, or condition occurred.

Logical fallacy   An error in reasoning. Assigning a causal relationship to a temporal one and reaching a general conclusion based on one example are both logical fallacies.

Post hoc reasoning   A logical fallacy in which a temporal relationship is mistaken for a causal one. The fact that one event preceded another only establishes a temporal not a causal relationship.

Primary cause   The most important cause or causes.

Secondary cause   The less important cause or causes.

Temporal relationship   Two or more events related by time rather than anything else.

▣ POINTERS FOR USING CAUSE AND EFFECT

Exploring the Topic

1. **Have you stated the topic as a question that asks why *X* happened?** What are the possible causes? The probable causes? Rank the causes in order of priority.

2. **Have you stated the topic as a question that asks what results from** *X?* What are the possible effects? The probable effects? Rank the effects in order of priority.

3. **Is a temporal relationship involved?** Review your lists of causes and effects and rule out any that have only a temporal relationship to your subject.

4. **Which do you want to emphasize, cause or effect?** Check to make sure your focus is clear.

5. **What is your point?** Are you trying to show that something is so or to explore your topic?

6. **What evidence can you use to support your point?** Do you need to cite authorities or quote statistics? If you depend on personal experience, are you sure your experience is valid, that is, representative of general experience?

7. **What does your reader think?** Does your audience have any preconceived ideas about your topic that you need to account for? What are they? How can you deal with them?

8. **What role do you want to play in the essay?** Are you an observer or a participant? Is your major intention to inform, to persuade, or to entertain? What point of view best serves your purpose?

Drafting the Paper

1. **Know your reader.** Figure out what attitudes your reader may have about your topic. If the cause-and-effect relationship you are discussing is unusual, you might want to shape your initial attitude so that it is as skeptical as your reader's. On the other hand, you may want to start with a short narrative that immediately puts the reader on your side. Consider how much your reader is apt to know about your topic. If you are the expert, make sure you explain everything that needs to be explained without being condescending.

2. **Know your purpose.** Adjust your tone and persona to suit your purpose. If you are writing a persuasive paper, make sure your persona is credible and that you focus your ideas so that they may change the mind of a reader who initially does not agree with you—or, short of that, that your ideas make the reader rethink his or her position. If you are writing an informative paper, choose a persona and tone that will interest the reader. Tone and persona are even more crucial to essays written to entertain, in which the tone can range from ironic to lighthearted.

3. **Emphasize a cause or effect.** Essays that focus on cause will more than likely cover a variety of probable reasons that explain the result. Though there may be only one effect or result, you may want to predict other possible effects in your conclusion. For instance, an essay that explores

the causes of violence may examine a number of reasons or causes for it, but may then conclude by speculating on the possible effects of a rising crime rate. On the other hand, essays that focus on effect will more than likely cover a number of possible effects that are produced by a single cause, though again you may want to speculate on other causes. If you are writing about the effects of smoking, at some point in the essay you may want to include other harmful substances in the air such as dust, hydrocarbons, and carbon monoxide.

4. **Check for validity.** Don't hesitate to include quotations, allusions, statistics, and studies that support your point. Choose your examples carefully to buttress the relationship you are trying to establish, and be sure you don't mistake a temporal relationship for a causal one.

5. **Make a point.** The cause-and-effect relationship you examine should lead to or stem from an assertion: video games not only entertain, they also stimulate the mind and improve coordination; video games are not only habit-forming, they are also addictive.

S|till a Mystery

Edna Buchanan

Although many people associate Edna Buchanan with mystery novels, those who read the Miami Herald *also know her as a Pulitzer Prize–winning crime reporter. That background has served her well. After writing one nonfiction book about her journalistic career in crime, Buchanan turned to the more structured world of fiction, creating Britt Montero, a* Miami Herald *police reporter who has now appeared in a series of adventures. The latest,* Act of Betrayal, *appeared in a paperback edition in 1997. The essay that follows was one of several published in an advertising supplement to the April 21, 1996,* New York Times Magazine *that announced the 1996 Edgar Allan Poe Awards. The supplement was compiled and edited for the Mystery Writers of America. As you read Buchanan's essay, ask yourself how much of it is explanation and how much is persuasion.*

WHAT TO LOOK FOR   *Buchanan's essay is a good example of how various patterns of organization can be used together. You'll find that although her main pattern is cause and effect, she also draws on definition, narration, description, process, and comparison and contrast. As you read the essay, try to spot where and how she uses these other modes.*

1   She looked like a broken doll, pale and naked, crumpled in a mangrove tangle at the water's edge. The little girl had been stolen from her bedroom during a dark and steamy Miami night.

2   Her murder, a quarter of a century ago, still haunts those who remember. The lead homicide detective never forgot. I sat at his bedside as he lay dying. During his final breaths, he spoke again of the case, still unsolved, still a mystery.

3   Too many disturbing mysteries weigh upon real life, the last pages forever elusive, frustratingly out of reach. In the case of that little girl I finally fashioned my own solution. I wrote about a similar child, a similar case. A central character in that novel was a dying detective, still obsessed by her fate. But this time there was closure, her murder was solved. Justice at last. Good therapy for me, for all of us. What joys there are in writing and reading mysteries.

More truth can be told in fiction than in real life. The writer can address society's problems, mirror the community, inform as well as entertain, expose wrongs and injustices and create characters who vent his or her own outrage. Fictional officials can be endowed with dedication, intelligence and common sense, so unlike most in real government.

4   Everybody is interested in mysteries, in crime. We are all touched by it. We are all fascinated by evil. We all yearn for resolution. Our system rarely provides it. Even if a crime is solved, even if there is an arrest and if—after hearing after hearing and deposition after deposition—there should be a conviction, it still never really ends. There are appeals and more appeals, basic gain time, incentive gain time, good time, pre-trial release, work release, conditional release and early release, to say nothing of furloughs, parole and probation—and escape. There is no last page.

5   Real life can be grim, unlike mystery fiction, where writers can wrap up those loose ends, solve the mysteries and best of all, write the last chapter, where the good guys win and the bad guys get what they deserve—so unlike real life.

6   The genre is an escape, a sanctuary, in an increasingly chaotic world overtaken by unresponsive government agencies, rush hour traffic, voice mail and other unspeakable torments. Mystery novels offer intellectual challenge, structure and the triumph of logic and order in a world where such comforts are increasingly rare.

7   Readers assume the role of detective, sharpening deductive skills and honing their talents for problem and puzzle solving. Mystery aficionados love logic and having the strands spun out of an original premise weave together satisfyingly at the end.

8   They experience wonderful literature, memorable characters, roller-coaster adventure, breathtaking suspense, and pumped up heart rates, all without exposing themselves to bullets, tear gas, rocks, bottles, or actual exercise.

9   The writer has even more fun.

10   We provide the only world in which our readers are certain to find swift and sure justice—or any real justice. We all need endings and it is a joy, as a novelist, for me to be able to give them to readers, and to myself.

11   Two fewer ghosts, one a little girl and the other an aging detective, haunt my dreams these dark and steamy nights. Who says there is no justice?

Thesis and Organization

1. Buchanan uses a framing device to open and close her essay. Explain whether you find it effective.
2. Which paragraphs focus on the writer of mysteries? What reasons does Buchanan give for writing mystery stories?
3. Which paragraphs focus on the reader of mysteries? What reasons does Buchanan give for reading mystery stories?
4. Paragraph 4 discusses the "system." What is Buchanan's point? How does it relate to the other ideas in the essay?
5. Consider what Buchanan has to say about why people write and read mysteries and how the world of fiction relates to the world of reality. In one sentence, state her thesis.

Technique and Style

1. Rewrite Buchanan's first sentence deleting the adjectives. What is gained? Lost?
2. The essay was one of several in an advertising supplement promoting the 1996 Edgar Allen Poe Awards in particular and mysteries in general. Analyze the degree to which Buchanan is "selling" mysteries.
3. Many people regard reading mystery stories as at best a waste of time, at worst a morbid interest. How does Buchanan counter that opinion?
4. What point is Buchanan making by comparing mystery fiction to real life crime? How valid do you find her opinion?
5. Quite intentionally, Buchanan chooses to have paragraph 9 consist of a single sentence. What reasons can you come up with for Buchanan's choice?

Suggestions for Writing

Journal

1. Explain why you read what you read. If you only read what is assigned for your classes, explain why you do not read for pleasure.
2. Buchanan states "We are all fascinated by evil. We all yearn for resolution." Explore the degree to which you think she is correct.

Essay

Almost everyone uses leisure time to relax by pursuing some form of pleasure. Think about what you do for day-to-day fun and make a list of what you come up with. Choose one subject and consider why you do it as well as its effects on you. Then draft an essay in which you explain what you do and why. You may want to emphasize cause rather than effect or vice versa.

T iffany Stephenson— An Apology

Bjorn Skogquist

Bjorn Skogquist came to Concordia College in Moorhead, Minnesota, with a firm interest in drama (having been in productions at Anoka High School that were recognized for excellence by the Kennedy Center for the Performing Arts) but a distinct aversion to writing. His freshman year, however, when his instructor, James Postema, encouraged him to "include anything I wanted, anything that I felt to be important," Skogquist "began to find it rather easy, and in a way, almost entertaining." He comments, "About halfway through, after I had written about various mishaps and comical incidents in my life, I decided to write about the things that a person would rather forget." The result is the essay that follows, although the name of the subject has been changed to Tiffany Stephenson. Skogquist relates "one of those things that I would rather forget, but instead of forgetting it, I apologized. It was something that I began and couldn't put down until I had finished."

WHAT TO LOOK FOR   *If you find yourself thinking about an incident that occurred to you and mulling over its effect, you may well be on the way to an essay that takes a personal narrative and reexamines it through the lens of cause and effect. That is what Bjorn Skogquist does with what happened to him in the fourth grade. As you read the essay, look for the ways he handles different time periods—what had been happening before he entered his new school, his first day there, the incident that occurred, and the present.*

1   When I was in the fourth grade, I moved from a small Lutheran school of 100 to a larger publicly funded elementary school. Lincoln Elementary. Wow. Lincoln was a big school, full of a thousand different attitudes about everything from eating lunch to how to treat a new kid. It was a tough time for me, my first year, and more than anything, I wanted to belong.

2   Many things were difficult; the move my family had just made, trying to make new friends, settling into a new home, accepting a new stepfather. I remember crying a lot. I remember my parents

fighting. They were having a difficult time with their marriage, and whether it was my stepfather's drinking, or my mother's stubbornness, it took an emotional toll on both me and my siblings. Despite all this, the thing that I remember most about the fourth grade is Tiffany Stephenson.

3   The first day of fourth grade at Lincoln Elementary School was an emptiness, and it felt enormous. I wasn't the only one who felt this way, but I was too absorbed in my own problems to notice anyone else's. I was upset that my father, my blood father, was in the hospital for abusing alcohol. Among other things, he was a schizophrenic. I was too young to understand these diseases, but I understood all too well that my daddy was very sick, and that I couldn't see him any more.

4   My first day at Lincoln was a very real moment in my life. The weather was both cloudy and intolerably sunny at the same time. Maybe it wasn't that the sun was so bright, maybe it was just that our eyes were still adjusted to morning shadows. It was one of those sequences that somehow stand out in my memory as unforgettable. I remember feeling gray inside. I think that all of us felt a little gray, and I would guess that most of us remember that first day as you might remember your grandmother's funeral, whether you liked it or not.

5   I walked in and sat near the back of the class, along with a few others. If you were different or weird or new, from another planet, you sat in the back because those were the only desks left. I sat at the far left of the room, in the back near the windows. For a while I just stared out into the playground, waiting for recess to come. Our teacher, Mrs. Bebow, came into the room and started talking to us. I don't remember exactly what she said that day, because I wasn't listening. I was numb to the world, concentrating solely on that playground. She seemed distant, far away, and I think that my whole day might have stayed numb if it weren't for a boy named Aaron Anderson.

6   Aaron, who sat to my right, leaned over and whispered, "My name's Aaron. And that's Tiffany Stephenson. Stay away from her. She's fat and ugly and she stinks." At that, a few others laughed, and I felt the numbness leaving me. Mrs. Bebow remarked that if we had something so terribly amusing to say, everyone had a right to know just what it was. Of course, we all quieted down. Then I asked which one was Tiffany, and Aaron pointed. There she was,

coloring contentedly, sitting alone in the corner, in the very back, just like me. She was not fat or ugly, and as far as I knew, she didn't stink either. I even remember thinking that she was cute, but I quickly dismissed the thought because I already had a new friendship, even though it was in the common disgust of Tiffany Stephenson.

7   While all this was happening, our teacher Mrs. Bebow managed to take roll, after which she proceeded to lecture the boys on good behavior and then the girls on being young ladies. Every time she turned her back, airplanes and garbage flew across the room at Tiffany, along with a giggle. I don't think Tiffany Stephenson thought too much of us, that day or ever.

8   A few days later, one of the girls passed Tiffany a note. It ended up making her cry, and it got the girl a half an hour of detention. I was too busy trying to fit in to notice though, or didn't notice, or was afraid to notice, or simply didn't care.

9   That fall, both the boys and girls would go up to Tiffany on the playground and taunt her. They made absurd accusations, accusations about eating boogers at lunch, or about neglecting to wear underwear that day. Interestingly, this was the only activity that we participated in where a teacher didn't command, "OK, boys and girls need to partner up!" What we did to Tiffany Stephenson was mean, but in using her we all became common allies. I wonder if the teachers knew what we were up to when we made our next move, or if they thought that we were actually getting along. I think they knew at first, but we got craftier as time passed. And Tiffany had quit telling the teacher what happened. She knew that when we were ratted on, her taunts got worse. And they did get worse. We were mean, but we kept on because there was no one to stand out and say, "Enough."

10   When I think about that year, and about Tiffany, I remember that she was almost always alone. Toward the second half of the year, a retarded girl named Sharon Olsen befriended her. Sharon and Tiffany were a lot alike. They spent most of their time together coloring and drawing pictures, and those pictures always found their way to the prize board at the end of the week. The teacher knew that they needed a little encouragement, but mostly that "encouragement" ended up making us hate them more. We picked on Sharon a lot too, but not as much as we targeted Tiffany.

11   Through the long winter, our taunts became hateful jeers, and our threats of pushing and shoving became real acts. We carried our threats out against Tiffany, but with no real reason to hate her. A couple of times when we walked down to lunch, we even pushed her around the corner to an area under the stairs. We knew that if no other classes followed us, we could get away with our plan, which was to tease her until tears flowed. We always asked her if she was scared. She never gave us the right answer. In a quiet voice she would reply, "No. Now leave me alone." Sometimes we left her alone, and sometimes we just laughed. Tiffany must have felt so very scared and alone, but she had more than us, she had courage. We didn't care. The more we could scare her, the better, the closer, the stronger knit we somehow felt.

12   One afternoon, heading for lunch, a few of us stayed behind and blocked the doorway. Tiffany was there, alone again, and cornered by three boys. Looking back, I realized why we began pushing her around. We felt unbelievably close, so close to each other through our hatred. It was a feeling that I have experienced only a few times since. And not only was the experience ours to cherish, it was a delight for Mrs. Bebow's entire fourth grade class. We were a purpose that afternoon, and we knew it. Looking back to that moment, I feel more remorse for my coldness than I have felt for any other passing wrong. But then, there, I felt alive, unafraid, and strangely whole.

13   That afternoon changed me forever.

14   By the time we sent Tiffany Stephenson to the green linoleum, she was no longer a person. Her full name, given to her at birth as a loving gesture, was now a fat, smelly, ugly title. There, on the green linoleum of Mrs. Bebow's fourth grade classroom, amidst the decorations and smell of crayfish aquariums, Tiffany Stephenson received many kicks, punches and unkind words. We didn't kick or punch her very hard, and the things we said weren't especially foul, but they were inhuman. This event was the culmination of the inhumane hate and vengeance that had been growing inside of us all year long. And yet, if any one of us stopped for a second to look, to really take a good look at who it was lying there on the ground, curled up in a ball crying, we would have realized that she was one of us.

15   At the beginning of the year, all of us had felt like we were in the back of the room. We were all unknowns. But somehow dur-

ing that year we had put ourselves above her by force, and I admit that for a long time I couldn't see my wrong. But I had wronged. I had caused someone pain for my own personal ambitions. I was now popular, and it was at Tiffany Stephenson's expense. I was a coward, stepping on her courage for one moment in the warm sunlight, above my own pale clouds.

16   Only recently do I realize my error. I wish I could have been the one to say, on that first fall afternoon, "Tiffany's not ugly, fat or stinky. She's just like you and me, and we're all here together." Really, I wish anyone would have said it. I know now that people need each other, and I wish I could tell the fourth grade that we could all be friends, that we could help each other with our problems. I wish that I could go back. But all I can do is apologize. So Tiffany, for all my shortcomings, and for sacrificing you for the sake of belonging, please forgive me.

Thesis and Organization

1. What paragraph or paragraphs introduce the narrative?
2. Trace the causal relationships in paragraphs 1–5. What does the author feel and why?
3. Trace the causal relationship in paragraphs 6–14. What does the author feel and why?
4. Paragraphs 15 and 16 sum up the incident that occurred "that afternoon." What did the author realize then? Now?
5. Consider all the cause-and-effect relationships in the narrative and state the thesis of the essay.

Technique and Style

1. Tiffany Stephenson's name first appears in paragraph 2 but not again until paragraph 6. Explain what is gained by the delay.
2. How does the author try to connect his experience with that of the reader? Why might he have chosen to do that?
3. In paragraph 15 Skogquist says "I was a coward, stepping on her courage for one moment in the warm sunlight, above my own pale clouds." What does he mean by "the warm sunlight, above my own pale clouds"?
4. Paragraph 13 consists of one sentence. Explain its function and effect.
5. Skogquist gives his audience a lot of information about his family. Explain why he may have chosen to do that and what it contributes to the essay.

Suggestions for Writing

Journal

1. Do you identify with the author or with Tiffany Stephenson?
2. If you were Tiffany Stephenson, would you forgive Skogquist? Why or why not?

Essay

Write your own personal narrative about an experience in which you explore the effect it had on you. Like Skogquist, you will probably want to have a dual perspective: the effects then and now. For a subject, consider your first

day at a new school
attempt at a sport
acquaintance with death
friendship
visit to the dentist or doctor or hospital

Wrestling with Myself

George Felton

*When not teaching writing and copywriting at the Columbus College
of Art and Design, George Felton is a freelance writer whose topics
cover the hot spots of popular culture—Richard Simmons, the
"Healthism" craze, not understanding how things work, and the like.
Here, he investigates his (and our) fascination with pro wrestling. The
essay was originally published in* Sun *Magazine, the supplement to
the* Baltimore Sun, *on November 11, 1990. Felton has also published
his work in the* New York Times, Newsweek, *and* Advertising Age
and has been a contributor to the Bread Loaf Writers' Conference.

WHAT TO LOOK FOR   *Felton's audience is composed of
readers who share his enthusiasm for pro wrestling, those who
regard it as silly or worse, and those who know little if anything
about it. At times, you may find yourself faced with a similar variety
of readers, which is when you can employ some of the techniques
Felton uses. As you read his essay, look for the ways he addresses the
attitudes of these various readers.*

1   It's Saturday morning, 11 a.m., right after the cartoons: time for
"The NWA Main Event." As I watch the ringside announcer set up
today's card, a huge wrestler—topless and sweating, wearing
leather chaps and a cowboy hat, carrying a lariat with a cowbell
on it—bursts into the frame, grabs the announcer by his lapels,
and, chunks of tobacco spraying out of his mouth, begins to
emote: "Well lookee here, this is just what eats in my craw. . . . I
don't care if you're the president or the chief of police, it don't
matter, I'm gonna do what I wanna do," and what he mostly wants
to do is wrassle somebody good for once—enough nobodies in
the ring, enough wimps running the schedule. As quickly as he
spills into camera, he veers out, having delivered exactly the 20-
second sound bite required. Our announcer blithely sends us to a
commercial, and another Saturday's wrestling hour has begun. I
feel better already.

2   I soon find out this cowboy's name is Stan Hanson, he's from
Border, Texas, and lately he's been getting disqualified in all his

matches for trying to kill his opponents and then "hogtying" them with his lariat. We get to watch a recent match in which he kicks some poor guy's stomach furiously with his pointed-toe cowboy boots and drop-slams his elbow into his neck and, after getting him down, hits him over the head with the cowbell, and first whips, then strangles him with his lariat. It's great stuff, with the bell ringing madly and the referee waving his arms, but Stan's already yanked the guy outside the ring onto the apron and he's still on top, trying to kill him.

3   Why do I love this? Why am I crazy about Stan Hanson, who's old and fat and a man the announcer warns us "ought to be in a straitjacket and chains"? Because he personifies the great redemption of pro wresting, the way it delivers me from civilization and its discontents. Not only is Stan Hanson mad as hell and not taking it anymore, but he's doing it all for me—getting himself disqualified so that I won't run the risk myself, but inviting me to grab one end of the rope and pull. He is my own id—the hairy beast itself— given a Texas identity and a push from behind, propelled out there into the "squared circle" where I can get a good look at it: sweat-soaked, mean, kicking at the slats, looking for an exposed neck. My heart leaps up, my cup runneth over.

4   Obviously I can't tell my friends about too much of this. If I even mention pro wrestling, they just stare at me and change the subject. They think I'm kidding. I am not supposed to like pro wrestling—its demographics are too downscale, its Dumb Show too transparent. They complain that it's fake and silly, which to me are two of its great charms. If it were real, like boxing, it'd be too painful to watch, too sad. I like knowing it's choreographed: the staged mayhem lets me know someone has studied me and will toss out just the meat the dark, reptilian centers of my brain require to stay fed and stay put. Sadomasochism? Homoeroticism? I am treated to the spectacle of Ric "The Nature Boy" Flair, astride the corner ropes and his opponent. His fist may be in the air, triumphant, but his groin is in the othe guy's face, and he keeps it there. For once the ringside announcers are speechless as we all stare, transfixed, at this clearest of symbolic postures. Consciously I am squirming, but my reptilian center feels the sun on its back.

5   Racism? Ethnocentrism? Am I unsettled about Japanese hegemony? No problem. There is, in the World Wrestling Federation, a tag team of scowling, unnervingly business-oriented Japanese

toughs—the Orient Express, managed by Mr. Fuji—who invite me to hate them, and of course I do. Their failure is my success, and I don't even have to leave the living room. Two oversized, red-trunked Boris types used to parade around the ring under a red flag and insist, to our booing, on singing the Russian national anthem before wrestling. Since the Cold War has become passé, however, I've noticed matches pitting Russians *against each other,* and that, as my newspaper tells me, is not passé. I hear groans of delight from below, as this reprise of Cain and Abel croons its libidinal tune.

6   I mean where else can I take my id out for a walk, how else to let it smell the sweaty air, root its nose through the wet leaves? Cartoons? No amount of Wile E. Coyote spring-loaded bounces, no pancakings of Roger Rabbit, none of the whimsical annihilations of Cartoonville can approximate the satisfactions of a real boot in a real belly, a man's head twisted up in the ropes, the merry surfeit of flying drop kicks, suplexes, sleeper holds, and heart punches, all landed somewhere near real bodies. Pro sports? I get more, not less, neurotic rooting for my teams—my neck muscles ache, my stomach burns with coffee, after enduring another four-hour Cleveland Browns loss on TV. The Indians? Don't even get me started. The violence of movies like *The Last Action Hero* and *Cliffhanger?* Needlessly complicated by storyline.

7   No, give it to me straight. Wrestling may be a hybrid genre—the epic poem meets Marvel Comics via the soap opera—but its themes, with their medieval tone, could hardly be simpler: warrior kings doing battle after battle to see who is worthy, women pushed almost to the very edges of the landscape, *Beowulf's* heroic ideal expressed in the language of an after-school brawl: "I wanna do what I wanna do. You gonna try to stop me?"

8   I also appreciate the pop-culture novelty of pro wrestling, its endearing way of creating, a little smudged and thick-fingered, but with a great earnest smile ("Here, look at this!") new *bêtes noires* for our consumption. One of the newest is something called Big Van Vader, a guy in a total upper torso headgear that looks like Star Wars Meets a Mayan Temple. He carries a stake topped with a skull and can shoot steam out of ventricles on his shoulders, but it looks like all he can do to keep from toppling over. He's horrifying and silly all at once, an atavistic nightdream wearing a "Kick Me" sign.

9   Such low rent Show Biz, this admixture of the asylum and the circus, is central to wrestling's double-tracked pleasure. Its emotional *reductio ad absurdum* taps my anger like a release valve, but its silliness allows me to feel superior to it as I watch. I can be dumb and intelligent, angry and amused, on all fours yet ironically detached, all at the same moment.

10   It's a very satsifying mix, especially since my life between Saturdays is such an exercise in self-control, modesty, and late twentieth-century angst. To my students I am the helpful Mr. Felton. To my chairman I am the responsible Mr. Felton. To virtually everybody and everything else I'm the confused and conflicted Mr. F. My violence amounts to giving people the finger, usually in traffic. When I swear I mutter. To insults I quickly add the disclaimer, "just kidding," a move I learned from watching David Letterman temper his nastiness. I never yell at people, threaten them, twist my heel into their ears, batter their heads into ring posts, or catch them flush with folding chairs. I don't wear robes and crowns and have bosomy women carry them around for me, either. In short, I never reduce my life to the satisfying oversimplification I think it deserves.

11   I'm a wimp. Just the sort of guy Cactus Jack or old Stan himself would love to sink his elbows into, a sentiment with which I couldn't agree more. And that brings us to the deepest appeal of pro wrestling: It invites me to imagine the annihilation of my own civilized self. When Ric Flair jabs his finger into the camera and menaces his next opponent with, "I guarantee you one thing— Junkyard Dog or no Junkyard Dog, you're going to the hospital," when another of the Four Horsemen growls, "I'm gonna take you apart on national television," the real thrill is that they're coming for me. And when Stan offers me one end of the rope, we both know just whose neck we're pulling on. Ah, redemption.

Thesis and Organization

1. What paragraph or paragraphs make up Felton's introduction? What are the reasons for your choice?
2. Paragraphs 4 and 5 rely heavily on examples. What ideas do Felton's examples illustrate?
3. Comparisons take up much of paragraphs 6 and 10. What are the comparisons? What are Felton's points in using them?

4. Where in the essay does Felton discuss the effect pro wrestling has on him? What reasons can you find for his placement of the effects?

5. Felton saves his most important reason till his last paragraph. Putting that reason together with the others in the essay, state Felton's thesis in your own words.

Technique and Style

1. Felton uses dashes in paragraphs 1, 3, and 7. After examining those examples, what conclusions can you draw about the proper function of dashes?

2. What impression do you have of Felton's persona? Explain whether it fits his self-description in paragraphs 10 and 11.

3. Both the first and last paragraph use dialogue. What does it add?

4. Paragraph 3 is riddled with allusions: to Freud's *Civilization and Its Discontents*, to the film *Network*, to a poem by Wordsworth, to the *Bible*. What do these allusions contribute to Felton's persona? To the essay as a whole?

5. Although the essay is written in first person, Felton uses *we* in paragraphs 2 and 11. Who does *we* refer to? What is gained or lost by switching pronouns?

Suggestions for Writing

Journal

1. Which category of readers do you belong to—wrestling fan, wrestling debunker, wrestling innocent, or some other? Evaluate the effectiveness of the essay from your perspective.

2. Felton maintains that pro wrestling appeals to the id, to "the hairy beast itself." What other sports can you think of that appeal to the id? Select one and detail its appeal.

Essay

Whether or not you are a fan, there's no arguing with the popularity of watching sports events. Select a sport that you enjoy or one that you cannot understand the appeal of, and use it as the subject for an essay in which you explain or speculate on its popularity. Suggestions:

    football or baseball
    tennis or golf
    racing (cars, horses, dogs)
    roller derby, amazon contests, demolition derby
    motocross

C ensoring Sex Information: The Story of *Sassy*

Elizabeth Larsen

If you've ever looked hard at a large magazine display, you have probably been surprised at the number of specialized magazines you saw, ones that fit almost every possible category. One category that is relatively new on the scene is aimed at young teenagers. Sassy *is such a magazine. When it was first published in 1987, its editorial policies—as the following essay explains—included a liberal attitude toward sex education, but its publishers quickly found out that the magazine had a dual audience, young teenagers and their parents. As hungry as the teenagers were for information about sex, the editors discovered that sex education doesn't sell. Elizabeth Larsen was on* Sassy's *editorial staff when that lesson became clear. She now works for the* Utne Reader, *where this essay was published in 1990. Since that time, attitudes toward sex have changed somewhat, at least in advertisements. As you read Larsen's article, you might think about how magazines sell sex.*

WHAT TO LOOK FOR *When dealing with causal relationships it's easy to fall into the habit of overusing transitions such as* therefore, so, because, consequently, thus, *and the like. You'll find that Larsen, in paragraphs 5–8, avoids these obvious transitions, so see if you can spot how she gets from one paragraph to another.*

1   At the first editorial meeting of *Sassy* magazine, in 1987, the staff sat around the editor-in-chief's office discussing how to make our new magazine different from other teenage publications. The unanimous first priority was to provide sex education: since we had read the competition during our own adolescence, we knew the sex information published by teen magazines was scarce and usually couched in judgmental terms.

2   We had a good reason to put this issue high on our agenda. The United States has the highest teen pregnancy rate of any similarly industrialized Western nation, and we felt this was not an issue that would go away by just telling teens to say no. The rock stars and athletes speaking out against drugs and drunk driving on TV weren't making any pitches for virginity. The situation had be-

come even more confusing for teenagers because of the attention that abstinence was getting as the only sure way to prevent AIDS. Our readers were left with a lot of unanswered questions that we felt were important to address.

3   *Sassy's* initial advertisers did not feel as strongly as its editors about leading the sex education of America's youth. Many were concerned about an article in the prototype issue entitled "Sex for Absolute Beginners," which had previously run in *Dolly, Sassy's* Australian counterpart. The article answered questions ranging from "Can I get pregnant?" and "What is an orgasm?" to "Am I homosexual?" and "Is masturbation wrong?" A few advertisers were offended by the thought of their own teenage daughters reading the information and decided not to advertise, while others reluctantly signed contracts, fearing that if the magazine were a huge success, they couldn't afford to be left out. It became clear to me later that their concerns were business rather than moral ones when I realized that many of the same companies who objected to "Sex for Absolute Beginners" in *Sassy* nevertheless advertised without complaint in *Dolly*—the most widely read teenage magazine in the world in terms of circulation per capita. For what the advertisers understood long before the editors did is that sex may sell billions of dollars of U.S. products every year, but responsible, direct information about sex directed toward U.S. teenagers would not.

4   In the first issue, *Sassy* printed an article entitled "Losing Your Virginity." We ran this because we felt that at least one reason so many teens were having sex was that the media had successfully convinced them that losing their virginity was going to be the biggest moment of their lives. Our strategy was to provide our readers with more realistic accounts to debunk the celluloid stereotype. After setting up some alternative scenarios, we left the moral decisions to the reader while providing detailed information about birth control and sexually transmitted diseases and answers to frequently asked questions such as, "Will it hurt?" "Can he tell I'm a virgin?" "What if I change my mind?" and "How long will it take?"

5   The reader response to this article was phenomenal. *Sassy* and the article's author received hundreds of letters saying that finally someone had spoken to them in a way with which they felt comfortable. Mail started pouring in to the "Help" column, which I wrote, making apparent that we had only scratched the surface of a teenager's reality. What was most disconcerting to us was the tone of fear and shame these letters portrayed. Many young women

were desperate for answers—we even received phone calls requesting advice. The next few articles we ran on sex were all in response to these frantic letters asking about pregnancy, abortion, incest, suicide, and homosexuality.

6   "The Truth About Boys' Bodies," "Getting Turned On," "And They're Gay," "My Girlfriend Got Pregnant," and "Real Stories About Incest" were articles written to let girls know that whatever choices they made about their sexuality weren't shameful as long as they were responsible about safe sex, birth control, and emotional self-care.

7   Much of our reader response was positive. Mothers and even grandmothers called to say that they had read our articles with their daughters and granddaughters and as a result felt closer to each other. There was also relief among some parents that we had explained something important they were uncomfortable communicating. On the other hand, there was also a fair share of irate screaming directed our way. Most of these callers felt the information we printed was "pornographic" and reeled off the old saw that information just encourages young women to have sex. Perhaps the most alarming phone call came from a father who screamed, "Anything my daughter learns about sex, she'll learn from me!" before he slammed down the receiver. These people canceled their subscriptions—a routine response to a publication one disagrees with and something we had counted on.

8   What we hadn't counted on was the mass reader/advertiser boycott led by a woman whose kids didn't even read *Sassy*. As a member of a group called Women Aglow was to show us, it is possible in this country for a vocal minority to bring about what amounts to censorship. Through the Jerry Falwell-supported publication *Focus on the Family,* Women Aglow organized a letter-writing campaign aimed at our major advertisers in which they threatened to boycott their products if those companies continued to advertise in *Sassy*. Within a matter of months *Sassy* had lost nearly every ad account, and we were publishing what we jokingly called *The Sassy Pamphlet.* We were told that to stay in business we must remove the "controversial" content from the magazine. That was reluctantly done, and today *Sassy* has regained its advertisers but not its detailed information on sex education.

9   Sadly, what was to a few young editors just a sobering lesson about the power of advertising was a great loss to young women, who need the information *Sassy* once provided.

Thesis and Organization

1. How does paragraph 1 answer the questions *who, where, when, why, how?*
2. What reasons does paragraph 2 state as what caused the editorial staff to focus on sex information?
3. How did that focus affect the advertisers? What primary cause lay behind that response?
4. Paragraphs 5–8 detail the readers' and advertisers' responses. What were they?
5. Reread paragraphs 3, 8, and 9. What do you conclude is the essay's thesis?

Technique and Style

1. How would you characterize the author's tone? Angry? Disappointed? Demoralized? What? On the whole, is it objective or subjective?
2. Given that tone, how would you describe the author's persona? Do you find it credible? Why or why not?
3. How would you define the author's purpose? Expressive, argumentative, informative, or some mixture? Explain.
4. What does the author gain by her use of the first-person plural, *we?*
5. What does the use of quotations add to the essay? What might be lost without them?

Suggestions for Writing

Journal

1. Recall the time when you were a young teenager. What would have been your response to the kinds of articles that *Sassy* originally published?
2. Consider the fine line between selling sex and selling information. Define what is and is not legitimate.

Essay

Think about times when you have met censorship head-on. What were the reasons behind it? What were its effects on you? Write an essay in which you explain what happened to you and why. No matter what incident you are writing about, you might start by looking up *censorship* in an unabridged dictionary. Suggestions:

> films you weren't allowed to see
> books you weren't allowed to read
> magazines you weren't allowed to have
> topics you couldn't discuss

You might also think of times when censorship was an issue in your family, church, or community. Or consider the reception of controversial films or the use of rating systems.

B lack Men and Public Space

Brent Staples

*Any woman who walks along city streets at night knows the fear
Brent Staples speaks of, but in this essay we learn how that fear can
affect the innocent. We see and feel what it is like to be a tall, strong,
young black man who enjoys walking at night but innocently terri-
fies any lone woman. His solution to his night walking problems
gives a delightful twist to nonviolent resistance.*

*The irony of Staples's situation was not lost on Jesse Jackson.
Speaking in Chicago in 1993, he pointed out an equally distressing
irony: "There is nothing more painful to me at this stage in my life
than to walk down the street and hear footsteps and start thinking
about robbery. Then [I] look around and see someone white and
feel relieved."*

*Brent Staples holds a PhD in psychology from the University of
Chicago and writes on politics and culture for the* New York Times
editorial board. His memoir, Parallel Time: Growing Up in Black
and White, *is published by Pantheon Books. The essay reprinted here
was first published in* Harpers *in 1986. He's still whistling.*

WHAT TO LOOK FOR   *Before you read the essay, look up the
dash in a handbook of usage so you'll be on the lookout for Staples's
use of it. He uses it in two different ways, but always appropriately.*

1   My first victim was a woman—white, well-dressed, probably in
her early twenties. I came upon her late one evening on a deserted
street in Hyde Park, a relatively affluent neighborhood in an otherwise mean, impoverished section of Chicago. As I swung onto the
avenue behind her, there seemed to be a discreet, uninflammatory
distance between us. Not so. She cast back a worried glance. To
her, the youngish black man—a broad 6 feet 2 inches with a beard
and billowing hair, both hands shoved into the pockets of a bulky
military jacket—seemed menacingly close. After a few more quick
glimpses, she picked up her pace and was soon running in
earnest. Within seconds she disappeared into a cross street.

2   That was more than a decade ago. I was 22 years old, a graduate student newly arrived at the University of Chicago. It was in
the echo of that terrified woman's footfalls that I first began to

know the unwieldy inheritance I'd come into—the ability to alter public space in ugly ways. It was clear that she thought herself the quarry of a mugger, a rapist, or worse. Suffering a bout of insomnia, however, I was stalking sleep, not defenseless wayfarers. As a softy who is scarcely able to take a knife to a raw chicken—let alone hold one to a person's throat—I was surprised, embarrassed, and dismayed all at once. Her flight made me feel like an accomplice in tyranny. It also made it clear that I was indistinguishable from the muggers who occasionally seeped into the area from the surrounding ghetto. That first encounter, and those that followed, signified that a vast, unnerving gulf lay between nighttime pedestrians—particularly women—and me. And I soon gathered that being perceived as dangerous is a hazard in itself. I only needed to turn a corner into a dicey situation, or crowd some frightened, armed person in a foyer somewhere, or make an errant move after being pulled over by a policeman. Where fear and weapons meet—and they often do in urban America—there is always the possibility of death.

3   In that first year, my first away from my hometown, I was to become thoroughly familiar with the language of fear. At dark, shadowy intersections, I could cross in front of a car stopped at a traffic light and elicit the *thunk, thunk, thunk, thunk* of the driver—black, white, male, or female—hammering down the door locks. On less traveled streets after dark, I grew accustomed to but never comfortable with people crossing to the other side of the street rather than pass me. Then there were the standard unpleasantries with policemen, doormen, bouncers, cabdrivers, and others whose business it is to screen out troublesome individuals *before* there is any nastiness.

4   I moved to New York nearly two years ago and I have remained an avid night walker. In central Manhattan, the near-constant crowd cover minimizes tense one-on-one street encounters. Elsewhere—in SoHo, for example, where sidewalks are narrow and tightly spaced buildings shut out the sky—things can get very taut indeed.

5   After dark, on the warrenlike streets of Brooklyn where I live, I often see women who fear the worst from me. They seem to have set their faces on neutral, and with their purse straps strung across their chests bandolier-style, they forge ahead as though bracing themselves against being tackled. I understand, of course, that the

danger they perceive is not a hallucination. Women are particularly vulnerable to street violence, and young black males are dras-
tically overrepresented among the perpetrators of that violence.
Yet these truths are no solace against the kind of alienation that
comes of being ever the suspect, a fearsome entity with whom
pedestrians avoid making eye contact.

6   It is not altogether clear to me how I reached the ripe old age of
22 without being conscious of the lethality nighttime pedestrians
attributed to me. Perhaps it was because in Chester, Pennsylvania,
the small, angry industrial town where I came of age in the 1960s,
I was scarcely noticeable against a backdrop of gang warfare,
street knifings, and murders. I grew up one of the good boys, had
perhaps a half-dozen fistfights. In retrospect, my shyness of combat has clear sources.

7   As a boy, I saw countless tough guys locked away; I have since
buried several, too. They were babies, really—a teenage cousin, a
brother of 22, a childhood friend in his mid-twenties—all gone
down in episodes of bravado played out in the streets. I came to
doubt the virtues of intimidation early on. I chose, perhaps uncon-
sciously, to remain a shadow—timid, but a survivor.

8   The fearsomeness mistakenly attributed to me in public places
often has a perilous flavor. The most frightening of these confu-
sions occurred in the late 1970s and early 1980s, when I worked as
a journalist in Chicago. One day, rushing into the office of a magazine I was writing for with a deadline story in hand, I was mistaken for a burglar. The office manager called security and, with
an ad hoc posse, pursued me through the labyrinthine halls,
nearly to my editor's door. I had no way of proving who I was. I
could only move briskly toward the company of someone who
knew me.

9   Another time I was on assignment for a local paper and killing
time before an interview. I entered a jewelry store on the city's affluent Near North Side. The proprietor excused herself and returned with an enormous red Doberman pinscher straining at the
end of a leash. She stood, the dog extended toward me, silent to
my questions, her eyes bulging nearly out of her head. I took a
cursory look around, nodded, and bade her good night.

10   Relatively speaking, however, I never fared as badly as another
black male journalist. He went to nearby Waukegan, Illinois, a
couple of summers ago to work on a story about a murderer who

was born there. Mistaking the reporter for the killer, police officers hauled him from his car at gunpoint and but for his press credentials would probably have tried to book him. Such episodes are not uncommon. Black men trade tales like this all the time.

11   Over the years, I learned to smother the rage I felt at so often being taken for a criminal. Not to do so would surely have led to madness. I now take precautions to make myself less threatening. I move about with care, particularly late in the evening. I give a wide berth to nervous people on subway platforms during the wee hours, particularly when I have exchanged business clothes for jeans. If I happen to be entering a building behind some people who appear skittish, I may walk by, letting them clear the lobby before I return, so as not to seem to be following them. I have been calm and extremely congenial on those rare occasions when I've been pulled over by the police.

12   And on late-evening constitutionals I employ what has proved to be an excellent tension-reducing measure: I whistle melodies from Beethoven and Vivaldi and the more popular classical composers. Even steely New Yorkers hunching toward nighttime destinations seem to relax, and occasionally they even join in the tune. Virtually everybody seems to sense that a mugger wouldn't be warbling bright, sunny selections from Vivaldi's *Four Seasons*. It is my equivalent of the cowbell that hikers wear when they know they are in bear country.

Thesis and Organizations

1. Reread paragraph 1. What expectations does it evoke in the reader? For paragraph 2, state in your own words what Staples means by "unwieldy inheritance." What effects does that inheritance have?
2. The body of the essay breaks into three paragraph blocks. In paragraphs 3–5, what effects does the author's walking at night have on others? On himself?
3. In paragraphs 6 and 7, Staples refers to his childhood. Why had he been unaware of his effect on others? What effect did the streets he grew up on have on him?
4. Staples uses examples in paragraphs 8–10. What do all three have in common? What generalization does Staples draw from them?
5. Summarize the causes and effects Staples brings out in paragraphs 11 and 12, and in one sentence, make a general statement about them. What does that statement imply about being a black male? about urban life?

about American culture? Consider your answers to those questions and in one sentence state the thesis of the essay.

Technique and Style

1. A large part of the essay's impact lies in the ironic contrast between appearance and reality. What details does Staples bring out about himself that contrast with the stereotype of the mugger?
2. In paragraph 1, Staples illustrates the two uses of the dash. What function do they perform? Rewrite either of the two sentences so that you avoid the dash. Which sentence is better and why?
3. Trace Staples's use of time. Why does he start where he does? Try placing the time period mentioned in paragraphs 6 and 7 elsewhere in the essay. What advantages does their present placement have? What is the effect of ending the essay in the present?
4. Examine Staples's choice of verbs in the second sentence of paragraph 5. Rewrite the sentence using as many forms of the verb *to be* as possible. What differences do you note?
5. Staples concludes the essay with an analogy. In what ways is it ironic? How does the irony tie into the essay's thesis?

Suggestions for Writing

Journal

1. All of us have been in a situation in which we felt threatened. Select an incident that occurred to you and describe its effect on you.
2. Think about a time when, intentionally or unintentionally, you threatened or intimidated someone. Describe either the causes or effects.

Essay

You can develop either of the journal ideas above into a full-fledged essay. Or, if you prefer, think about a situation in which you have been stereotyped and that stereotype determined your effect on others. Among the physical characteristics that can spawn a stereotype are

    age
    race
    gender
    physique
    clothing

Reform Should Make Room for Dad

Joseph Perkins

In this essay, Joseph Perkins examines the problems faced by young unmarried fathers, single-mother households, and the welfare system. Combining the three, he traces both their causes and effects on his way to proposing changes that he believes will not only provide more "stable, intact families in America's inner cities," but less poverty as well. Joseph Perkins is a columnist for the San Diego Union-Tribune, *and this piece was reprinted in the* Rocky Mountain News, *June 23, 1993. Since that time, the welfare laws have tightened considerably, but the problems Perkins identifies remain the same. Some would argue that the changes have worsened those problems.*

WHAT TO LOOK FOR   *Getting started, that first sentence or paragraph, is often the hardest part of writing an essay, particularly one on a difficult subject such as the one Perkins tackles. A brief narrative, however, not only provides human interest but can also serve as an example. That's how Perkins starts his essay.*

1   Olie Mann was only 17 years old when he got a girl pregnant. At the time, the Cleveland youth hardly fit anyone's idea of a model father. "I was in a gang," he remembers. "I sold drugs. I was very promiscuous."

2   The teen-age mother of his child was whisked away to Texas by her mother, who wanted to put as much distance as possible between her daughter and incorrigible young Olie. But Olie wanted to have his child near him.

3   He turned to the National Institute for Responsible Fatherhood and Family Development, a Cleveland-based organization that began 10 years ago as a local support program for teen fathers.

4   Since its inception, the institute has reached almost 2,000 young fathers like Olie. The program is built on expectations: That the young dads will legitimize their children by acknowledging paternity. That they'll finish school. That they'll hold down a steady job.

265

5   The caseworker assigned to Olie, who himself had been through a similar experience, encouraged the young man to clean up his act. Olie went back to school and earned his high-school equivalency degree. He dropped out of the gang. He gave up drugs.

6   Now, three years later, he is married to the mother of his child. The family lives happily in Cleveland.

7   There are hundreds of thousands of young men like Olie in inner cities throughout the country. They want to be real fathers to their children, but most are unable to take advantage of the kind of program that helped Olie get on the straight and narrow.

8   While there are myriad public and private programs that provide aid and comfort to unwed mothers, there are precious few that support unwed fathers. That's because our culture tends to view the role of fathers in family life as less important than mothers.

9   Just look at television and film, says psychologist Jane Myers Drew, author of *Where Were You When I Needed You Dad?* "There often is such a sense of Dad being the fool, or not important, or that he's sort of a throwaway, or we can get along without him."

10   Ultimately, Drew says, the marginalization of fathers is detrimental to the development of children. "Dads have so much to do with building self-esteem, setting values, encouraging a child to find his or her place in the world," she says. "Without Dad there, it leaves a real gap."

11   This "gap" is probably even more pronounced in poor families. Not only are such families deprived of a breadwinner, they also lack a positive role model who can imbue poor young men, like Olie Mann, with character and a sense of responsibility.

12   The welfare system is no help. It tilts decidedly in favor of single mothers, at the expense of poor, young fathers. In California, for example, an unmarried mom may receive $500 to $600 a month through Aid to Families with Dependent Children, another $100 in food stamps, plus free medical care. If she has a man at home, she risks losing all of this.

13   The government's subsidy of single motherhood contributes mightily to the devaluation of fatherhood in poor families. In poor homes, the government acts as surrogate for the father, providing most of the family's material support. Poor children are virtual wards of the state.

14   The perverse irony is that by supporting unmarried mothers, and thereby marginalizing fathers, the government actually perpetuates poverty. Roughly half of all poor families are headed by unmarried mothers. Such families have a staggering 650% greater probability of being poor than families with a husband and wife present.

15   Moreover, the diminished role of fathers in poor families almost certainly has contributed to the rise of the various social pathologies that afflict many inner-city communities.

16   Teen pregnancies, school dropouts, drug and alcohol abuse, juvenile delinquency all are symptomatic of the breakdown of the family. If the welfare system were reformed to encourage family cohesion—or at least to not discourage poor mothers and fathers from getting and staying married—many of these social problems would improve.

17   Alas, for all the high-sounding blather about welfare reform emanating from the Clinton administration, the proposals floated will only perpetuate the status quo.

18   The Clintons hope to break the "cycle of dependency" by getting welfare moms off the rolls and into jobs. So they plan to offer poor moms government day care and job training and transportation and other such support.

19   But what welfare mothers really need are husbands and fathers. Whereas one in three female-headed families is poor, only one in 20 married-couple families falls below the poverty line.

20   If the government provided all poor men the kind of moral and material support that Olie Mann received from the National Institute for Responsible Fathers and Family Development, there would be far more stable, intact families in America's inner cities. In the long run, there would be fewer poor, too.

Thesis and Organization

1. The essay begins with the particular, the story of Olie Mann. At what point does it turn to the general?
2. Perkins points out that few programs are designed to help unwed fathers. What reasons does he cite for that fact?
3. What are the effects of the "marginalization of fathers" and the present welfare system?

4. What reforms does Perkins call for? What are their predicted effects?
5. Consider the problems Perkins addresses, the causes he cites, the reforms he proposes, and the effects he predicts. What is the essay's thesis?

Technique and Style

1. How does the story of Olie Mann relate to Perkins's thesis?
2. The paragraphing in the essay is typical of a newspaper format, one that calls for short paragraphs that can be read quickly. If you were to reformat the essay according to the paragraphing typical of books or magazines, what paragraphs would you combine and why?
3. Drew, the expert cited in paragraph 9, points her finger at television and film for their portrayal of fathers. In your experience, do you find her accusation accurate?
4. What is the irony in paragraph 14?
5. A glance at the vocabulary Perkins uses shows it to be formal. Choose a paragraph that uses formal diction and change it to a more conversational level. What is gained? Lost?

Suggestions for Writing

Journal

1. Perkins quotes a psychologist who maintains that the image of the father portrayed on television and in film is one in which "There often is such a sense of Dad being the fool, or not important, or that he's sort of a throwaway, or we can get along without him." Evaluate this statement in terms of your own experience.
2. The example of Olie Mann is certainly a success story. Yet Perkins glosses over the struggle Mann went through to achieve a happy life (paragraph 5). Explore whether the essay is weaker or stronger for not depicting Mann's struggle.

Essay

Make a list of problems and then pick the one you find most interesting. Think about it and jot down possible causes and possible effects. Select either cause or effect and write an essay explaining that part of the problem. If you want to write an essay closer to Perkins's, then consider other problems and the agencies designed to deal with them:

career choice and your institution's counseling service
crime and neighborhood watch groups

dieting and Weight Watchers
problem children and Tough Love
the homeless and the Salvation Army
alcoholism and Alcoholics Anonymous

The odds are that any research you have to do will be easy; these groups and others like them usually publish material that will provide you with the necessary facts and information, though you will need to evaluate that information for bias.

Argument

*U*p to this point, this book has focused on patterns of organization that can be used singly and in combination for various aims—to express how you feel, to explain, and, to a lesser extent, to argue. Those modes or patterns are the means to an end, ways to achieve your goal of self-expression, exposition, or argument. This chapter directly addresses the goal of argument, but because book after book has been written on the art of argument, think of what you have here as a basic introduction. In this chapter you will discover how to construct a short argumentative essay and how the various modes are used to support that aim. It's only appropriate, therefore, that the discussion start with a definition.

In everyday speech, ***argument*** is so closely associated with *quarrel* or *fight* that it has a negative connotation, but that connotation does not apply to the word as it is used in the writing of essays. If you were to analyze an essay by examining its argument, you would be looking at the writer's major assertion and the weight of the evidence on which it rests. That evidence must be compelling, for the aim of all argumentative writing is to move the reader to adopt the writer's view. In writing argumentative papers, you might want to go further than that and call for a particular action, but most of the time you'll probably work at convincing your reader to at least keep reading and at best share your position on the issue. Many of the subjects of argumentative essays are ones your readers already have an opinion about, so if all you accomplish is having someone who disagrees with your thesis keep reading, you have constructed a successful argument.

Because an argumentative essay bases its thesis primarily on reason, the word *logic* may pop into your mind and raise images of mathematical models and seemingly tricky statements stringing together sentences beginning with *if*s and leading to one starting with *therefore*. Don't worry. The kind of argumentative essays you will be asked to write are simply an extension of the kinds of essays you've written all along: your thesis is the heart of your argument, and examples, definitions, descriptions and the like provide your supporting evidence.

It's useful to distinguish between self-expression and argument. Open your local newspaper to the editorial pages, and you'll probably find examples of both. If you found a letter to the editor that rants about the "sins" of the Democratic Party and describes the "sinners" as "dishonest, lying, cheats," it's unlikely that the letter will be read all the way through by a Democrat. The writer was letting off steam rather than trying to argue a point, and the steam was based on emotion, not reason. But if there's an editorial on the same page on the same general subject, you'll find it uses reason to support its point as it argues in favor of specific reforms in the laws governing campaign contributions. Such an editorial may well state that although the media's focus highlights abuses within the Democratic party, the Republicans are not altogether innocent. Both Democrats and Republicans are apt to read the editorial all the way through, and many from both parties may come to agree with the editor's thesis.

Slipping from argument into self-expression, relying on emotion instead of reason, is easy to do, particularly if you're writing about a subject you feel strongly about. One way to avoid that trap is to start work on your topic by brainstorming on the subject as a whole, not your position on it. Phrase the subject as a question and then list the pros and cons. If you are writing on gambling, for instance, you would ask, "Should gambling be legalized?" Then you would define your terms: Who would be legalizing it—the federal government, the state, the county, the city? What kind of gambling is involved—betting on horse races, on sports? playing games such as bingo, video poker, slot machines, roulette? buying tickets for a lottery? Answering those kinds of questions will help you to draw up your pros and cons more easily because your focus will be more specific. Once you've listed the arguments that can be used, you can then sort through them, noting the evidence you can cite and where to find it. Having done all that, you then are in a position to choose which side you wish to take, and you know the arguments that can be used against you.

The next step is to think about the ways in which you can appeal to your readers. Citing facts and precedents will appeal to their reason;

exploring moral issues will appeal to their emotions; and presenting a persona that is thoughtful and therefore credible will appeal to their sense of fairness.

Reason is the primary appeal in most argumentative writing, and to use it successfully, you may need to do some research on your subject (each of these appeals—reason, emotion, and persona—is discussed in greater detail following this overview). Once your argument begins to take shape, however, you will find that dealing with one or two of the opposing views will not only strengthen your own case but will also earn you some points for fairness.

Argumentative writing ranges from the personal to the abstract and draws on the various patterns that can be used to structure an essay. For instance, waiting tables in a restaurant may have convinced you that tips should be automatically included in the bill. To make the case that the present system is unfair to those in a service trade, you might draw primarily on your own experience and that of others, though you need to make sure that your experience is representative. If you don't, your reader may discount your argument, thinking that one example isn't sufficient evidence. A quick check among others who are similarly employed or a look at government reports on employment statistics should show that your example is typical and therefore to be trusted.

The technical term for an entire argument based on only one example is **hasty generalization,** one of many logical fallacies that can occur in argumentative writing. **Logical fallacies** are holes or lapses in reasoning and therefore to be avoided. If you were to argue that the reader should consider only the present system of tipping or the one you propose, you will be guilty of **either-or reasoning**, which is false because it permits no middle ground such as requiring a minimum tip of five percent. Quote Darryl Strawberry on the subject and you will be citing **false authority**; he knows baseball but not the restaurant industry. And obviously, if you call a ten-percent tipper a cheap idiot, you will be accused quite rightly of name-calling, the **ad hominem** (to the person) fallacy.

Say you noticed one evening that as closing time loomed, your tips got smaller. Is that because people who dine late tip minimally or because your customers felt rushed or because someone miscalculated the tip or some unknown reason? If you conclude that people who dine late are poor tippers, you may well be mistaking a temporal relationship for a causal one. Two events may occur at times close to each other (small tip, late hour) without implying a valid cause and effect relationship. To confuse the two is called **post hoc reasoning**.

Often the best topic for an argumentative essay is the one you come up with on your own, but at times you may be assigned a topic. If that happens, you may find your chances for success increase if you shape the topic so that you have a direct connection to it. Because you already know something about the subject, you have done some thinking about it instead of having to start from scratch or to use second-hand opinions. Even abstract topics such as euthanasia can be made concrete and will probably be the better for it. Though you may have never been confronted directly by the issue of mercy killing, you probably have had a member of your family who was terminally ill. Would euthanasia have been an appropriate alternative? Should it have been? In addition to using your own experience, consider using your local newspaper as a resource. Newspaper accounts and editorials can also help give form and focus to an abstract issue, and in addition to the book and periodical sources you may consult, they will help you delineate your topic more clearly.

AUDIENCE AND PURPOSE   Audience plays a greater role in argument than in any other type of writing, and therein lies a problem: you must adapt both form and content to fit your audience, while at the same time maintaining your integrity. If you shape your argumentative position according to its probable acceptance by your readers rather than your own belief, the result is propaganda or sensationalism, not argument. Knowingly playing false with an audience by omitting evidence or shaping facts to fit an assertion or by resorting to logical fallacies are all dishonest tricks. For example, imagine that you are on the staff of your campus newspaper and have been given the assignment of investigating the rumors that the Dean of the College of Business is going to resign. You know that the dean has been fighting with the president of your university, arguing that the College of Business is "grossly underfunded," a phrase you found in an earlier story on university finances. But you also read an interview with the dean and know that she has close ties to the local business community and may be offered a job heading a local company. Add to that your suspicion that not many colleges of business have deans who are women, a suspicion borne out by statistics you can quote, and you begin to scent a story. If you choose to write one that plays up the conflict with the president and implies sexism while ignoring the possibility of the dean's being hired away from the university, you are not being true to your evidence and are therefore misleading your readers.

Within honest bounds, however, you have much to draw on, and a sense of what your audience may or may not know and of what the audience believes about a topic can guide you. Even if your topic is familiar, what you have to say about it will be new information. Censorship is a tired subject, but if you were to write on the banning of a particular book from a particular public school library, you would probably give the topic a new twist or two. A concrete example, often in the form of a short introductory narrative, makes an abstract issue more accessible and is apt to keep your reader reading.

If your subject is one many readers know little about, then you can begin by explaining the issue and its context. If your classmates are your readers, for example, they will know little about your personal life. And if you have an aunt whose health insurance was cancelled after her cancer returned, the action may compel you to research an insurance company's right to drop those it insures. Put your indignation together with what you discovered through your research and what your classmates don't know, and you have all the makings of a successful argumentative paper protesting what you see as an injustice.

Whether you start with what your audience does or does not know or with a narrative that illustrates the general situation and makes it concrete, your aim is to convince your readers to adopt your convictions, perhaps even to act on them. Not all readers will be convinced, of course, but if they at least respond, "Hmm, I hadn't thought of that" or "Well, I may have to rethink my position," you will have presented an effective argument.

ARGUMENTATIVE APPEALS   When you write an argumentative essay, you will find that you are appealing to the reader's emotions and reason by creating a credible persona, the ethical appeal. Reason, however, is the most important. To present a logical pattern of thought, you will probably find yourself drawing on one or more modes, particularly definition, comparison, and cause and effect. If, for instance, you have a part-time job at a fast-food franchise, you may have noticed that most of the other employees are also part-time. The situation may strike you as exploitive and you want to write about it.

You might start sketching out a first draft with the example of your job, then define what part-time means, using cause and effect to argue that franchise companies that depend primarily on part-time labor exploit their workers to create greater profits for the company. As you work, you will find that you are laying out a line of reasoning, the assertions—probably the topic sentences for paragraphs or paragraph clusters—that support your thesis. You will also have to do some research so that you place your example in a larger context, showing that it is clearly typical. Then, armed with some facts and figures, you can test each of your supporting sentences by first asking "Am I making an assertion?" If the answer is yes, then you can test your line of reasoning and hence your appeal to reason by asking "Is it supported by evidence?" and "Is the evidence sufficient?"

Logical thinking must undergird all argumentative essays, even those that stress an emotional appeal, an appeal that often rests on example, description, and narration. In the example of the essay about health insurers, you would be using an emotional appeal if you began your essay with a brief narrative of your aunt's battle with cancer and the crisis caused by her loss of health insurance. And although the bulk of the essay would be taken up with the essay's appeal to reason, you might choose to close with an emotional appeal, perhaps reminding your readers of the number of people who cannot afford any kind of medical insurance and calling for a general reform of health care.

But the emotional appeal has its dangers, particularly when you are close to the subject. You would not want your description of your aunt's problems to slide into the melodramatic, nor would you want create so powerful an impression that anything that comes after, which is the heart of your argument, is anticlimactic. Emotional appeals are often best left to snagging the reader's attention or calling for action, relatively small roles, than serving a primary function in the essay. Emotion will have an impact, but reason will carry the argument.

The appeal of **persona,** known in classical rhetoric as *ethos* (which translates somewhat ambiguously as "the ethical appeal"), is more subtle than the others; the writer is not appealing directly to the reader's emotions or intellect but instead is using his or her persona to lend credence to the essay's major assertion. The point gets tricky. A fair and honest writer is one who is fair and honest with the reader. Such a writer takes on a persona, not like donning a mask to hide behind but like selecting a picture to show those elements in the personality that represent the writer at his or her best.

For a good example of how persona functions, think of the last time you took an essay test. What you were writing was a mini-argument maintaining that your answer to the question is a correct one. Your persona, which you probably didn't even think about, was intended to create a sense of authority, the idea that you knew what you were writing about. You are so used to writing within an academic context, that the elements of your persona come naturally. The tone you use for essay tests is more formal than informal, which means that your choice of words, your diction, is more elevated than conversational. And if a technical vocabulary is appropriate—the vocabulary of physics, sociology, the arts, and the like—you use it. Successful essay answers also use evidence and are tightly organized so that the line of thought is clear and compelling, all of which comes under the appeal of reason, but don't underestimate the appeal of persona. If two test answers contain the exact same information, the one that is written in the more sophisticated style that implies a more thoughtful response will receive the higher grade.

LOGICAL FALLACIES   Logical fallacies abuse the various appeals. The introduction to this chapter has already pointed out the more obvious ones—hasty generalization, false authority, name-calling, post hoc and either-or reasoning—but there are many others as well. Advertising and political campaigns are often crammed with them. If you receive a flyer asking you to vote for a candidate for the school board because he is a Vietnam veteran who has a successful law practice, the logic doesn't follow, a literal translation of the Latin term **non sequitur**: the claim leaves you wondering what being a veteran and an attorney have to do with the duties of a member of the school board. And if the flyer goes on to maintain that because the candidate has three children he can understand the problems of students in the public schools when you know that his three children go to private schools, then you've spotted a **false analogy**, a double one—public and private schools are quite different, and three children from the family of a professional are not representative of the public school student population.

Such a flyer is also guilty of **begging the question**, another fallacy. The main question for a school board election is "Can this person make a positive contribution?" Being a Vietnam veteran and the father of three children doesn't answer that question. A **shift in definition** is another form of begging the question. If this hypothetical candidate also claims to be a "good citizen" and then goes on to define that term by example, citing service to his country and fatherhood as proof, then as a voter, you're left with a very narrow definition. Good citizenship involves much more.

Often when you read or hear about the holes in an argument, you may also hear the term **straw man**. With this technique (yet another form of begging the question), your attention is drawn away from the main point, and instead the argument focuses on a minor point with the hope that by demolishing it, the main one will also suffer. Imagine that there's a move to increase local taxes, and you want to argue against it in a letter to the local paper. As you consider the points you can make, you come up with a short list: that the taxes are already high, that existing funds are not being spent wisely, and that all that the taxes support—schools, roads, government and the like—while not outstanding are adequate. You start to gather information to use as evidence for each of these points (probably discovering several more) and run across a news story about a large amount of local taxpayers' money having been spent on rebuilding a bridge on a back road that averaged all of three cars a day. If you were to stop there and construct a thesis arguing taxes should not be raised because of waste in government, then making your case by basing it on the example of the building of the bridge, you would be constructing a straw man argument, one that avoids the major issues.

THESIS AND ORGANIZATION   The thesis of an argumentative essay should be readily identifiable: it is the conviction that you want an audience to adopt. Sometimes the thesis may be stated in the title, but more often you will state your position early on, then back it up with evidence in the body of your essay. If you organize your ideas by moving from the general (the thesis) to the particular (the evidence), you are using **deductive reasoning**. Most of the argumentative essays you run across will be using this kind of logical organization. As for the order in which you choose to present the evidence on which your thesis rests, you'll probably arrange it from the least important to the most important so that the essay has some dramatic tension. Putting the most important first doesn't leave you anywhere to go, rather like knowing from the start that the butler did it.

Along those same lines, you usually don't want to put your thesis as your first sentence; instead, lead up to it, *introduce* it in the literal sense. Starting right off with the thesis will probably strike the reader as too abrupt, too sudden. Often an argumentative essay will begin with a narrative or some explanation, ways of setting the scene so that when the thesis appears, it seems natural. As for the ending, you may want to return to the same narrative or information you started with or call for action or point out what may happen unless your view is adopted. Remember, by the time your reader finishes reading what you have to say, if all you have done is make the person reconsider ideas and re-think the argument, you will have succeeded. It's rare, though not impossible, for one essay to change a person's mind.

Now and then, you'll find yourself reading an argument that is organized by moving from the particular to the general, from evidence to thesis. What you have then is called **inductive reasoning**, and it's usually more difficult to write because it demands tight focus and control. Think of the essay's organization as a jigsaw puzzle. Your reader has to recognize each piece as a piece, and you have to build the evidence so that each piece falls into a predetermined place. The completed picture is the thesis. If you want to construct an essay using inductive reasoning, you may find it easier to do if in your first draft you state your thesis at the beginning, baldly, just so you stay on track. Then, when you've shaped the rest of the paper, you simply move the thesis from the beginning to the last paragraph, perhaps even the last sentence.

You'll find that the essays in this section represent both kinds of organization, so you'll have a chance to see how others have developed their ideas to argue a particular point.

USEFUL TERMS

Ad hominem argument   Name-calling, smearing the person instead of attacking the argument. A type of logical fallacy. Smearing the group the person belongs to instead of attacking the argument is called an *ad populum* logical fallacy.

Appeal to emotion   Playing or appealing to the reader's emotions.

Appeal to persona   The appeal of the writer's moral character that creates the impression that the writer can be trusted and therefore believed.

Appeal to reason   Presenting evidence that is logical, well thought out, so as to be believed.

Argument   The writer's major assertion and the evidence on which it is based.

Begging the question   Arguing off the point, changing direction. A type of logical fallacy.

Deductive reasoning   Reasoning that moves from the general to the particular, from the thesis to the evidence.

Either-or reasoning   Staking out two extremes as the only alternatives and therefore excluding anything in between. A type of logical fallacy.

False analogy   An analogy that does not stand up to logic. A type of logical fallacy.

False authority   Citing an expert on one subject as an expert on another. A type of logical fallacy.

Hasty generalization   Reasoning based on insufficient evidence, usually too few examples. A type of logical fallacy.

Inductive reasoning   Reasoning that moves from the particular to the general, from the evidence to the thesis.

Logical fallacy   An error in reasoning, a logical flaw that invalidates the argument.

Non sequitur   Literally, it does not follow. No apparent link between points. A type of logical fallacy.

Persona   The character of the writer that comes through from the prose.

Post hoc reasoning   Assuming a causal relationship where a temporal one exists. A type of logical fallacy.

Shifting definition   Changing the definition of a key term, a form of begging the question. A type of logical fallacy.

Straw man   Attacking and destroying an irrelevant point instead of the main subject.

▧ POINTERS FOR USING ARGUMENT

Exploring the Topic

1. **What position do you want to take toward your subject?** Are you arguing to get your audience to adopt your thesis or to go further and take action? What is your thesis? What action is possible?

2. **How is your audience apt to respond to your assertion if you state it baldly?** How much background do you need to provide? Do you need to use definition? What arguments can the reader bring against your assertion?

3. **What examples can you think of to illustrate your topic?** Are all of them from your own experience? What other sources can you draw on?

4. **How can you appeal to your readers' emotions?** How can you use example, description, and narration to carry your emotional appeal?
5. **How can you appeal to your readers' reason?** How can you use example, cause and effect, process, comparison and contrast, analogy, or division and classification to strengthen your logic?
6. **What tone is most appropriate to the kind of appeal you want to emphasize?** Does your persona fit that tone? How can you use persona to support your argument?

Drafting the Paper

1. **Know your reader.** Estimate how familiar your reader is with your topic and how, if at all, the reader may react to it emotionally. Keeping those ideas in mind, review how the various patterns of development may help you contend with your audience's knowledge and attitudes, and decide whether your primary appeal should be to emotion or reason. Description, narration, and example lend themselves particularly well to emotional appeal; process, cause and effect, comparison and contrast, analogy, example, and division and classification are useful for rational appeal. Use definition to set the boundaries of your argument and its terms as well as to clear up anything the reader may not know.
2. **Know your purpose.** Depending on the predominant appeal you find most appropriate, your essay will tend toward persuasion or argument; you are trying to get your reader not only to understand your major assertion, but also to adopt it and perhaps even to act on it. Short of that, a successful writer of argument must settle for the reader's "Well, I hadn't thought of it that way" or "Maybe I should reconsider." The greatest danger in argumentative writing is to write to people like yourself, ones who already agree with you. You need not think of your audience as actively hostile, but to stay on the argumentative track, it helps to reread constantly as you write, playing the devil's advocate.
3. **Acknowledge the opposition.** Even though your reader may be the ideal—someone who holds no definite opposing view and indeed is favorably inclined toward yours but hasn't really thought the topic through—you should bring out one or two of the strongest arguments against your position and demolish them. If you don't, the reader may, and there goes your essay. The ideal reader is also the thinking reader who says, "Yes, but . . . ."
4. **Avoid logical pitfalls.** Logical fallacies can crop up in unexpected places; one useful way to test them is to check your patterns of development. If you have used examples, does your generalization or assertion follow? Sometimes the examples are too few to support the assertion, leading to a hasty generalization; sometimes the examples don't fit,

leading to begging the question or arguing off the point or misusing authority; and sometimes the assertion is stated as an absolute, in which case the reader may think of an example that is the exception, destroying your point. If you have used analogy, double-check to see that the analogy can stand up to scrutiny by examining the pertinent aspects of the things compared. If you have used cause and effect, you need to be particularly careful. Check to see that the events you claim to have a causal relationship do not have a temporal one instead; otherwise, you fall into the post hoc fallacy. Also examine causal relationships to make sure that you have not merely assumed the cause in your statement of effect. If you claim that "poor teaching is a major cause of the high dropout rate during the freshman year in college," you must prove that the teaching is poor; if you don't, you are arguing in a circle or begging the question. Non sequiturs can also obscure cause-and-effect relationships when an element in the relationship is missing or nonexistent. Definition also sets some traps. Make sure your definition is not only fully stated but also commonly shared and consistent throughout.

5. **Be aware of your persona.** The ethical appeal, the rational appeal, and the emotional appeal are fundamental concepts of argument, and it is the persona, together with tone, that provides the ethical appeal. To put it simply, you need to be credible. If you are writing on an issue you feel strongly about and, for example, are depending primarily on an appeal to reason, you don't want to let your dispassionate, logical persona slip and resort to name-calling (formally known as arguing ad hominem or ad populem). That's obvious. Not so obvious, however, is some slip in diction or tone that reveals the hot head behind the cool pen. Your reader may feel manipulated or use the slip to discount your entire argument, all because you lost sight of the ethical appeal. Tone should vary, yes, but never to the point of discord.

6. **Place your point where it does the most good.** Put each of your paragraphs on a separate piece of paper so that you can rearrange their order as you would a hand of cards. Try out your major assertion in different slots. If you have it at the beginning, try it at the end and vice versa. Or extend the introduction so that the thesis comes closer to the middle of the paper. See which placement carries greater impact. You may want to organize your material starting with examples that lead up to the position you wish to attack and to the conviction you are arguing for; in that case your thesis may occur somewhere in the middle third or at the end of the paper. On the other hand, you may want to use deduction—starting with the opposition, stating your position, and then spending ninety percent of the remaining essay supporting your case. Remember that you want to win your reader over, so put your thesis where it will do the greatest good.

O ld-Fashioned Housing for Simcity

Amber Kucera

If you've had any experience with computer games, you're probably familiar with Simcity, a game that lets you play the various roles involved in the planning and running of a modern municipality. A similar idea undergirds the assignment for the essay that follows. Jill Feldkamp, who teaches English at Wartburg College in Waverly, Iowa, asked her students "to read and interpret the background concerning a contemporary land use debate" and then to write a proposal that argues for a specific kind of development. The intended audience was the Zoning Commission, and using the MLA system of documentation, students were encouraged to rely on both logical and emotional appeals and to assume a persona that fit the proposal and audience. As you will discover, that persona is a long way from the real Amber Kucera, who wrote the essay and who is a biology major at Wartburg. Raised on a small farm in Iowa, Kucera based her argument "on similar problems that developed in [her] hometown." Although she had a hard time deciding which side to take, she "enjoyed the debate [the] class held concerning the Simcity controversy," finding that it "made the paper a worthwhile experience." Like Kucera, you will find that debate and discussion help clarify ideas and increase motivation.

WHAT TO LOOK FOR   *While all your other papers also involved persona, argumentative ones call for particular and careful attention to the way you present yourself as writer to your readers. You need to convince your audience that you are credible, a fair person presenting a fair position. In this argument, Kucera assumes the persona of a developer, the head of a business that builds entire residential communities, not just a house or two. As you read the paper, note the various ways Kucera creates a persona, not just by what is said but also by how it is said.*

1   The controversy concerning the four hundred plus acres of land willed to Simcity has formed a complex debate. Much discussion has arisen concerning three different sides, all of which seem to support worthwhile views. By zoning the land commercial,

needed businesses would be promoted. Another possible zoning assignment could be environmental. Just allowing the land to run wild would preserve the land for years to come. Although these are relevant possibilities, both seem to concentrate on only one concern. I feel that by zoning the land residential, all points of importance can be covered. The benefits acquired as a result of residential zoning would greatly help the town expand publicly and financially.

2   My private corporation, called Old-Fashioned Design, which was started in 1989, is interested in purchasing the willed land from Simcity. Old-Fashioned Design can devise a fitting residential district for the town. Simcity would make a substantial amount of money with the sale of four hundred plus acres of land. With the money made from selling the land, an addition to the hospital could be made or new equipment could be purchased to keep it up to date. Simcity definitely needs to make sure the current hospital doesn't close its doors. When an accident occurs, driving sixty miles to the nearest hospital should not be the only possibility. The money acquired from the sale of the acreage could definitely help maintain satisfaction with health care in Simcity.

3   The land, willed by Alexandra Sim, the great great granddaughter of the founder, should be turned into an intentional old-fashioned housing development. It would consist of Victorian style houses, looking like those from the 1900s. The easiest picture to formulate is a narrow street consisting of two-story homes surrounded by big yards and white picket fences. A picture such as this is far from the scene occurring in large metropolitan cities. There the streets are so wide and busy that children can't even cross alone. The houses are all identical in style and located very close together. In the new development, additions such as pitched roofs, dormers, shutters, front porches, and bay windows will bring a touch of charm to the neighborhoods. This style of architecture has recently been named "the traditional family values neighborhood," and *People* magazine has termed the development as a "new American way of life" (Rybczynski 14). These "traditional" design homes are one of the hottest new ideas on the market since the condominium.

4   Each Victorian home would be surrounded by a lush, green lawn and a multitude of trees and bushes. The houses would be situated on straight, narrow streets, and nestled between approximately every twenty homes would be a park. This park would

consist of a small playground for children to enjoy, benches and paths for taking leisurely walks, and plenty of flowers, bushes, and trees for beauty.

5   This development is designed for commuters working in nearby towns and the larger metropolitan city. The price range was created for middle- to upper-class lifestyles, but if a less-expensive model is desired, the plans can be reduced. The finished product will be both desirable and valuable on the financial market. It will be particularly inviting for expanding families who are looking for affordability as well as a wholesome upbringing for their children.

6   These old-fashioned homes are also designed to attract families that believe urban life is having a unfavorable impression on their children. Today the level of crime is extremely high in urban cities. With parents working so much, children who used to go to the playground or sitter after school are now causing trouble in their neighborhoods. The educational level of the urban schools has also declined due to the high numbers of registered students. In schools such as these, children who need extra help are not always receiving it, and parents are getting upset with the system. Parents who earlier felt that big-city schooling was the way to go are now finding out that smaller schools and smaller neighborhoods are better options. The buyers of the housing development would probably want their children to go to the smaller school in Simcity because of the rise in violence and trouble in larger schools. The growing concern for children's needs has sent the desire for traditional neighborhood developments to the top of the market. By living in the new "old-fashioned" development, parents would be giving their children a quieter, safer environment to grow up in.

7   The plans for developing the land also include restoring the one hundred-year-old Sim mansion. Using creative zoning techniques, a team of workers with Old-Fashioned Design have considered many possible ideas. They have found a land use amendment that was recently passed in Delaware, and they believe it could possibly be passed in Simcity. This amendment would allow properties to be used as commercial space, while retaining residential zoning. Under the Delaware amendment, properties must have dwellings of at least five thousand square feet, be at least fifty years old, and have historical or architectural significance. The grounds must be at least ten acres, sixty percent of which must be open space (Milford 24). This type of creative zoning is needed, in this case, because Alexandra Sim wanted the entire sum of land to be zoned

the same way. The Sim mansion fits all of the requirements, so it could be used commercially. If the amendment passed, it could be used as a museum/bed and breakfast. The museum could outline the history of the Sim family and the growth of Simcity. This would benefit the community by bringing in tourism and providing possible jobs, while preserving the historical mansion, as closely as possible, to the original.

8   Once the land is sold to my company, Simcity can concentrate its attention on bringing in needed businesses. I feel that by having this new housing development, many more people will be attracted to the town. It is the belief of Old-Fashioned Design that for a sound business strategy to exist, an understanding of the community's needs and objectives must also develop (Milford). The current businesses need to concentrate on keeping their customers, and the city council needs to concentrate on bringing in needed businesses. With additional people joining your community and working in your businesses, it is a firm opinion of Old-Fashioned Design that the current companies will flourish and more businesses will come into town.

9   The controversy over the willed land can be solved if it is purchased by Old-Fashioned Design. This will bring much into the Simcity community. Not only will the town be better off financially, but also more people from the metropolitan area will join the community. These new residents will choose Simcity because of the new housing district and flourishing hospital, which are all a result of selling the land. The growth of business in the town will expand, making your city an important part of continuing the American way of life.

WORKS CITED

Braccidiferro, Gail. "Year-Rounders for a Resort." *New York Times* 4 July 1993: R9.

Milford, Maureen. "Creative Zoning for Delaware's 'Chateau Country'." *New York Times* 26 Mar 1995, sec. R6: 24–25.

Rybczynski, Witold. "This Old House." *New Republic* 8 May 1995, sec. 19: 14–16.

Thesis and Organization

1. Paragraph 1 serves as an introduction. Reread it and note exactly what the introduction contains.
2. What paragraph or paragraphs use cause and effect? How? Given the argument, what does this mode add?

3. Where in the paper do you find comparison and contrast? How does it bolster the writer's position?

4. Paragraph 4 uses description. How does that description fit the writer's purpose? How persuasive is the description?

5. How would you describe the function of paragraph 9, the conclusion? What other alternatives can you think of for a conclusion?

Technique and Style

1. The paper uses all three kinds of appeals—reason, emotion, and persona. Which one dominates? What evidence can you find to support your answer?

2. Where in the essay do you find an emotional appeal? How effective is it?

3. How would you characterize the persona Kucera assumes? How is it created?

4. How would you evaluate the success of the persona? Is it believable? Why or why not?

5. Analyze the argument in terms of its effectiveness. Would you be persuaded? Why or why not?

Suggestions for Writing

Journal

1. A formal proposal would need much more in the way of facts and figures, but if you were on the Zoning Commission, would you vote for or against the concept behind this proposal?

2. Setting up a realistic concept for an assignment can be interesting. Outline an assignment similar to the one here, specifying an audience and an immediate context.

Essay

Place yourself in a specific role and write an argument in response to the proposal. Make up your own persona and feel free to invent information and sources (though they have to be believable). Suggestions:

> a developer of a business park
> a spokesperson for an environmental group
> a developer of a theme park
> the head of a nearby and physically cramped community college
> the staff member of the Zoning Commission charged with evaluating
> > the proposal

*L*ast Rites for Indian Dead

Suzan Shown Harjo

Writing as a Cheyenne, Suzan Shown Harjo points to a problem that affects Native Americans and, she argues, that raises an ethical issue for the rest of us. Her essay, which appeared on the editorial page of the Los Angeles Times *in September of 1989, is a good example of deductive reasoning.*

> ***WHAT TO LOOK FOR***   *Conclusions are often difficult to write, but one way of ending an argumentative essay is to call for a specified action. That is what Harjo does for her essay, and it's a technique you can adapt for your own arguments.*

1   What if museums, universities, and government agencies could put your dead relatives on display or keep them in boxes to be cut up and otherwise studied? What if you believed that the spirits of the dead could not rest until their human remains were placed in a sacred area?

2   The ordinary American would say there ought to be a law—and there is, for ordinary Americans. The problem for American Indians is that there are too many laws of the kind that make us the archaeological property of the United States and too few of the kind that protect us from such insults.

3   Some of my own Cheyenne relatives' skulls are in the Smithsonian Institution today, along with those of at least 4500 other Indian people who were violated in the 1800s by the U.S. Army for an "Indian Cranial Study." It wasn't enough that these unarmed Cheyenne people were mowed down by the cavalry at the infamous Sand Creek massacre; many were decapitated and their heads shipped to Washington as freight. (The Army Medical Museum's collection is now in the Smithsonian.) Some had been exhumed only hours after being buried. Imagine their grieving families' reaction on finding their loved ones disinterred and headless.

4   Some targets of the Army's study were killed in noncombat situations and beheaded immediately. The officer's account of the decapitation of the Apache chief Mangas Coloradas in 1863 shows the pseudoscientific nature of the exercise. "I weighed the brain

and measured the skull," the good doctor wrote, "and found that while the skull was smaller, the brain was larger than that of Daniel Webster."

5   These journal accounts exist in excruciating detail, yet missing are any records of overall comparisons, conclusions or final reports of the Army study. Since it is unlike the Army not to leave a paper trail, one must wonder about the motive for its collection.

6   The total Indian body count in the Smithsonian collection is more than 19,000, and it is not the largest in the country. It is not inconceivable that the 1.5 million of us living today are outnumbered by our dead stored in museums, educational institutions, federal agencies, state historical societies and private collections. The Indian people are further dehumanized by being exhibited alongside the mastodons and dinosaurs and other extinct creatures.

7   Where we have buried our dead in peace, more often than not the sites have been desecrated. For more than 200 years, relic hunting has been a popular pursuit. Lately, the market in Indian artifacts has brought this abhorrent activity to a fever pitch in some areas. And when scavengers come upon Indian burial sites, everything found becomes fair game, including sacred burial offerings, teeth and skeletal remains.

8   One unusually well-publicized example of Indian grave desecration occurred two years ago in a western Kentucky field known as Slack Farm, the site of an Indian village five centuries ago. Ten men—one with a business card stating "Have Shovel, Will Travel"—paid the landowner $10,000 to lease digging rights between planting seasons. They dug extensively on the 40-acre farm, rummaging through an estimated 650 graves, collecting burial goods, tools and ceremonial items. Skeletons were strewn about like litter.

9   What motivates people to do something like this? Financial gain is the first answer. Indian relic-collecting has become a multimillion-dollar industry. The price tag on a bead necklace can easily top $1000; rare pieces fetch tens of thousands.

10   And it is not just collectors of the macabre who pay for skeletal remains. Scientists say that these deceased Indians are needed for research that someday could benefit the health and welfare of living Indians. But just how many dead Indians must they examine? Nineteen thousand?

11   There is doubt as to whether permanent curation of our dead really benefits Indians. Dr. Emery A. Johnson, former assistant surgeon general, recently observed, "I am not aware of any current medical diagnostic or treatment procedure that has been derived from research on such skeletal remains. Nor am I aware of any during the 34 years that I have been involved in American Indian . . . health care."

12   Indian remains are still being collected for racial biological studies. While the intentions may be honorable, the ethics of using human remains this way without the full consent of relatives must be questioned.

13   Some relief for Indian people has come on the state level. Almost half of the states, including California, have passed laws protecting Indian burial sites and restricting the sale of Indian bones, burial offerings and other sacred items. Representative Charles E. Bennett (D-Fla.) and Sen. John McCain (R-Ariz.) have introduced bills that are a good start in invoking the federal government's protection. However, no legislation has attacked the problem head-on by imposing stiff penalties at the marketplace, or by changing laws that make dead Indians the nation's property.

14   Some universities—notably Stanford, Nebraska, Minnesota and Seattle—have returned, or agreed to return, Indian human remains; it is fitting that institutions of higher education should lead the way.

15   Congress is now deciding what to do with the government's extensive collection of Indian human remains and associated funerary objects. The secretary of the Smithsonian, Robert McC. Adams, has been valiantly attempting to apply modern ethics to yesterday's excesses. This week, he announced that the Smithsonian would conduct an inventory and return all Indian skeletal remains that could be identified with specific tribes or living kin.

16   But there remains a reluctance generally among collectors of Indian remains to take action of a scope that would have a quantitative impact and a healing quality. If they will not act on their own— and it is highly unlikely that they will—then Congress must act.

17   The country must recognize that the bodies of dead American Indian people are not artifacts to be bought and sold as collectors' items. It is not appropriate to store tens of thousands of our ancestors for possible future research. They are our family. They deserve to be returned to their sacred burial grounds and given a chance to rest.

18   The plunder of our people's graves has gone on too long. Let us rebury our dead and remove this shameful past from America's future.

Thesis and Organization

1. Paragraphs 1 and 2 introduce the essay by presenting a "what if" situation. Why might Harjo have chosen this kind of opening?
2. Summarize the examples Harjo presents in paragraphs 3–8.
3. Paragraphs 9–12 explain why people dig up Indian burial sites. What reasons does Harjo give?
4. Harjo explains what is being done and what needs to be done about the situation in paragraphs 13–18. What solution does she call for?
5. Considering the situation Harjo describes, the steps that are being taken to address that situation, and what remains to be done, what is the thesis of the essay?

Technique and Style

1. Describe the audience the essay is aimed at as precisely as you can. What evidence do you base your description on?
2. How would you characterize the diction Harjo uses in connection with her examples? Choose one or two examples and substitute more or less loaded words. What is gained? Lost?
3. Based on the way the essay is written, what kind of person does Harjo appear to be? How would you describe her?
4. To what extent does the essay rest its appeal on Harjo's persona? on emotion? on logic? Which appeal predominates?
5. The essay concludes with a call for action. Evaluate its effectiveness.

Suggestions for Writing

Journal

1. Imagine that you are on the board of a museum that owns Indian skeletons. Explain your response to Harjo's essay.
2. Explain whether you would like to meet Harjo.

Essay

Think of an action that was considered acceptable in the past but today is either questionable or unacceptable. Fifty years ago, for instance, no one thought much about the hazards of smoking, nor of cholesterol levels, nor of needing to inspect meat. Segregation was acceptable, as were other forms of racism. Choose a subject and think about the ethics involved and how present knowledge has changed how we live. Other suggestions:

the sale of cigarettes
the advertising of alcoholic beverages
the popularity of natural foods
the sale of diet products

G ay Marriages: Make Them Legal

Thomas B. Stoddard

What is traditional is not always what is right; so Thomas B. Stoddard argues in the essay that follows. He calls for a redefinition of marriage that accommodates the legal status of matrimony to the present times. Stoddard is an attorney and executive director of the Lambda Legal Defense and Education Fund, a gay rights organization. Stoddard's essay was published as an opinion piece in the New York Times *in 1989. Since that time, the narrative Stoddard opens with has developed a different ending: Kowalski's parents stopped paying the bills for the nursing home, and she was then released into the care of Karen Thompson.*

WHAT TO LOOK FOR   *Definition is a key element in argument. Note how careful Stoddard is to define* marriage *in paragraphs 4 and 5. When you write your own argumentative paper, you'll probably find it helpful first to identify the most important term and then make sure early on in your paper that you define it carefully.*

1   "In sickness and in health, 'til death do us part." With those familiar words, millions of people each year are married, a public affirmation of a private bond that both society and the newlyweds hope will endure. Yet for nearly four years, Karen Thompson was denied the company of the one person to whom she had pledged lifelong devotion. Her partner is a woman, Sharon Kowalski, and their home state of Minnesota, like every other jurisdiction in the United States, refuses to permit two individuals of the same sex to marry.

2   Karen Thompson and Sharon Kowalski are spouses in every respect except the legal. They exchanged vows and rings; they lived together until November 13, 1983—when Ms. Kowalski was severely injured when her car was struck by a drunk driver. She lost the capacity to walk or to speak more than several words at a time, and needed constant care.

3   Ms. Thompson sought a court ruling granting her guardianship over her partner, but Ms. Kowalski's parents opposed the petition and obtained sole guardianship. They moved Ms. Kowalski to a

nursing home 300 miles away from Ms. Thompson and forbade all visits between the two women. Last month, as part of a reevaluation of Ms. Kowalski's mental competency, Ms. Thompson was permitted to visit her partner again. But the prolonged injustice and anguish inflicted on both women hold a moral for everyone.

4   Marriage, the Supreme Court declared in 1967, is "one of the basic civil rights of man" (and, presumably, of woman as well). The freedom to marry, said the Court, is "essential to the orderly pursuit of happiness."

5   Marriage is not just a symbolic state. It can be the key to survival, emotional and financial. Marriage triggers a universe of rights, privileges and presumptions. A married person can share in a spouse's estate even when there is no will. She is typically entitled to the group insurance and pension programs offered by the spouse's employer, and she enjoys tax advantages. She cannot be compelled to testify against her spouse in legal proceedings.

6   The decision whether or not to marry belongs properly to individuals—not the government. Yet at present, all 50 states deny that choice to millions of gay and lesbian Americans. While marriage has historically required a male partner and a female partner, history alone cannot sanctify injustice. If tradition were the only measure, most states would still limit matrimony to partners of the same race.

7   As recently as 1967, before the Supreme Court declared miscegenation statutes unconstitutional, 16 states still prohibited marriages between a white person and a black person. When all the excuses were stripped away, it was clear that the only purpose of those laws was, in the words of the Supreme Court, "to maintain white supremacy."

8   Those who argue against reforming the marriage statutes because they believe that same-sex marriage would be "antifamily" overlook the obvious: marriage creates families and promotes social stability. In an increasingly loveless world, those who wish to commit themselves to a relationship founded upon devotion should be encouraged, not scorned. Government has no legitimate interest in how that love is expressed.

9   And it can no longer be argued—if it ever could—that marriage is fundamentally a procreative unit. Otherwise, states would forbid marriage between those who, by reason of age or infertility, cannot have children, as well as those who elect not to.

10   As the case of Sharon Kowalski and Karen Thompson demonstrates, sanctimonious illusions lead directly to the suffering of others. Denied the right to marry, these two women are left subject to the whims and prejudices of others, and of the law.

11   Depriving millions of gay American adults the marriages of their choice, and the rights that flow from marriage, denies equal protection of the law. They, their families and friends, together with fair-minded people everywhere, should demand an end to this monstrous injustice.

Thesis and Organization

1. Paragraphs 1–3 present an example that holds a "moral for everyone." What is it?
2. Paragraphs 4 and 5 define marriage. What point does Stoddard make about marriage?
3. Paragraphs 6–9 are aimed at countering arguments that can be used against Stoddard's view. Summarize them.
4. What is the effect of paragraph 10? What other paragraphs does it connect with?
5. The essay concludes with a statement of thesis and a call to action. Who should demand what, and how?

Technique and Style

1. What paragraph or paragraphs appeal to the reader's emotions?
2. What paragraph or paragraphs appeal to the reader's reason?
3. Where in the essay can you identify an ethical appeal, an appeal based on the author's persona?
4. Stoddard cites the arguments that can be used against his. Does he cite obvious ones? Is his treatment of them fair? How so?
5. Stoddard's subject is a sensitive one and his views may not be shared by many readers. Where in the essay can you find evidence that he is aware of his readers and their potential sensitivity to the issue he writes about?

Suggestions for Writing

Journal

1. Stoddard's subject is an explosive one. What do you think about this issue?
2. Select one of the points Stoddard makes and either support or refute it.

Essay

Think of an issue that ought to be covered by a law or one that is governed by law and should not be. The best place to start is probably with your own experience and what irks you, but after that you'll need to do some research so that you can present your position in a more objective and reasoned way. The use of outside sources will lend more weight to your ideas. Suggestions for laws that do exist but that some think should not:

the given speed limit
the legal drinking age
particular zoning or IRS regulations
banning of prayers in public schools

Suggestions for laws that some think should exist but don't (varies by state):

car insurance
automobile safety seats for infants
helmets for motorcycle riders
neutering of pets

*A*merica Needs Its Nerds and Responses

Leonid Fridman, David Lessing, David Herne, and Keith W. Frome

Leonid Fridman's opinion piece appeared in the New York Times *on January 11, 1990, as part of a continuing series of essays called "Voices of the New Generation." Appropriately enough, Fridman is a founding member of the Society of Nerds and Geeks, an organization that began at Harvard University where, at the time the piece was written, Fridman was enrolled in the doctoral program in mathematics. The reaction was immediate. The very same day, Keith W. Frome, a member of Harvard's faculty, fired off a response, and one day later, two Harvard freshmen, David Lessing and David Herne, also rose to the battle. The essay and the two letters reacting to it are reprinted below. Fridman's essay was accompanied by the drawing that Frome describes and attacks.*

WHAT TO LOOK FOR   *Although Fridman announces his stance toward his subject in his first paragraph, you can make a good case that he reserves his thesis for his conclusion. As a result, the reasoning in the essay is more inductive than deductive. As you read it, keep track of the line of reasoning and see if you can recognize the logical fallacies the letters to the editor accuse him of. You'll be able to judge for yourself whether their charges are just.*

America Needs Its Nerds
Leonid Fridman

1   There is something very wrong with the system of values in a society that has only derogatory terms like nerd and geek for the intellectually curious and academically serious.

2   A geek, according to *Webster's New World Dictionary,* is a street performer who shocks the public by biting off heads of live chickens. It is a telling fact about our language and our culture that someone dedicated to pursuit of knowledge is compared to a freak biting the head off a live chicken.

3   Even at a prestigious academic institution like Harvard, anti-intellectualism is rampant: Many students are ashamed to admit, even to their friends, how much they study. Although most students try to keep up their grades, there is a minority of undergraduates for whom pursuing knowledge is the top priority during their years at Harvard. Nerds are ostracized while athletes are idolized.

4   The same thing happens in U.S. elementary and high schools. Children who prefer to read books rather than play football, prefer to build model airplanes rather than get wasted at parties with their classmates, become social outcasts. Ostracized for their intelligence and refusal to conform to society's anti-intellectual values, many are deprived of a chance to learn adequate social skills and acquire good communication tools.

5   Enough is enough.

6   Nerds and geeks must stop being ashamed of who they are. It is high time to face the persecutors who haunt the bright kid with thick glasses from kindergarten to the grave. For America's sake, the anti-intellectual values that pervade our society must be fought.

7   There are very few countries in the world where anti-intellectualism runs as high in popular culture as it does in the U.S. In most industrialized nations, not least of all our economic rivals in East Asia, a kid who studies hard is lauded and held up as an example to other students.

8   In many parts of the world, university professorships are the most prestigious and materially rewarding positions. But not in America, where average professional ballplayers are much more respected and better paid than faculty members of the best universities.

9   How can a country where typical parents are ashamed of their daughter studying mathematics instead of going dancing, or of their son reading Weber while his friends play baseball, be expected to compete in the technology race with Japan or remain a leading political and cultural force in Europe? How long can America remain a world-class power if we constantly emphasize social skills and physical prowess over academic achievement and intellectual ability?

10   Do we really expect to stay afloat largely by importing our scientists and intellectuals from abroad, as we have done for a major portion of this century, without making an effort to also cultivate a pro-intellectual culture at home? Even if we have the political will to spend substantially more money on education than we do now,

do we think we can improve our schools if we deride our studious pupils and debase their impoverished teachers?

11   Our fault lies not so much with our economy or with our politics as within ourselves, our values and our image of a good life. America's culture has not adapted to the demands of our times, to the economic realities that demand a highly educated workforce and innovative intelligent leadership.

12   If we are to succeed as a society in the 21st century, we had better shed our anti-intellectualism and imbue in our children the vision that a good life is impossible without stretching one's mind and pursuing knowledge to the full extent of one's abilities.

13   And until the words "nerd" and "geek" become terms of approbation and not derision, we do not stand a chance.

Responses

1   While "America Needs Its Nerds" (Op-Ed, Jan. 11) by Leonid Fridman, a Harvard student, may be correct in its message that Americans should treat intellectualism with greater respect, his identification of the "nerd" as guardian of this intellectual tradition is misguided.

2   Mr. Fridman maintains that anti-intellectualism runs rampant across this country, even at the "prestigious academic institution" he attends. However, he confuses a distaste for narrow-mindedness with anti-intellectualism. Just as Harvard, as a whole, reflects diversity in the racial, ethnic and religious backgrounds of its students, each student should reflect a diversity of interest as well.

3   A "nerd" or "geek" is distinguished by a lack of diverse interests, rather than by a presence of intellectualism. Thus, a nerd or geek is not, as Mr. Fridman states, a student "for whom pursuing knowledge is the top priority" but a student for whom pursuing knowledge is the sole objective. A nerd becomes socially maladjusted because he doesn't participate in social activities or even intellectual activities involving other people. As a result, a nerd is less the intellectual champion of Mr. Fridman's descriptions than a person whose intelligence is not focused and enhanced by contact with fellow students. Constant study renders such social learning impossible.

4   For a large majority at Harvard, academic pursuit is the highest goal; a limited number, however, refuse to partake in activities other than study. Only these select few are the targets of the geek label. Continuous study, like any other obsession, is not a habit to be lauded. Every student, no matter how "intellectually curious," ought to take a little time to pursue social knowledge through activities other than study.

5   Mr. Fridman's analysis demonstrates further flaws in his reference to Japan. He comments that "in East Asia, a kid who studies hard is lauded and held up as an example to other students," while in the United States he or she is ostracized. This is an unfair comparison because Mr. Fridman's first reference is to how the East Asian child is viewed by teachers, while his second reference is to how the American child is viewed by fellow students. Mr. Fridman is equating two distinct perspectives on the student to substantiate a broad generalization on which he has no factual data.

6   Nerdism may also be criticized because it often leads to the pursuit of knowledge but not for its own sake, but for the sake of grades. Nerds are well versed in the type of intellectual trivia that may help in obtaining A's, but has little or no relevance to the real world. A true definition of intellectualism ought to include social knowledge.

7   While we in no way condone the terms "nerds" and "geeks" as insults, we also cannot condone the isolationist intellectualism Mr. Fridman advocates.

                                        David Lessing, David Herne

1   I am disturbed by Leonid Fridman's article (Op-Ed, Jan. 11) and its accompanying collage. The collage displays a huge football player saying, "I read a book once." He is adored by a diminutive cheerleader, who sports a pennant that reads "Yea."

2   The picture is, of course, sexist and a silly and immature insult. Then, both the article and the picture commit the fallacy of bifurcation, otherwise known as the black-or-white fallacy. According to Mr. Fridman, one is either a jock, who neither reads nor writes and who spends time away from the field house punishing intellectuals, or a nerd, who totally devotes his time to learning at the expense of "social skills and physical prowess."

3   This is reductive. Mr. Fridman's analysis ignores the marvelous and rich field of humanity that lies between these poles. Rarely, if ever, is a student one way or another.

4   I am an adviser, teacher and administrator at Harvard (the only school Mr. Fridman mentions). I also live with 22 freshmen. Many of my students are dedicated athletes, but they are in no way jocks in Mr. Fridman's bifurcated sense of the word. The athletes I advise and teach are reflective, hard working, polite and, yes, intellectual. They read and discuss books, and even ideas.

5   In my expository-writing class, a hockey player has just handed in a rigorously constructed essay on law, ethics and religion. He is one of the best writers in the class. Another student, who plays football for Harvard, just spent an afternoon in my study discussing the metaphysical poets.

6   I could tell many more anecdotes of student-scholars I have taught and from whom I have learned. But the point is this: our pedagogic goal ought not to be to produce nerds or jocks, but human beings who are thoughtful, healthy and socially adept.

Keith W. Frome

Thesis and Organization

1. What paragraph or paragraphs constitute Fridman's introduction? What reasons can you give for your opinion?
2. Trace Fridman's use of examples. Explain whether you find them valid.
3. Where in the essay does Fridman use comparison and contrast? In what way does it support his argument?
4. Fridman also uses comparison and contrast to further his argument. Explain whether you find his comparisons accurate.
5. Combine the ideas contained in the title, the first paragraph, and the last paragraph. In your own words and in one sentence, state Fridman's thesis.

Technique and Style

1. Fridman's essay obviously elicited strong reactions. Reasoning aside, why do you think the letter writers responded as they did?
2. Lessing and Herne fault Fridman's reasoning, accusing him of shifting definition, false analogy, and hasty generalization. Are their criticisms valid?

3. Frome accuses Fridman of either-or reasoning, calling it the "fallacy of bifurcation, otherwise known as the black-or-white fallacy." Explain whether the charge is accurate.
4. Explain the extent to which the letter writers agree with Fridman's view that "a good life is impossible without stretching one's mind and pursuing knowledge to the full extent of one's abilities."
5. To what extent do all three pieces use the ethical appeal? Which one uses it most effectively?

Suggestions for Writing

Journal

1. Define and describe a nerd, and the extent to which the term is or is not derogatory.
2. Write a response to one of the three arguments.

Essay

Although the characteristic Fridman attacks is anti-intellectualism, and the examples he uses are the negative terms used for the "intellectually curious and academically serious," he is hardly alone in decrying our society's "system of values." Consider other subjects that our society appears to value or not value and draft an argumentative essay stating your position. You may well find that it's easier to start with examples and follow them to their subjects. Suggestions:

single-family homes
fast food
gadgets
television commercials
pets

Why I Hunt and Why I Don't Hunt and Why We Hunt

Dan Sisson, Steve Ruggeri, and Humberto Fontova

The three essays that follow were published in Sierra, *the magazine of The Sierra Club, an organization that promotes the conservation of wildlife, flora and fauna, and their surrounding ecosystems. Together with another essay (on hunting as an ethnic rite), they appeared along with a longer, expository essay that presented the various issues and groups involved in hunting. These three essays, however, are clearly argumentative. Their authors' backgrounds are as different as their immediate environments and reveal their positions on the subject: Dan Sisson lives in Oregon where he writes a regular column for* Field and Stream; *Steve Ruggeri works for Friends of Animals, an organization based in Newport, Rhode Island, and directs the group's wildlife policy; Humberto Fontova lives in Louisiana, where he works as a freelance writer, publishing his articles in magazines focusing on the outdoors.*

WHAT TO LOOK FOR   *Depending on where you live, hunting may or not be a hot issue, but for these three writers it's a flaming one. As you read each of their essays, play devil's advocate and read each as though you belonged to the opposite camp. Reading antagonistically will reveal how each of the writers deals with a reader's preconceived attitude and how each combats it. Look for concessions to the opposite view. Noting how these writers handle opposition can help you to use some of the same techniques.*

Why I Hunt
Dan Sisson

1   Hunting implies a relationship between man and animal, and as in any relationship, the layers of meaning that make it unique cannot be reduced to a single proposition or a simple-minded set of clichés.

2   Yet that is what has happened in the United States, where the debate between hunters and anti-hunters has been reduced to one question: How can anyone justify killing any animal?

3   As a hunter, I have felt hostility from people I know and respect who are anti-hunters. I have been told that killing any animal, except in self-defense, is immoral; and I have been characterized as a social leper who belongs to a more primitive age.

4   But this view of the hunter as an anachronism ignores the histories of science and of humankind. It conveniently blots out the fact that in nature every species, no matter how big or small, is either predator or prey, the hunter or the hunted. This—not the preservation of all life at any cost—is the dynamic of existence on our planet.

5   In all predator–relationships there is an inequality between the hunter and the hunted. The belief that all creatures have an equal right to life, and that therefore all killing is immoral, is a fallacy without precedent in science or the natural world.

6   The conviction of the anti-hunter that killing any animal is wrong may be based on the misguided concept that equality between hunter and hunted is the corollary of equality before the law. The equality of men and their right to life are *artificial* constructs of constitutional government and hold true only in the most civilized nations.

7   For me the essence of hunting is not the indulgence of the instinct to kill, nor is it to be found in the instant one kills. In fact, killing is no more necessary to a successful hunt than catching a fish is to a good fishing trip. If every hunt ended in a successful kill, hunting would be both boring and banal.

8   The essence of hunting for me is to pursue the animal ethically and in a manner that makes the possibility of killing or capturing it a genuine challenge. There is no certainty of killing when I hunt. Indeed, the *uncertainty* is what makes the sport interesting.

9   I accept limits on my ability to kill. The hunting seasons are carefully constructed so as to make the wit of the hunter and the cunning of the animal more truly competitive.

10   That is why we limit seasons to several days or weeks a year, limit the use of baits to lure unwary animals and birds, and limit the number of animals we kill, their size and age and sex. We limit our behavior by law in order to pursue game ethically and to make the challenge even more difficult. These odds I take on happily, knowing the elk herds will continue to flourish. Those who

refuse to accept the odds—the poachers—are not hunters, they are outlaws.

11   Hunting is a complex activity involving undercurrents that are rarely articulated, but that nevertheless form the basis for one's actions. One of these unstated values is the attempt to establish a strong ethical position in life. Few activities in this world test ethical standards as does hunting.

12   There are no witnesses in the wilderness. The hunter knows in his conscience whether he has compromised the sportsman's standards. For an ethical hunter, hypocrisy and hunting are incompatible.

13   I have asserted that hunting involves much more than the act of killing. I hunt to nourish my aesthetic appreciation of nature; being in the field six months a year allows me to experience, personally, the most beautiful parts of America.

14   I hunt for food, and I do not choose to delegate my right to obtain it to a slaughterhouse. My friends go to supermarkets and buy packaged beef and lamb. I go into the wilderness and kill elk, venison, and wildfowl. Is there a moral difference between a cow being killed for market and a deer for my freezer?

15   I hunt because it deepens my relationship with my son. We have literally spent years in duck blinds, on deer stands, and around campfires—talking. I would not trade those conversations for anything on Earth.

16   I hunt because I can contribute to conservation directly. Last year I raised 5,000 valley quail. I killed 49 of them. This reflects a traditional value of giving more to the land and the environment than you take from it. How many anti-hunters can make a similar claim?

17   I hunt to simplify my life, away from the noise and the pollution of urban environments. What better way to ponder John Muir's axiom that every star is connected to every other star in the universe than by starlight after a day in the wilderness?

18   All this is why I hunt.

Why I Don't Hunt
Steve Ruggeri

1   Why did I hunt? From the time I was 12 until shortly after my 18th birthday, I pumped lead at the furred and feathered from

Maine to Pennsylvania. I was the youngest member of the New-port Rifle Club in Rhode Island, where I was trained and disci-plined as a small-bore competitive shooter. I was tutored by mas-ters of the art, and I was given numerous opportunities to engage in my sport.

2   Despite my enthusiasm, I sought diversion from the rigors of competitive shooting. Trap and skeet shooting introduced me to moving targets, but I was anxious to sight down a barrel at ani-mate ones. I looked forward to the pleasure of seeing birds plum-met earthward. I knew I would delight in the contortions of small game, the end-over-end tumbling after the rabbit felt the sting of my .22. And I was confident that I would shrug and say, "Better luck, next buck," should I miscalculate shot placement and merely blow the lower jaw completely off a deer.

3   I didn't disappoint myself. I reveled in killing, maiming, bloodletting, and gutting. Never did I have the slightest thought regarding carrying capacity, overbrowsing, population dynamics, or any other game-management concept. The arguments that hunters advanced in defense of their sport were alien to me. I hunted in order to kill; I did not kill in order to have "the hunt-ing experience."

4   Why did I stop? Social expedience: My pastime was deemed un-acceptable by a circle of high-school mates from whom I sought acceptance. Would I have ever experienced an after-kill crisis of conscience of such emotional magnitude that I would hurl my weapon into the nearest lake? No, I was incapable of the visceral compunction that has triggered the moral rebirth of many who for-merly exploited animals.

5   A couple of years after my guns had been silenced by peer pressure, I was dining on a hamburger so rare that the blood still appeared to be coursing through the animal tissue. While hurrying to finish so as not to be late for my cat's appointment with the vet, I was seized by the realization of how utterly inconsistent it was for me to be so solicitous of a cat, yet have no regard for the cow I was devouring.

6   Pain is pain, I reasoned, whether felt by the family feline or by the unknown steer shackled and hoisted above the killing-room floor. It became morally imperative for me to end my complicity in the infliction of any gratuitous pain and suffering upon either wild or domesticated animals. This ethical awakening led to extensive

research and reading that enlightened me further as to the magnitude of our exploitation of nonhuman animals, and reaffirmed my resolve to embrace an ethic of moral consideration for all animal species. I recognized that my decision to stop hunting years earlier had been correct, though made for the wrong reason.

7   Why don't I hunt? I could allude to the fruits of exhaustive research into the ecological and biological consequences of hunting, and to the collective insight of biologists, ecologists, and naturalists who challenge the prevailing wildlife-management dogma. Yet, fundamentally, the answer can be expressed in simple moral terms: Hunting is wrong, and should be acknowledged to be so not only by those who espouse the strict precepts of the animal-rights credo, but by those who hold a common sense of decency, respect, and justice. When we have exposed the specious reasoning of the hunters' apologists and stripped their sport of its counterfeit legitimacy, the naked brutality of hunting defines itself: killing for the fun of it.

8   Although my current occupation requires attention to a wide array of animal issues, the subject of hunting is the predominant focus of my work. If I find my energy or motivation waning during the course of a day's work, I merely conjure up the image of my former self as a slayer of wildlife. The memory of stalking targets on the hoof or wing infuses me with renewed vigor in my labor against blood sports.

9   But obviously, no amount of dedication or energy expanded will atone for the suffering and death I visited upon the scores of animals I wantonly killed.

Why We Hunt
Humberto Fontova

1   Just once. My God, just once, I'd like to see hunters face up to the primal instinct that motivates us. But no, all I hear is:

2   "We're the top conservationists in the country."

3   "We put our money where our mouths are."

4   "We're nature lovers."

5   Hell, we'll pat ourselves on the back all day.

6   Yes, hunters are actually all these things. But no one (from our ranks, anyway) seems to want to point out that essentially we are

killers of animals in the most direct way, and that what distin- guishes us from everyone else who indirectly causes animals to die is that we take delight in it.

7　"Don't you eat meat?"

8　"How much did you contribute to conservation this year, Mr. Birdwatcher?"

9　Oh, how we love to retort to the anti-hunters. But they do have a point: If we're attracted by the beauty of nature, surely it's just as beautiful without a gun in hand. If the challenge is the key, why not sneak up on a bull elk and take a picture of it? If tradition and camaraderie are the inspiration, why pull the trigger?

10　And, of course, we all rush afield on opening day enraptured by the prospect of culling excess animals. The sleeplessness of the night before and the hollow stomach that morning are obviously caused by this opportunity to do our part for sound game-management.

11　I've never bought the classic hunting argument about the in- significant part that actual killing plays in the sport. If this were true, there would be no reason for the vitriol we hurl at the anti- hunters. These mushheads aren't out to stop us from walking in the woods and embracing nature. They're not out to deny us the challenge of stalking an animal. They're not out to prevent the friendship and the card games at the cabin. They're out to stop one thing: the killing. If it's such a tiny part of the total hunting picture, why are we in such a lather about the anti-hunters?

12　Let's face it: After we cut through all the embellishments, the one thing that distinguishes a canoeing trip or a nature walk from the hunt is the prospect of killing.

13　We *like* to kill animals. I can no more explain this predatory in- stinct to the satisfaction of Friends of Animals than anyone else can. But I won't throw up a smokescreen of rationalizations when confronted with this unnerving but unavoidable fact.

14　For a hunter to admit that there's something enjoyable about killing an animal is considered fantastic. The outdoor magazines are a perfect example: Their editorials constantly harp on sports- manship, challenge, conservation ethics, nature worship, tradition, and camaraderie. These are showcased as the most genuine ratio- nales for our sport; the killing is merely incidental—the "We kill in order to have hunted" syndrome. According to these editorials, it's the grueling hours of scouting, stalking, and honing our woods- manship that count. We're led to believe that only a small minority of slob hunters forsake these principles.

15   Then the rest of the magazine's pages are filled with stories of guided hunts where, almost literally, all the hunter does is pull the trigger.

16   After a night of good-timing, the biggest challenge for the Texas deer "hunter" is to huff and puff his way to the top of a deer tower and keep his balance on the revolving seat. The "hunting" is a matter of gazing out over the corn-baited landscape and picking out which deer he wants.

17   The tycoon who roams over the African bush in a Land Rover, gets out, walks 500 yards, and kills a 60-year-old animal pointed out by a professional guide is not out to stock his freezer or display his woodsmanship. I know that this gentleman, with what he paid for licenses and trophy fees, probably contributed more toward the conservation of elephants than any of the do-good organizations, but still, he killed the elephant. And he enjoyed it.

18   I see absolutely nothing wrong with any of these scenarios, but let's recognize them for what they aren't and for what they are. They do not show the behavior of the conservationist, adventurer, master woodsman, naturalist, or philosopher of hunting-magazine mythology. Hunters are simply guys who get a thrill out of killing animals.

19   Yes, the love of the outdoors contributes to my urge to hunt. The challenge is definitely part of it. Studying the nature of the terrain and my quarry's habits, and then ambushing him fair and square, makes the kill more rewarding. Sometimes the fellowship is nice, although I usually hunt alone. Feeding my family year-round on what I kill gives a certain bounce to the step. But mostly, I recognize the urge as a predatory instinct to kill. Man is a predator—has been for tens of thousands of years. It's going to take a while to breed that out of us, and thank God I won't be around by then.

Thesis and Organization

1. Identify the thesis of each essay and its placement. What differences do you note?
2. Consider the body of evidence each essay presents. What pattern of organization does each rely on? Which do you consider the most reasoned?
3. Considering the thesis and its placement, which of the arguments would you label inductive? Why?

4. Which argument would you call deductive? Why?
5. Examine the last sentence in each essay. Which do you find the most effective and why?

Technique and Style

1. Identify the most prominent appeal for each of the essays. Which appeal do you find the most effective and why?
2. All three essays deal with the issue of killing. What does each say about it? Which do you find the most compelling and why?
3. To what extent does the subject of ethics enter the arguments of the essays? What reasons can you find for bringing up the subject?
4. What logical fallacies do the writers point out? Are their charges valid?
5. Examine the essays for any logical fallacies the writers themselves might have fallen into. What do you find?

Suggestions for Writing

Journal

1. Before you read the essays, did you have a position on hunting? If so, briefly explain it. If not, jot down what you associate with hunting and then judge whether those associations are negative or positive.
2. Explain which of the arguments you find most compelling and why.

Essay

Environmental issues have the potential to affect us all, and no matter whether the issues are large or small, they are debated. Choose an issue that interests you, find several recent articles on it (ones that consider various perspectives on the subject), and write an essay that argues for your position. Suggestions:

 global warming
 depletion of rain forests
 mining
 timber cutting
 Endangered Species Act
 wetlands

*P*utting Africa at the Center and Beware of the New Pharaohs

Molefi Kete Asante and Henry Louis Gates, Jr.

Both Asante and Gates are scholars who specialize in Afro-Ameri-can studies, yet as these two essays point out, their approaches to their field are quite different. Asante sees "cultural stability" as the crucial goal, but Gates finds it to be "free inquiry." Asante's view concentrates on African Americans; Gates welcomes all comers. What they have in common is a belief in Afrocentricity, but the simi-larity stops there. The two essays appeared side by side in the Septem-ber 23, 1991, issue of Newsweek *as part of a larger story on the black experience.*

Asante chairs the Department of African American Studies at Temple University and is the author of a number of books, includ-ing The Afrocentric Idea *(1988),* Afrocentricity *(1990),* Malcolm X as Cultural Hero and Other Afrocentric Essays *(1993), and* African Intellectual Heritage: A Book of Sources *(1996). Gates chairs Afro-American Studies at Harvard University where he holds the posi-tion of W. E. B. Du Bois Professor of the Humanities. Gates has written a number of scholarly books, of which the best known is probably* The Signifying Monkey *(1989). Most recently, however, he has edited the* Norton Anthology of African American Literature *(1996) and written for a more general audience in* Loose Canons: Notes of the Culture Wars *(1992), his autobiography,* Colored People: A Memoir *(1993), and* Thirteen Ways of Looking at a Black Man *(1997). He is also a regular contributor to the* New Yorker *magazine.*

WHAT TO LOOK FOR *The vocabulary in Asante's essay may put you off at first, but bear with it for he is using the specialized diction of academic prose.* Subject *and* object *take on special meanings here. A group or person in the* subject *position commands center stage as the one who acts, does, causes things to happen; conversely, a group or person in the* object *position is a bit player who is acted on or done to. Once you think about it, the terms make*

*sense. Gates's vocabulary is also formal, academic. As you read the
essays, figure out whether the specialized language is necessary.*

Putting Africa at the Center
Molefi Kete Asante

1   Afrocentricity is both theory and practice. In its theoretical aspect it consists of interpretation and analysis from the perspective
of African people as subjects rather than as objects on the fringes
of the European experience. When Afrocentric methods are used
to explain an issue, the aim is to look for areas where the idea or
person is off-center in terms of subject position and suggest appropriate solutions. For example, young African-American males who
may be engaged in violent behavior are often off-center. It is the
aim of Afrocentric intervention to relocate them in a place of values and cultural stability.

2   Since Africans in America have been dislocated—that is, taken
off their own terms for the past 345 years—we seldom operate as
the subjects of our own historical experiences. We often operate
based on an illusion that creates disillusionment and self-alien-
ation, the most fundamental alienation a person can have. Afrocentricity is a struggle against extreme misorientation, where many
of us believe that we share the same history as whites; indeed, that
we came across on the Mayflower.

3   In its practical implications, Afrocentricity aims to locate African-
American children in the center of the information being presented
in classrooms across the nation. Most African-American children sit
in classrooms, yet are outside the information being discussed. The
white child sits in the middle of the information, whether it is literature, history, politics or art. The task of the Afrocentric curriculum
is finding patterns in African-American history and culture that
help the teacher place the child in the middle of the intellectual
experience. This is not an idea to replace all things European, but
to expand the dialogue to include African-American information.
An Afrocentric curriculum covers kindergarten through 12th grade
in every subject area. It can then be infused into an academic program cleansed of pejoratives like "Bushman" and "wild Indian" in
order to have a truly multicultural curriculum.

4   Afrocentricity is neither racist nor anti-Semitic; it is about placing African people within our own historical framework. In none of the major works of Afrocentricity has there ever been a hint of racism, ethnocentrism or anti-anybody. Indeed, Afrocentricity believes that in order to have a stable society, we must always have a society that respects difference. One cannot argue that there is no difference—or that difference necessarily means hostility. One may be alien and yet not hostile. We only have to witness "E.T." to see the truth of that proposition.

5   **Imitative history:** Recent African-American history has shown that we have frequently been imitative of whites, following in the path of Europeans without understanding our own identities. Few African-American students or adults can tell you the names of any of the African ethnic groups that were brought to the Americas during the Great Enslavement; and yet prior to the Civil War there were no African-Americans, merely enslaved Africans. We know European ethnic names, but not these names, because we have seldom participated in our own historical traditions.

6   Afrocentricity resonates with the African-American community because it is fundamental to sanity. It is the fastest growing intellectual and practical idea in the community because of its validity when tested against other experiences. What could be any more correct for any people than to see with their own eyes?

Beware of the New Pharaohs
Henry Louis Gates, Jr.

1   There's a scene in Woody Allen's "Bananas" in which the luckless hero, played by Allen, bemoans the fact that he dropped out of college. "What would you have been if you'd have finished school," a co-worker asks him. "I don't know," he sighs, "I was in the black-studies program. By now, I could have been black."

2   The truth is, too many people still regard African-American studies primarily as a way to rediscover a lost cultural identity—or invent one that never quite existed. And while we can understand these impulses, those in our field must remember that we are scholars first, not polemicists. For our field to survive, we need to encourage a true proliferation of rigorous methodologies, rather

than to seek ideological conformity. African-American studies should be the home of free inquiry into the very complexity of being of African descent in the world, rather than a place where critical inquiry is drowned out by ethnic fundamentalism.

3   We need to explore the hyphen in African-American, on both sides of the Atlantic. We must chart the porous relations between an "American" culture that officially pretends that an Anglo-American *regional* culture is the true, universal culture, and the black cultures it so long stigmatized. We must also document both the continuities and discontinuities between African and African-American cultures, rather than to reduce the astonishing diversity of African cultures to a few simple-minded shibboleths. But we should not lay claim to the idea of "blackness" as an ideology or religion. Surely all scholars of Africa and its diaspora are, by definition, "Afrocentric," if the term signals the recognition that Africa is centrally in the world, as much as the world is in Africa. But this is a source of the problem: all Afrocentrists, alas, do not look alike.

4   In short, African-American studies is not just for blacks; our subject is open to all—to study or to teach. The fundamental premise of the academy is that all things ultimately are knowable; all are therefore teachable. What would we say to a person who said that to teach Milton, you had to be Anglo-Saxon, Protestant, male . . . and blind! We do nothing to help our discipline by attempting to make of it a closed shop, where only blacks need apply. On the other hand, to say that ethnic identity is the product of history and culture is not to say that it is any less real. Nor is it to deny our own personal histories, to pretend that these are not differences that make a difference.

5   Nobody comes into the world as a "black" person or a "white" person: these identities are conferred on us by a complex history, by patterns of social acculturation that are both surprisingly labile and persistent. Social identities are never as rigid as we like to pretend: they're constantly being contested and negotiated.

6   For a scholar, "Afrocentrism" should mean more than wearing Kente cloth and celebrating Kwanzaa instead of Christmas. (Kwanzaa, by the way, was invented in Los Angeles, not Lagos.) Bogus theories of "sun" and "ice" people, and the invidious scapegoating of other ethnic groups, only resurrects the worst of 19th-century racist pseudoscience—which too many of the pharaohs of "Afrocentrism" have accepted without realizing.

7   We must not succumb to the temptation to resurrect our own version of the thought police, who would determine who, and what, is "black." "Mirror, mirror, on the wall, who's the blackest one of all?" is a question best left behind in the '60s.

Thesis and Organization

1. How do Gates's and Asante's definitions of Afrocentricity differ?
2. How do the two writers view the Afro-American culture?
3. Both essays contain attacks. Who is attacking what?
4. Who is defending what?
5. Both writers argue for changes in curriculum. What does each want?

Technique and Style

1. The audience for *Newsweek* can be described as college educated, middle-class, predominantly white, and male. Which essay is apt to have more appeal to that audience? To an African American audience?
2. Select a paragraph that uses formal vocabulary and rewrite a sentence or two, using more conversational words. What is gained? Lost?
3. Which of the essays makes better use of the appeal to reason? Cite examples from the texts to make your point.
4. What examples can you think of that fit Asante's statement that "Most African-American children sit in classrooms, yet are outside the information being discussed"?
5. How does the term *New Pharaohs* fit Gates's essay?

Suggestions for Writing

Journal

1. If you could fit such a class into your studies, use your journal to explain whether or not you would take it.
2. Of the two writers, which would you rather take a class with and why?

Essay

Gates maintains that "Nobody comes into the world as a 'black' person or a 'white' person: these identities are conferred on us by a complex history, by patterns of social acculturation that are both surprisingly labile and persistent." Write an essay in which you argue for or against requiring a college course that focuses on how cultural identities are formed. If that idea doesn't appeal to you, consider your college and argue for a change. Suggestions:

drop a specific requirement (name it)
add a specific course (name and explain it)
drop a specific sport
ban or promote fraternities/sororities
raise or lower admission standards

Credits

Index